THE
RAILWAY
PRESERVATION
REVOLUTION

THE
RAILWAY PRESERVATION REVOLUTION

A HISTORY *of* BRITAIN'S HERITAGE RAILWAYS

JONATHAN BROWN

PEN & SWORD
TRANSPORT

First published in Great Britain in 2017 by
Pen & Sword Transport

An imprint of Pen & Sword Books Ltd
47 Church Street, Barnsley, South Yorkshire S70 2AS

ISBN 978 1 47389 117 3

Pen & Sword Books Ltd incorporates the imprints of Pen & Sword
Archaeology, Atlas, Aviation, Battleground, Discovery, Family History,
History, Maritime, Military, Naval, Politics, Railways, Select, Social History,
Transport, True Crime, and Claymore Press, Frontline Books, Leo Cooper,
Praetorian Press, Remember When, Seaforth Publishing and Wharncliffe.

For a complete list of Pen & Sword titles please contact
Pen & Sword Books Limited
47 Church Street, Barnsley, South Yorkshire S70 2AS England
E-mail: enquiries@pen-and-sword.co.uk
Website: www.pen-and-sword.co.uk

Design and typesetting
by Juliet Arthur, www.stimula.co.uk

Printed and bound in India by Replika Press Pvt. Ltd.

CONTENTS

List of tables

List of figures

ABBREVIATIONS

AcoRP	The Association of Community Rail Partnerships
AIR	Association of Independent Railways
ARPS	The Association of Railway Preservation Societies
BR	British Railways/British Rail
CVR	Churnet Valley Railway
DVR	Dart Valley Railway
ELR	East Lancashire Railway
FR	Ffestiniog Railway
GCR	Great Central Railway
HLF	Heritage Lottery Fund
HRA	Heritage Railway Association
KESR	Kent and East Sussex Railway
KWVR	Keighley and Worth Valley Railway
LCGB	Locomotive Club of Great Britain
LMS	London Midland and Scottish Railway
LNER	London and North Eastern Railway
LNWR	London and North Western Railway
M&GN	Midland and Great Northern
NR	Network Rail
NVR	Nene Valley Railway
NYMR	North Yorkshire Moors Railway
ORR	Office of Rail Regulation/Office of Rail and Road
RHDR	Romney Hythe and Dymchurch Railway
SRA	Strategic Rail Authority
SRPS	Scottish Railway Preservation Society
TR	Talyllyn Railway
TRPS	Talyllyn Railway Preservation Society
UDC	Urban District Council
WHR	Welsh Highland Railway
WSR	West Somerset Railway

PREFACE

It was while riding on one of the preserved railways that the thought came: there's already a fifty-year history to these railways that deserves study. On sharing this thought with my wife, she said, 'That seems like a project for you.' Fifty years since the foundation of the first preserved railway became sixty, sixty-five and more, so this book has had a gestation similar in length to most preservation schemes.

There are now several preserved or heritage railways that have been in operation for forty years or more – a remarkable achievement in itself – but for many the longest period of settled ownership in their history. It's longer than the time they were part of British Railways, and longer than the period of the grouped railways. In the 1950s these preserved railways were curiosities, but now they are part of the fabric of British social and economic life. They are part heritage attraction alongside the stately homes and ancient monuments, part leisure activity, good for a day out with Thomas the Tank Engine, part form of transport, and for some a thriving business, generating millions for the local economy.

These railways are about preserving our history. Yet, characteristically, their own history has had little attention. The exception is the Welsh narrow-gauge railways – the pioneers on the Talyllyn and Ffestiniog, for example. The revival of the Welsh Highland Railway was such an epic struggle that already half a dozen books have been written about it. Elsewhere though, coverage is patchy, so I hope my attempt to draw together some of the broad themes of the railway preservation story will stimulate attention.

There's plenty of scope. I haven't covered anything like the range of social and economic aspects alluded to earlier. And this story is drawn almost entirely from the published record, mostly in magazines, with a small amount of oral history mixed into that. The magazines do not give all the story, however, and that includes the journals of the preservation societies.

This story is about the preserved railways as operational entities. It does not detail the locomotives, coaches and other artefacts preserved on the railways, although they enter the story at appropriate points. I also do not cover railway museums and centres, independent workshops and engineering establishments for the preserved railways. Even with such exclusions, there's still some blurring around the edges of defining what is a preserved (or heritage) railway. I have not worried about such things. There are probably slight discrepancies between figures for numbers of railways derived from different sources; otherwise the effect is limited.

My father introduced me to the concept of preserved railways many years ago. He was a great supporter of the Talyllyn Railway in many ways – a few of his photographs are included here. As this project got going he did a lot of research, checking references. He died a few years ago, so unfortunately hasn't seen the end result. My brother is among several people who have read drafts of the text, including my wife Patricia and Peter Bosley; he provided photographs as well as helpful comment. I am grateful, too, to Mark Casson, who provided a forum at the Centre for Institutional Performance in the University of Reading, where I presented a paper trying out some of the arguments contained in this book; the comments by members of that conference were further help. John Scott-Morgan has been a stimulating and supportive editor. He came up with the title as well. Peter Waller of the Online Transport Archive was a great help in finding photographs. Finally my thanks go to all those staff and volunteers on the railways I have visited during the course of research and writing, for sharing their enjoyment of working on these lines. In many ways this is their book.

INTRODUCTION

More than sixty years ago a small group of enthusiasts took over the running of a railway. They formed a railway preservation society to make sure that this line, which was threatened with closure, was saved for posterity. It was a small railway in mid-Wales, of narrow gauge, and sufficiently obscure to have been passed over by government when it grouped the railways into four large companies in 1923, and again when it nationalised the railways in 1948. Small though it was, and quaint, this was a real railway running for nearly seven miles; a serious undertaking.

For a band of volunteers to operate such a railway was a bold move, and one that introduced a new approach to preservation. There had been moves to preserve canals before, and other aspects of industry, but an industrial museum or preserved waterway did not involve public service in the same way that preserving a railway could. The possible closure of the Talyllyn was not the first occasion that railway preservation had been mooted – talk of saving the Southwold Railway in the 1930s came to nothing. The success of the Talyllyn's preservers proved an inspiration. Before long that first group had been joined by others taking over and restoring more small narrow-gauge railways. Then a few years later, the movement spread to the purchase and revival of railway lines that British Railways was discarding.

From then on, it seems, there was no holding back. More and more railway lines were taken over and revived by preservation groups, until by 2011 there were 108 in operation with 536 miles of line, a total greater than the London Underground system. The 44 railways of standard gauge accounted for nearly 300 miles. The longest individual line was 25 miles. These railways maintain the Talyllyn's tradition as volunteer-run, with more than 18,000 volunteers; they are the biggest employers of volunteer labour in the leisure and tourist sector – more than museums, heritage centres and gardens. They have paid staff as well – 2,200 of them in 2011. In that year more than 7.1 million

The modern preserved railway epitomised: crowds streaming off the train at Pickering.

passenger journeys were made on the lines, and their total income was £92 million.[1] Some of them had become considerable businesses. The North Yorkshire Moors Railway has an annual turnover of about £5 million, as do the West Somerset Railway and the combined Ffestiniog and Welsh Highland railways. The contribution of the railways to their local economies is significant. Some places are now 'heritage railway towns', so great is the impact of the railway, with its passengers and its volunteers. The Severn Valley Railway is worth an estimated £10 million to local trade; when it was closed for eight months because of flooding some businesses closed as a result. The estimated total value of this new industry of heritage railways to the British economy is £248 million.[2]

It might seem that there was inexorable progress about the growth of railway preservation. However, many preservation schemes failed, and for others there was a long period of struggle before the first trains ran on the revived line. It took thirteen years for the Kent & East Sussex Railway Society to open the first stretch of its line, and that was typical of many. It is easy to be seduced by the stories of large sums of money raised, but for most railways finances have often been tight. Without the incalculable benefit of volunteer support hardly any would have survived.

It would be equally misleading to run away with the romantic notion that the railway preservation story has been one of doughty warriors battling to get their lines going. It cannot be turned into a simple tale either of struggle or of inevitable growth and success. For the most part reviving a railway has required a mixture of ingenuity, entrepreneurship and mundane slog.

Preserved railways embrace a wide range of different types in organisation and character. Some are narrow gauge, others standard gauge. Some are very short lines, others quite long. Some are steam railways, others have diesel traction, some even electric stock, although no lines, so far, are electrified. Some railways operate every day, at least in high summer, others at weekends only. All share a reliance on tourism and leisure for the bulk of their business. Some are very commercial operations, others less so, run by dedicated volunteers. Some promote themselves more to their local communities than others. Recent years have seen greater cross-fertilisation between the preserved railways and the privatised national network, especially those characterised as 'new generation' lines, with a greater emphasis on running community services. All in all, the preservation movement has added a diverse, colourful, even at times innovative element to Britain's railways.

From the beginning railway preservationists faced the question: what exactly is it we are trying to preserve? Was it a historic artefact in all its detail, or a form of railway transport that could grow and develop? At the first meeting in Birmingham from which the Talyllyn Railway Preservation Society was formed, this question entered the debate. One contributor suggested that the best way to maintain the Talyllyn should be to electrify it, using local hydroelectric power supplies. Tom Rolt, who had founded the preservation society, entertained rebuilding the railway to the 15 inch gauge, following the precedent of the Ravenglass & Eskdale Railway, which had been converted from the 3ft gauge. Most members wanted to preserve the railway as it was, except that they did not mean it should remain in the decrepit state in which they found it. A working compromise was argued then, and was still being presented more than fifty years later: 'the purpose of a preservation society is to preserve the historic character and maintain the original appearance of its locomotives and rolling stock.'[3]

The debate continued: where should one draw the line between historical accuracy and efficiency in running an active railway? Should traditional bullhead rail be used always or continuous welded rail, which is cheaper and easier to maintain? Compromise is usually managed – traditional track at stations where the crowds gather, and continuous welded rail along the main route. Authenticity has been one of the watchwords among railway preservationists. It has been defended vigorously throughout the preservation years, in no area more so than locomotives and rolling stock. 'Correct' liveries for locomotives and coaches has been an emotive issue. Rebuilding and alteration to locomotives has similarly been contentious. Compromise and adaptation were necessary to keep old locomotives running, but debate raged as to how far that should go. Conversion of some of the Ffestiniog Railway's locomotives to oil fuel was met with protests. On the Ffestiniog, again, the withdrawal of the Fairlie locomotive *Earl of Merioneth* and the use of its bogies for *Merddyn Emrys* in 1972 caused concern.[4] This type of argument prompted Allan Garraway, General Manager of the Ffestiniog Railway, to write to the HM Railway Inspectorate on 22 May 1970: 'I think that people are getting the message that we are operating a very busy railway and not a working museum.'[5] He was not entirely correct: defenders of authenticity have continued to look askance at some choices of locomotive, carriages and other aspects of a preserved railway's operation. When the revived Lynton and Barnstaple Railway opened with diesel locomotives hauling the inaugural trains of new coaches, the view was publicly expressed that this was 'dishonest'.[6] Whereas many have been concerned about preserving the authenticity of their railway, for some the preservation of the railway as a provider of transport has been uppermost. This was strong in the thinking of the 1960s and early 1970s, when large numbers of railway lines were being closed, often to great local protest. Some believed that preservation groups had a major part to play in restoring local transport links. O.H. Prosser, one of the Talyllyn's founders, saw in the 1960s considerable scope for the transfer of branch lines from British Railways to preservation groups so that their value as feeder lines might be maintained.[7] A number of preservation projects started out with that intent, but the reality turned out differently. The interval, usually of several years, that elapsed between the closure of the line by British Railways and reopening by the preservation group meant the local population got used to life without it and bought cars. The preserved railways had to take a different approach, leading one correspondent to the *Railway Magazine* in 1972 to bemoan 'Gaily-painted locomotives [going] from nowhere to nowhere. … Is there any hope in the future that lines will be reopened providing regular feeder services to BR and that they will be run on *real* railway principles, not like a fairground amusement?'[8]

These questions of what the railway should be preserving and how have proved contentious, provoking rows in the boardroom and between different groups associated with the railway. The ways in which different railways have resolved the tensions account for some of their range of character. A tiny number of preserved railways have maintained themselves as museum lines. Some that set out with that intent have been drawn away from it by the demands of balancing the books. They have kept a museum side to their activities, as have many

Restoring a wagon, Isle of Wight.

other railways that never thought of themselves solely as museums. Such railways have usually gained registered status for their museum work, together with lottery grants for restoration and educational projects. But the museum work has usually been managed as a static display, with, perhaps, vintage trains run on special occasions.

Most lines have tried to preserve the 'character' or 'spirit' of the railway, but even that is open to a wide range of interpretations. The pioneers of the Kent & East Sussex Railway Society were keen to preserve the character of their line as 'the Farmer's Line' typical of the light railways run by Colonel Stephens, which this had once been. Making that aim compatible with operating a service for tourists and railway enthusiasts has inevitably meant compromise. The Bluebell Railway, a different sort of railway from the outset, pragmatically recreated the steam age, but re-examined its steam-only policy in 2004 when it was offered a diesel-electric railcar.[9] Pragmatic interpretations of 'character' have been necessary, for the branch lines that most preserved railways run never had catering establishments, gift shops, museum displays or covered sheds for a dozen locomotives and twenty or more coaches. Indeed, most of these railways are arguably not so much preserved as recreated. They have had to be rebuilt on closed branch lines, and although they might have preserved artefacts, the railway itself is something different altogether.[10] The emergence of the term 'heritage railway' arose naturally from the realities of preserved railway operation.

These widely differing characteristics means that they can only be defined loosely. What, for example, differentiates the steam centre or museum that has a running line from the operational railway? What distinguishes the private pleasure line from the public preserved railway? The Heritage Railway Association website provides one definition: 'railways offering regular passenger rides between two or more stations'. Another clear demarcation is that the operating railway will do so under the statutory authority of a Light Railway Order, a Transport & Works Act Order, or occasionally an Act of Parliament, whereas the steam centre is unlikely to need such authorisation. Light Railway Orders have, however, been used for a variety of operations, making definition not necessarily any clearer. In this

book I have not made a hard and fast definition, although inevitably that means some will disagree with the choices of railways included or excluded.

In March 2015 a plaque was unveiled on the wall of 84 High Street, Banbury. This was where Bill Trinder had a shop selling gramophones and records in the mid-twentieth century. He was well-known to his customers and the membership of his church, but elsewhere little recognised. Except that he was one of the founders of the Talyllyn Railway Preservation Society. It is people like him – 'unsung heroes' – who have made the story of railway preservation. They have fought to get their project off the ground; they have built up the railways once they were open. Each generation of volunteers made its mark, giving heritage railways their differences in character. This is the story of how that has come about. It is far from the complete story, but an initial gathering of material from the published accounts in magazines, newspapers and books, with some archives and interviews added. There is much more to be learned about how people created and developed preserved railways, and gradually more is being brought to light, especially in the society journals.

The Cholsey & Wallingford Railway train scurries past by the field path. The locomotive was Robert Stephenson & Hawthorn saddle tank No.7386 on 29 August 2011.

LOCATION MAP OF HERITAGE RAILWAYS IN THE BRITISH ISLES

1. Alderney Railway (not shown)
2. Alford Valley Railway
3. Aln Valley Railway
4. Amerton Railway
5. Avon Valley Railway
6. Bala Lake Railway
7. Barry Tourist Railway
8. Battlefield Line
9. Bluebell Railway
10. Bo'ness and Kinneil Railway
11. Bodmin and Wenford Railway
12. Border Union Railway
13. Bowes Railway
14. Brecon Mountain Railway
15. Bure Valley Railway
16. Caledonian Railway
17. Cambrian Heritage Railways
18. Cavan and Leitrim Railway
19. Chasewater Railway
20. Chinnor and Princes Risborough Railway
21. Cholsey and Wallingford Railway
22. Churnet Valley Railway
23. Cleethorpes Coast Light Railway
24. Colne Valley Railway
25. Corris Railway
26. County Donegal Railway
27. Dartmoor Railway
28. Dartmouth Steam Railway
29. Dean Forest Railway
30. Derwent Valley Light Railway
31. Downpatrick and County Down Railway
32. East Kent Railway
33. East Lancashire Railway
34. East Somerset Railway
35. Ecclesbourne Valley Railway
36. Eden Valley Railway
37. Elsecar Railway
38. Embsay and Bolton Abbey Railway
39. Epping Ongar Railway
40. Fairbourne Railway
41. Ffestiniog Railway
42. Fintown Railway
43. Foxfield Railway
44. Giant's Causeway and Bushmills Railway
45. Gloucestershire Warwickshire Railway
46. Great Central Railway
47. Great Central Railway (Nottingham)
48. Groudle Glen Railway
49. Gwili Railway
50. Helston Railway
51. Isle of Man Railways
52. Isle of Wight Steam Railway
53. Keighley and Worth Valley Railway
54. Keith and Dufftown Railway
55. Kent and East Sussex Railway
56. Kirklees Light Railway
57. Lakeside and Haverthwaite Railway
58. Lartigue Monorailway

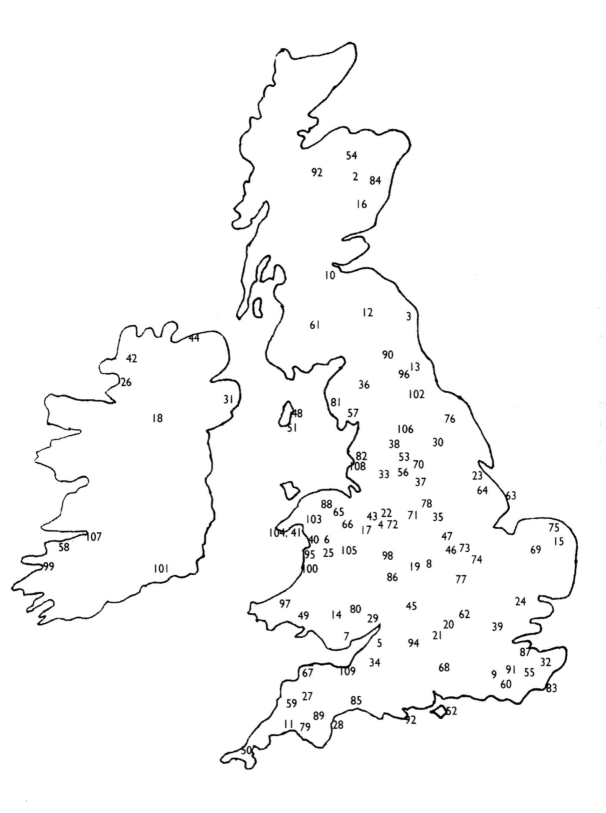

59. Launceston Steam Railway
60. Lavender Line
61. Leadhills and Wanlockhead Railway
62. Leighton Buzzard Railway
63. Lincolnshire Coast Light Railway
64. Lincolnshire Wolds Railway
65. Llanberis Lake Railway
66. Llangollen Railway
67. Lynton and Barnstaple Railway
68. Mid-Hants Railway
69. Mid-Norfolk Railway
70. Middleton Railway
71. Midland Railway Butterley
72. Moorland and City Railway
73. Mountsorrel Railway
74. Nene Valley Railway
75. North Norfolk Railway
76. North Yorkshire Moors Railway
77. Northampton and Lamport Railway
78. Peak Rail
79. Plym Valley Railway
80. Pontypool and Blaenavon Railway
81. Ravenglass and Eskdale Railway
82. Ribble Steam Railway
83. Romney, Hythe and Dymchurch Railway
84. Royal Deeside Railway
85. Seaton Tramway
86. Severn Valley Railway
87. Sittingbourne and Kemsley Light Railway
88. Snowdon Mountain Railway
89. South Devon Railway
90. South Tynedale Railway
91. Spa Valley Railway
92. Strathspey Steam Railway
93. Swanage Railway
94. Swindon and Cricklade Railway
95. Talyllyn Railway
96. Tanfield Railway
97. Teifi Valley Railway
98. Telford Steam Railway
99. Tralee and Dingle Railway
100. Vale of Rheidol Railway
101. Waterford and Suir Valley Railway
102. Weardale Railway
103. Welsh Highland Railway
104. Welsh Highland Heritage Railway
105. Welshpool and Llanfair Railway
106. Wensleydale Railway
107. West Clare Railway
108. West Lancashire Light Railway
109. West Somerset Railway

Part One

GETTING STARTED:
The 1950s

Portmadoc 1959. (Les Folkard/Online Transport Archive) (LF7-2)

Chapter 1

PIONEERS ON THE NARROW GAUGE

Bill Trinder's radio and gramophone shop in Banbury was where he used to get together with fellow railway enthusiasts in the late 1940s. Jim Russell, a photographer, was one, freelance writer L.T.C. (Tom) Rolt another. Among their discussions was the future of the Talyllyn Railway in mid-Wales. This narrow-gauge railway was unusual. It had escaped nationalisation in 1948, and was owned by a sole proprietor, Sir Henry Haydn Jones, MP for Merionethshire. Because of this it had survived when logic suggested it should have closed. The quarries it had been built to serve closed in 1946, but despite the fact that he was making a loss, Haydn Jones continued to run the trains for summer holiday-makers and a handful of local passengers. Rolt was in earnest about saving the Talyllyn, and he went with Trinder to visit Haydn Jones in the summer of 1949. Rolt had an established background in what would now be called heritage projects. He had been involved in the Vintage Sports Car Club, and in 1946 was a founder of the Inland Waterways Association to campaign for the greater use and better maintenance of the nation's canal system.[11] He had visited the Talyllyn Railway in the 1940s, and when he observed that the government had forgotten to nationalise it, the idea formed of it being maintained as a free and independent organisation. He was not the first to propose the idea of enthusiasts taking over a railway. Arthur E. Rimmer had published a letter in *Modern Tramway* in September 1941 suggesting that volunteers should revive the Welsh Highland Railway, which had closed in 1936. Further back, there had been attempts to revive the Southwold Railway in Suffolk as a tourist railway in 1929.[12] Rolt first articulated preserving the Talyllyn Railway in September 1949. An article was published in the *Birmingham Post* lamenting the sorry state of the Talyllyn and appealing for the government to do something. Rolt wrote a letter to say that, far from looking to the state, people should 'consider whether we might not be doing something about it ourselves'.[13] Other responses followed supporting saving the railway, including one from Owen Prosser, who suggested the formation of a society to preserve the railway.[14]

When Haydn Jones died in July 1950, Rolt and his friends were ready to act. Rolt proposed to the executors of Haydn Jones' estate that a voluntary society should run the railway and asked them to stay any decision on its future until the outcome of a public meeting he had called for 11 October 1950. This meeting in the Imperial Hotel, Birmingham, attracted a good attendance, boosted by front-page publicity in the *Birmingham Post*, which found the idea of volunteers running a railway most newsworthy. At the meeting there was enthusiastic support for the immediate formation of the Talyllyn Railway Preservation Society, and a committee was formed immediately, chaired by Trinder. The Imperial Hotel was demolished several years ago, so no plaque records its place in the foundation of the railway preservation movement.[15]

The committee was based in Birmingham, with prominent members of the Birmingham Loco Club on it, among them Pat Whitehouse and Pat Garland, who was a valuable recruit. He was a chartered accountant, who steered the society through financial technicalities, and set up Talyllyn Holdings Ltd as the vehicle for holding the railway company's shares. Talyllyn Holdings provided the legal means by which the railway continued operating under its original Act of Parliament, without the need to seek any new statutory authorisation. Its shares were owned by the preservation society, which made sure that the volunteers had absolute control and decision-making power. Not all preservation groups were able to emulate that, and had to accept the role of supporters' organisation to a railway owned by someone else.[16] Rolt and his colleagues were fortunate in gaining the support of Edward Thomas, the manager of the railway under Haydn Jones. Through him the co-operation and support of the Haydn Jones family was secured. He acted as representative of the family on the railway company's board in the preservation era. As a result of this support, the transfer to society ownership was relatively smooth, and the Talyllyn could be proud of its boast that it never closed. A talented team worked on the railway, including David

Curwen (Chief Mechanical Engineer), Pat Whitehouse and John Snell, a student spending his summer at Towyn before going to Oxford University. He was the fireman on the first train run by the society. Some among the Talyllyn pioneers developed other preserved railways. Whitehouse was one, as were Allan Garraway and Bill Harvey, who went on to the Ffestiniog Railway. Snell was the first chairman of the North Norfolk Railway, and, from 1972 to 1999, general manager of the Romney Hythe & Dymchurch Railway.[17]

The Talyllyn had been built in 1865 to bring slate from quarries at Bryn Eglwys in the inland mountains to the coast at Towyn (now spelled Tywyn). It was built to the unusual gauge of 2' 3". A passenger service was also operated, and the continuing use of the original locomotives and coaches had given the line the appearance of quaintness by the 1930s, when more tourists discovered it, sending picture postcards featuring the 'toy' railway. Nevertheless, it was a real railway, incorporated under Act of Parliament in the same way as the main-line railways. Its operation was no mean undertaking for a voluntary group.

The railway they took over was badly run down. Its track was in terrible condition. 'I had never seen a working line in such an appalling state', Alan Holmes recalls of his first visit in 1949. The office at the Wharf station at Towyn was a real museum piece. The two locomotives, built in 1866, were in a poor way. No.1 *Talyllyn* was now unsteamable, in need of a complete overhaul. That left No.2 *Dolgoch* to handle all the traffic; she astounded everybody by the way she soldiered on, but was in need of a good rest and recuperation. It was because of this poor state that Rolt thought the best chance for the railway lay in converting it to miniature gauge, drawing inspiration from the successful conversion of the Ravenglass & Eskdale Railway in Cumberland from a mineral line of 3ft gauge to a 15 inch gauge tourist line back in 1915. Rolt's friends persuaded him that this idea would not attract much support, and he dropped it before the public meeting was held in Birmingham.[18]

One of the first acts of the new society was a search for additional motive power. The surviving locomotives from the closed Corris Railway, of the same narrow gauge, were bought from British Railways at Swindon. That was not a simple solution, however, for one of the new engines, No.3, could not

ride the poor-quality track, and the second, No.4, needed a new boiler before she could relieve *Dolgoch* in the 1952 season.[19]

L.T.C. Rolt's own account of the first two seasons operating the preserved Talyllyn Railway portrays the pioneering spirit of those times: the multitudinous difficulties; the fortuitous encounters that brought forth generous donations of time and equipment; the good humour of the passengers: all added to the impression of an organisation characteristic of the British amateur tradition.[20] To the outsider it all seemed delightfully eccentric. This was a theme taken up by two films. *Railway with a Heart of Gold*, a lovingly romantic portrayal of the railway's work, was filmed in 1953 by the American Carson Davidson. That remained a little-known documentary for many years, whereas Ealing Studios' comedy, *The Titfield Thunderbolt*, which was shot in 1952, inspired by the publicity given to the Talyllyn pioneers, was on general release in cinemas, and a firm favourite on television

The Earl of Northesk was president of the Talyllyn Railway Preservation Society from 1952 to 1963, and was always willing to pose for his photograph. 27 September 1958.

(Gordon Brown)

thereafter. In that film a motley group of local people take over a standard-gauge branch line that is threatened with closure. The producers must have known something was in the air.

Although they were preserving a picturesque railway, whose ramshackle nature added to its quaintness, the volunteers of the society knew that they were engaged in a serious business. They were involving themselves in a new, growing tourist market. The society ran its first train on 14 May 1951, from Towyn to Rhydryrhonen. Services over the whole line began on 4 June. In that first season of preservation, lasting until 28 September, the Talyllyn carried 15,000 passengers, a record for the line, and this was exceeded the following year, when 22,000 passenger bookings were taken. All this was achieved in the short operating season of that time, from May to September, with a handful of staff (between five and seven) and a small number of volunteers, and with a severe shortage of motive power, poor track and other difficulties.[21]

Behind that achievement lay the serious volunteer effort keeping the track in order and the rolling stock in operation. Despite the number of times the poor track failed to support the trains, causing derailments, good fortune followed the society's efforts. Useful track was found, another locomotive was given to the line and army exercises were arranged in 1953 and 1954 to allow complete relaying of the track to be undertaken. Some of the quality was not good, but in 1953 the army laid as many sleepers in two weeks as the small band of volunteers would have managed in two years.[22]

Many of the railway's supporters were young, enthusiastic and, after years in wartime service, looking for adventure. The remoteness of the Talyllyn could cause problems. Most of the society members lived and worked in the Midlands, the North West, Yorkshire and London. James Boyd, of the North West area, hit upon the idea of organising regular working parties for team efforts and pooling transport to mid-Wales, and other regional groups soon followed. The working parties undertook maintenance and renewal of track, signalling, rolling stock and other less public parts of the railway. The society soon had a regional structure, and members remote from the railway took on home-work projects, and engaged in local fundraising and publicity. Until well into the 1960s, even the most local of model

Inside Pendre works, Talyllyn
Railway. The locomotive is No.4
Edward Thomas. 27 June 1959.

(Gordon Brown)

A working party of volunteers repairing a landslip on the embankment near Dolgoch, Talyllyn Railway. It took months of mainly manual effort to repair. Locomotive No.1 has brought a works train alongside. 23 August 1958.

(Gordon Brown)

railway shows was considered worth attending with a sales stand. It might seem very homespun from today's perspective, but it brought a sense of engagement with a worthwhile enterprise to the lowliest and most distant of supporters. In many ways the society set a pattern of activity that was to be emulated by almost every railway preservation society, at least in its early years, for the succeeding three decades.

The circumstances that led to the initial meeting being held in Birmingham proved fortuitous. The society's committee was made up mainly of men with local family businesses – Pat Whitehouse had a building firm, for example – and they mobilised their contacts in Midlands industry to provide goods to the nascent preservation society at little or no cost. Tom Hunt's foundry in Oldbury was one of these benefactors. So was John Wilkins, who supplied Servis washing machines and had bought the Fairbourne Railway in Wales in 1946. However, the 'Birmingham Committee' taking most business decisions could seem remote from those at work day by day on the railway, and there was friction between them and Rolt.[23]

The new venture expanded. The society had 700 members by the end of 1951. Traffic had almost doubled in volume by 1954, and trains were often full. Another locomotive was acquired, and, to cater for extra passengers, a second train set was introduced in the 1953 peak timetable. This put pressure on the supply of coaching stock, especially after the use of goods wagons for passengers was given up after a derailment. By 1956 the number of passenger bookings had reached 37,000, and the next year traffic almost doubled, boosted by publicity received from a television programme in May 1957.[25]

Chapter 2

MORE ACTION IN WALES

It might seem as if there was a natural, almost inevitable, progression in the moves that allowed the Talyllyn Railway to continue operating and become the first preserved railway. That was far from true. For some preservationists, the period charm characteristic of the Talyllyn was an attraction, but for others it repelled. The latter group saw that the Talyllyn could be a nightmare to keep going. Even after a few years of operation by the society, the condition of the track was far worse than that of the Ffestiniog Railway, which had been lying derelict since the line closed in August 1946.[26] This alone was enough for some, among them Allan Garraway, to divert their attention to the Ffestiniog.[27] This railway a few miles further north in Wales had many supporters who thought the line a more worthy candidate for preservation than the Talyllyn. It had historical claims as the first narrow-gauge railway, built in 1836; the first to use steam; and a pioneer in the use of articulated locomotives designed by Robert Fairlie, many of which survived. Although the line had closed, the Festiniog Railway Company was unable to dismantle it without a new Act of Parliament, so it was sitting more or less intact. By the early 1950s it needed a good deal of work to bring it back to working order, but it was still in better shape than the Talyllyn, because it had been built and operated to high standards.[28] The Ffestiniog always did think of itself as a main line in miniature, and was never allowed to decline into the ramshackle quaintness of the Talyllyn. The fact that the owners and manager wanted to see the line continue operating gave the Talyllyn the edge with a smooth transition to new ownership, whereas buying the Ffestiniog was more problematic.

The closure of the Ffestiniog Railway attracted the attention of enthusiasts, among whom the railway was probably better known than the Talyllyn. Soon there were proposals to take over the FR and reopen it, some time before the TRPS was formed. Like the Talyllyn, the Ffestiniog was an independent business.

There had been no trains for some years, but the railway company was still trading, receiving rent from property and business from the slate quarries at Blaenau Ffestiniog. Unlike the Talyllyn, there were many shareholders, and this caused difficulties for the preservationists trying to buy the shares. On the positive side, it meant that nobody else had gained a controlling interest before them, and the dispersed ownership and poverty of the company had stopped it seeking the statutory powers to demolish the line. However, the general manager of the FR, Robert Evans, did not have the immediate sympathy with preservationists that Edward Thomas had. Evans thought the difficulties in restoring the line would be too great for a preservation group. When the preservation society was founded he kept aloof for some time.[29]

The first approach to the Festiniog Railway Company seems to have been from J.K. Firth, a pupil at Radley College in October 1946. That was followed a few months later, in 1947, by another from Bill Broadbent and Michael Low, two employees of the London, Midland and Scottish Railway (LMS) at Crewe. Neither approach came to anything. Nor did that of James Boyd, who in 1950–51 tried to stir up Portmadoc Urban District Council to lead a revival of the Ffestiniog. The local authority was aware of the railway's potential for bringing in tourist traffic (it had carried 65,000 passengers in 1936), and had discussed saving the line with the company and other councils in 1946. However keen to have an operating railway, the council was short of money and smarting from having invested in the Welsh Highland Railway, and was not persuaded.[30]

Leonard Heath Humphrys was another teenaged railway enthusiast who was drawn to the plight of the Ffestiniog. When he heard in 1950 of what was happening on the Talyllyn, he wrote to other enthusiasts interested in the FR, to the railway company, to the railway press and to anyone whose interest in reviving the railway might be stimulated. Then he advertised a meeting to be held in Bristol on 8 September 1951, to 'forward the Festiniog Railway Preservation Scheme'. A dozen people came to this inaugural meeting, among them Allan Garraway and Vic Mitchell, who became leaders in the FR's management in preservation. There were some notable people among those who apologised and expressed interest, including George Dow and Pat Whitehouse. The meeting resolved to establish a Ffestiniog Railway society with the aim of reopening the line. Shortly afterwards Heath Humphreys dropped out of the organisation for a couple of years to undertake his national service, but others pressed forward to gain control of the railway company.

The leaders of this new society needed patience and persistence, for negotiations to take control of the Festiniog Railway Company were difficult. The fundraising ability of a small society was limited: money was coming in by the few pounds and shillings. Although the sums quoted for buying a controlling shareholding, at about £4,000, might seem modest, in these conditions for fundraising the prospect of achieving that was somewhat distant. Meanwhile, procedures had been initiated to allow the dismantling of the line. Without some substantial backing this railway might be lost. Salvation came in the form of Alan Pegler, a young businessman, who, with some associates, agreed to buy the majority shareholding in the company. This meant that the Ffestiniog society, unlike the Talyllyn's, was denied control of the railway it wished to run. Society members were upset, and the relationship between society and company remained sensitive for some time. The society's financial support was vital, as the railway lived a hand-to-mouth existence under new ownership. But the amount the society could put in was not enough to give it power over the company's board of directors. Some years later Pegler's shares were vested in a new Ffestiniog Railway Trust, to create a 'triangular' structure of company, trust and society. Nominally this gave greater control to the voluntary side of the railway.[31]

On 24 June 1954 ownership of the Festiniog Railway Company was transferred. Pegler, with the major interest, was elected chairman. Inspections by the railway inspectorate confirmed that the ways and works of the railway were basically sound. The biggest obstacle to immediate reopening was the condition of the locomotives and carriages. They had deteriorated considerably since the line was last operated. Finance for their repair and restoration was extremely limited. A Simplex petrol-engined locomotive with two coaches operated the first trains over the first mile to be reopened, from Portmadoc to Boston Lodge, starting on 29 July 1955. Intensive

Not a sight for today's safety officers to behold. Children inspect *Prince* at Tanybwlch, Ffestiniog Railway in April 1959.

(Gordon Brown)

work allowed the first steam locomotive, *Prince*, to run from the beginning of August. By the end of the first season, on 24 September, 11,371 people had made 20,000 journeys. Allan Garraway was appointed full-time manager. He held the post, regraded as general manager in 1958, until he retired in 1983. By then his clear-sighted management had overseen the rebuilding of the complete railway.[32]

Services to Minffordd, an additional mile's journey, started on 19 May 1956. In that season 38,629 passengers were carried, and the following year 53,000 after the line had been extended to Penrhyn in April. Traffic receipts at £3,000 were seventy per cent greater than those for 1956.[33] A further extension was made to Tanybwlch in 1958, formally opened on 23 May, making the railway 7½ miles long. At this point these regular extensions halted. The company's board decided it must consolidate operations while preparations were made for the deviation route around the Trawsfynedd power station, resisting the temptation, and the pressure from some of the enthusiastic supporters, for immediate additional extensions. Garraway was very firm on the need to pause: the availability of motive power and coaching stock needed stabilising, and he had a long list of sections of line that needed bringing up to standard. In the first season of working to Tanybwlch passenger journeys reached a new record of 60,323.[34]

A third Welsh narrow-gauge railway to become the subject of a preservation scheme was the Welshpool & Llanfair Light Railway. This line, of 2' 6" gauge, had opened in 1903 to provide passenger and goods services between two small towns in mid-Wales. It did that until the Great Western Railway, then owners of the line, withdrew the passenger service in 1931. The goods service continued, and even revived in wartime conditions after 1939. The line thus survived to be nationalised, but its future was far from secure. With the successful preservation of the Talyllyn as inspiration, Eric Cope, of the Narrow Gauge Railway Society, floated the idea of a society taking the Welshpool line over in 1952. British Railways informed him that the line was not immediately to close, but, when it did, they would not be averse to selling to preservationists. Cope did not receive such a positive response from Welshpool Council, however. By the time complete closure of the line came in 1956, when British Railways withdrew the remaining goods services, interest in preservation was already growing. There had been some correspondence on the issue in the railway press in 1955, and Llanfair Parish Council supported the idea of a voluntary group taking over the line. Further away, in London, William Morris canvassed support for a preservation society. He published a letter in the *Railway Magazine* appealing for support, organised a special train over the line and a meeting at Welshpool in September, out of which a preservation society was formed. By the time BR ran its final

The Earl at Llanfair Caereinion, Welshpool & Llanfair Railway, 26 August 1965.

(Les Folkard/Online Transport Archive) (LF111-26)

train on 5 November the society was on the way to formal constitution and in a position to negotiate.[35]

Such rapid moves did not presage a speedy transfer of the line to new ownership, for there were many obstacles. Whereas Llanfair Parish Council was keen for the railway to be taken over, there was less enthusiasm from the town councillors at Welshpool, who were not happy at the prospect of trains continuing to run through the town streets. This was the first preservation group that had to deal with British Railways, but, with the two previous examples, progress was reasonably smooth. By 1959 basic agreement had been reached with BR for a lease, society members were allowed access to undertake track clearance work, and the society was reconstituted in 1960 as a company limited by guarantee so that it could be the responsible body to operate the railway. By the end of that year the society was hoping to reopen the first section, from Llanfair to Heniarth, during 1961, but that proved optimistic. The society, like those on the Talyllyn and Ffestiniog, was penurious, trying to save a railway that many said had no prospects, being remote from holiday resorts and centres of population. Despite that, under the invaluable guidance of the chairman, Sir Thomas Salt, they made quiet progress. The return of the railway's two original locomotives, *The Earl* and *The Countess*, in 1961–62, gave the preservation group a fillip, and coaches and a diesel locomotive were acquired.

Reward came on 6 April 1963, when *The Earl* pulled the reopening train out of Welshpool. After that, regular weekend services operated four miles between Llanfair and Castle Careinion. In August 1963 Welshpool Borough Council took over the track through the town; after a final special train along the route, the track was lifted. When the railway finally extended regular operation to Welshpool, it was to Raven Square on the edge of town, not the main station.[36]

Chapter 3

NEW STANDARDS: THE BLUEBELL AND THE MIDDLETON

The story of preserved railways is one of ever-expanding horizons. Saving a couple of little narrow-gauge railways might have been enough, and there were many who were satisfied with that. But in the 1950s there were already standard-gauge branch lines being closed or threatened with closure both by British Railways and industrial owners, and enthusiasts thought that there should be no reason why the lessons of the Talyllyn and Ffestiniog should not be applied to these lines. By the end of the 1950s the first societies had been founded to preserve standard-gauge steam railways. Branch-line preservation introduced a new element. The Welsh narrow-gauge lines had been entities in themselves, whereas the Bluebell Railway and its successors had to create a new operating organisation, even though some harked back to once-independent companies.

The most high-profile of these preservation schemes was the Bluebell Railway, born out of a *cause celebre* in the annals of railway closure. In 1954 British Railways announced that they would close the railway from Lewes to East Grinstead, Sussex. There was fierce opposition from local residents, but closure went ahead on 28 May 1955. The opponents refused to give in. They mounted legal challenges to keep open the 'Bluebell line', as it had been christened by a local journalist (that was not the first use of the term: 'Bluebell and Primrose' line had existed before the First World War and the campaigners regularly used that name). Leading the protesters was Miss Madge Bessemer, granddaughter of Henry Bessemer, inventor of the steel-making process named after him. She discovered in the original Act of Parliament authorising construction of the line a clause stating that four trains were to be run daily over the route, and that these could not be withdrawn without further parliamentary sanction. No later legislation affecting the operators of the line had repealed that clause. Miss Bessemer successfully challenged BR with failure to fulfil its statutory obligations. The line was reopened and operated by BR with bad grace and a minimal, inconvenient service until the British Transport Commission obtained a new Act repealing the clause in the original legislation. This allowed the line to be closed from 17 March 1958. The immense national publicity surrounding the closure meant that the final train consisted of nine overcrowded coaches instead of the usual one or two.[37]

It was perhaps not surprising that preservation proposals followed, but the audacity of four teenaged students – Chris Campbell, David Dallimore, Martin Eastland and Alan Sturt – in calling a public meeting in March 1959 does seem remarkable. The founding generation of railway preservationists in the 1950s and early 1960s was, however, predominantly young. Reasoning that what had worked on the Welsh narrow gauge could work in Sussex, this quartet founded the Lewes and East Grinstead Railway Preservation Society.[38] Bernard Holden, a railwayman working at Liverpool Street, was appointed chairman, as someone over 21 was needed. The Bluebell name coined by journalists and closure protesters stuck, and the preservationists soon adopted it: the society was renamed the Bluebell Railway Preservation Society, and the business entity Bluebell Railway Limited was set up in February 1960. The original intention was to reopen the whole of the route, and to run a commercial service using one of the former Great Western Railway diesel railcars. These plans soon foundered. Once the furore over the original closure had died down, the new group found there was little local enthusiasm for a revived railway service – in contrast to many later preservation schemes, which had local supporters at their heart. Failure to raise enough funds to buy the whole line sealed the fate of the original scheme. Instead, the line was to be run as a steam museum railway over the portion of the route between Horsted Keynes and Sheffield Park.

British Railways at Waterloo had no experience of people wanting to buy railway branches, and did not take the society seriously when they approached, their opinion swayed by the leaders' youth. Once this scepticism had been overcome, dealings proceeded remarkably smoothly. The freehold of the line was offered for £34,000; when it became clear that such a sum would take some raising, a lease for five years, at a rent of £2,250 a year, was agreed in December 1959, with the purchase option kept open. This allowed the line to be brought into operation quickly, with a Light Railway Order granted in July 1960, meaning the society could run its first trains on 7 August between Sheffield Park and Bluebell Halt, south of Horsted Keynes, a distance of five miles. From then until the end of October 1960 trains were run every weekend. The hand-to-mouth nature of the railway was evident in that there were only two coaches available and two locomotives, acquired not long before reopening, in contrast to most later preserved railways that had built up a yard full of locomotives and rolling stock by the time trains ran. The locomotives were former London, Brighton and South Coast Railway (LBSCR) 'Terrier' tank engine No.55 *Stepney* and South Eastern and Chatham Railway (SECR) class P No.323, given the name *Bluebell*. Trains were run with an engine at each end as there were no run-round loops. Despite all the handicaps, traffic in that short operating season reached more than 15,000 passengers, far more than expected. The close season was spent in acquiring additional stock: four former Metropolitan Railway coaches dating from 1898–1900, and another P class locomotive, No.31027, to which the name *Primrose* was applied. Enthusiasts complained about the inauthentic names given to the locomotives, but they were popular with the general public, and the money they paid over was vital to the society.[39]

The *Railway Magazine* had noted that the Bluebell's greater accessibility to London than the Welsh railways 'should go far towards stimulating interest in its preservation'. But these were not easy times for raising money, and the railway society continued to be strapped for cash. The preservation fund raised enough for the society to buy a few more locomotives and coaches, including London and South Western Railway (LSWR) tank engine No.488, but shortage of funds meant the society couldn't buy some items it hoped to acquire, such as an LBSCR class K 2-6-0, which had been kept aside for it. Other locomotives did eventually come to the line, after being kept aside by sympathetic railway officials: a North London Railway tank engine was one.[40] Traffic receipts from the first season yielded £1,136 19s 5d, with additional contributions of £297 from refreshment sales and £255 from the bookstall, rather less than the rent for the line. The rental under the lease agreement increased to about £3,000 a year from 1963, when the railway was granted full access to Horsted Keynes station. Meanwhile, the society was trying to raise the funds to buy the line. When the original five-year lease ended in 1965, British Railways had changed policy and would not grant an extension. It was purchase or nothing, as far as BR were concerned, and they threatened to close the line. The Bluebell management persuaded BR that such a move would reflect badly on them, and an agreement was reached for a down payment of the £23,500 the Bluebell had in their purchase fund, the remainder to be paid in quarterly instalments of £1,000 over five years. By 1968 the society had raised £20,000, but by then the purchase price agreed with BR had been increased to £43,500. However, with this purchase agreement, the prospects for the Bluebell felt more secure.[41]

Despite the difficulties the railway grew rapidly. It carried 91,000 passengers in its first full season in 1961. For a brief period the railway had a connection with British Railways,

A quiet afternoon at Horstead Keynes, Bluebell Railway in April 1966 as No.2650 waits with its train.

which allowed it to run its trains into the main station at Horsted Keynes in 1962. The following year, however, BR services to Horsted Keynes were withdrawn, leaving the Bluebell isolated again, but able to take the whole station on lease. Traffic was building up: by 1965 there were 200,000 passenger journeys.[42]

The museum aspect of the railway was taken very seriously. A preservation committee was set up in 1961 to develop a preservation strategy, and not to have an ad hoc assemblage of locomotives, rolling stock and equipment. Although not every aspect could be adhered to, such an approach has stood the line in good stead. The railway acquired one of the best collections of locomotives and stock with southern connections. A founding principle of the line was that it should be a steam-only operation. It was not until 2007 that this was relaxed, when a diesel locomotive was brought in for works trains in connection with the northern extension.

Its public profile was higher, but the Bluebell was pipped to the post by the Middleton Railway for the title of first preserved

The Plymouth Railway Circle booked a special train on the Bluebell Railway on 18 April 1972. Locomotive No.3217 took the train and is seen at Horsted Keynes.

(Les Folkard/Online Transport Archive) (LF266-71)

standard-gauge railway. The Middleton ran its inaugural passenger train on 20 June 1960, a few weeks before the Bluebell opened. The train was an event of Leeds University's rag week and was formed of the odd combination of a former LMS diesel shunter and a double-deck tram from the Swansea & Mumbles line. The Middleton was the first of another important strand in the development of preserved railways – the industrial railway. Although it was a public railway, which could trace its origins to the first Act of Parliament authorising railway construction, it was relatively unknown, for its business had been as a freight railway serving the industries of Hunslet, in Leeds. The Act of Parliament was passed in 1758, giving the line the claim to be the oldest railway in continuous operation in the country. It was the site of Matthew Murray's experiments with locomotives using Blenkinsop's rack and pinion mechanism. On historical grounds alone it had a strong case for preservation. These impeccable credentials were not enough to guarantee survival. What really saved the Middleton Railway was that it found a doughty champion in Dr Youell, of Leeds University.

During the nineteenth century, the Middleton Railway was owned and operated by the local collieries. When the coal industry was nationalised in 1948, the railway passed into the hands of the Middleton Fireclay Company, which leased the surviving sections to the National Coal Board. As well as serving its own collieries, the NCB provided freight services for other businesses from their private sidings to the main railway network. Shortly after bicentenary celebrations were held for the line in 1958, however, the NCB decided the line was losing money and should close. Only a short section to Middleton Park Colliery would be retained. At this point Dr Youell stepped in, with members of Leeds University Railway Society. They decided late in 1959 to preserve the railway, which would also be a home for the society's tramcar collection. Dr Youell and the students formed the Middleton Railway Preservation Society in January 1960. Their initiative attracted very little public support or publicity, even in the railway press, and no backing from their university. They were fortunate to win the cooperation and support of some of the businesses along the line and of British Railways. Two of the businesses, Clayton, Son & Co. and Robinson & Birchill Ltd, bought the trackbed of the railway,

handing it over to the society to operate. After a very short interval, therefore, the railway reopened with the operation of a temporary passenger service in June 1960, and the regular freight services were relaunched in September. Four firms with private sidings provided the bulk of the traffic, mostly of steel and scrap metal. The Middleton thus became the only railway operated entirely by volunteers providing a year-round freight service. Traffic carried in 1961 amounted to about 12,500 tons. About 10,000 tons a year were being carried in the late 1960s. As the revived railway became established, additional sections were reinstated, such as the Moor End branch in 1964 to connect with an additional factory.[43]

Students made up the bulk of the volunteers at first, but others joined, helping to maintain services during holidays. The Middleton Railway introduced 'visitors' days' in the mid-1960s

The yard at Middleton Railway on a miserable February afternoon in 1971. Behind stacks of rail, steel and timber stand three of the railway's locomotives. The nearest, Sentinel No.54, was one of the first acquisitions of the preserved railway, arriving in 1961.

on the first Sunday of each month between April and September, when the public could see operations. As freight traffic declined during the late 1960s, the Middleton turned again to passenger services. The track between Hunslet Moor and Middleton Park was rebuilt to higher standard for services to begin running from 30 June 1969. Clayton, the last freight customer, closed in 1983, since when the Middleton has been a passenger-only railway, with headquarters at a much-enhanced Moor Park station.[44]

The Middleton Railway has remained at heart an industrial line and has inspired other industrial preservation projects, such as the Foxfield Railway in Staffordshire and the Tanfield Railway, County Durham. Even before the Bluebell had opened, a society had been formed to preserve parts of the Midland & Great Northern Railway. In the years that followed, the number of projects to preserve lines closed by British Railways grew steadily.

Part Two

GETTING ESTABLISHED:
The 1960s and 1970s

Selling tickets, Bala Lake.

Chapter 4

EXPANSION AGAINST THE ODDS, 1960s AND 1970s

Once the Bluebell Railway had shown it was possible to reopen a line closed by British Railways, the number of preservation proposals grew rapidly. At times it seemed as though hardly a branch line was closed without someone proposing that it should be preserved. Some were concerned: complaints about the 'proliferation' of preservation schemes were numerous (see below, p. 264-7). There were certainly plenty of branch lines available, for this was the time of closure on a large scale under Dr Beeching's rationalisation of BR. Not only branch lines: some long-distance, regional cross-country and main line routes were closed, such as the Midland & Great Northern routes in Norfolk, the Waverley route in the Scottish borders and the Great Central main line. Many of them did not go quietly. There were angry protests and campaigns to 'save our railway'. They hoped to restore regular services, and many preservation schemes arose. The end of steam on BR prompted activity to save locomotives, and a ban on the operation of privately owned steam locomotives on the main line forced enthusiasts to concentrate on their own railways.

Despite this activity, progress, in terms of getting new projects to the operating stage, was slow. Members of preservation societies had to be patient while negotiating the financial terms, raising the money and then obtaining Light Railway Orders. Persistence and enthusiasm carried them through. Tom Salmon, one of the founding group of the North Yorkshire

TABLE 1 Preservation projects and openings, 1960-1979	
Railway	Opening, first section
Welshpool & Llanfair	1963
Dart Valley	1967
Leighton Buzzard	1968
Keighley & Worth Valley	1968
Chasewater	1970
Severn Valley	1970
Seaton Tramway	1970
Sittingbourne & Kemsley	1971
Isle of Wight	1971
Llanberis	1971
Bala Lake	1972
Dart Valley, Kingswear	1972
North Yorkshire Moors	1973
Lakeside & Haverthwaite	1973
Kent & East Sussex	1973
North Norfolk	1973
Battlefield	1973
West Somerset	1976
Bowes	1976
Mid-Hants	1977
Nene Valley	1977
Battlefield	1978
Strathspey	1978
Swanage	1979
Alford Valley	1979
Bristol Suburban (Avon Valley)	1979

Moors Railway, led, it was said, 'a society with very little money and only a surge of local enthusiasm.'[45] At the end of the 1960s the number of operational preserved lines had not reached double figures. Only two standard-gauge lines were opened during the 1960s to join the Bluebell and Middleton. The following ten years saw a more than doubling in the number of lines operating, as projects launched in the 1960s, some even the 1950s, came to fruition. More preservation projects were launched during the 1970s, but for a while growth in the preservation movement was slowing with fewer new groups joining the Association of Railway Preservation Societies.[46]

Large numbers of projects were abandoned (table 2). Whereas most put in a fleeting appearance in the local and railway press, some had a high profile for a while. The Westerham Valley Railway in Kent was one of the first to follow in the footsteps of the Bluebell. It launched on 3 March 1962, and gained a strong local following for plans involving a commuter service supported by weekend steam trains.[47] The Hayling Island was a celebrity branch line among enthusiasts for its long-lived 'Terrier' class locomotives hauling trains across the wooden viaduct to the island. After the line closed, the Hayling Light Railway Society

TABLE 2
Some unsuccessful preservation projects, 1960-1979

Railway	Location	Date
Southwold	Suffolk	1960
Westerham Valley	Dunton Green –Westerham, Kent	1962-65
Hayling Island	Sussex	1965-66
Weston Clevedon & Portishead	Somerset	1950s
Clevedon & Yatton	Somerset	1965
Vectrail	Isle of Wight	1966-70
Longmoor	Liss, Hampshire	1968-71
South Devon	Moretonhampstead	1959
Kingsbridge	Devon	1963
Somerset & Dorset		
Swansea & Mumbles	South Wales	1960s-1970s
Sandy & Potton	Bedfordshire	1968-69
Stour Valley	Sudbury – Haverhill, Essex –Suffolk	1968. Became East Anglian Rail Museum
Lowestoft-Yarmouth	Norfolk	1960s
Horsham & Guildford	Surrey	1965
Bristol-Warmley		1970
North Devon	Barnstaple – Ilfracombe	1975
Meon Valley	Hampshire	1961-64
Rushden	Northamptonshire	
Jersey Railway	Channel Islands	

achieved prominence with plans to revive the line, electrified and using former Blackpool tram No.11, which was seen by many parked in a siding by the main line until the project was abandoned.[48] Preservation of the Longmoor Military Railway at Liss in Hampshire was supported by the Association of Railway Preservation Societies and leading members of the railway preservation movement, such as Allan Garraway, and a lease was signed in April 1970. Local residents, district councils and the MP for Petersfield, Miss Joan Quennell, campaigned against the project on traffic and planning grounds, and their opposition eventually put the Ministry of Defence off the idea.[49]

Perhaps some projects were too ambitious and deserved to fail. Several of the projects arising out of campaigns to save the local branch line wanted to provide local transport for commuters, shoppers and others, to replace the service withdrawn by BR, and this proved beyond their reach. The Horsham & Guildford Direct Railway Society opened negotiations with BR for the 15½ mile route from Guildford via Bramley and Slinfold to Horsham. 'To make the line a paying proposition,' the society announced, it hoped to run 'a fast modern diesel car to serve the commuter and shopping public on weekdays', and there would be a steam service at weekends. 'It was felt that a private society, able to operate the line under a Light Railways Act, would enjoy more flexibility of operation,' the statement added. Unfortunately, these ideas proved too ambitious, and this society soon disappeared.[50] The Clevedon & Yatton Railway Society, formed in 1965, proposed to become a 'new operating authority' for a branch line that had not yet closed, but was under threat. The society took seriously the government's policy published in a white paper, *Transport Policy*, and the subsequent Transport Act 1968, which made provision for local authorities to provide community support for railway services. Real experience proved different, and soon both branch line and railway society closed.[51]

Some of the railways that did get established had similar ambitions. The West Somerset Railway was to run diesel commuter services into Taunton, and the Swanage Railway aimed to run to Wareham. Both had to cut back their ambitions. Those railways that started running faced very rocky early years. Both the North Yorkshire Moors Railway and West

Somerset Railway, now regarded as 'premier league' heritage railways, were not far from folding at times in the 1970s.

Such experiences underlined the fact that these were not easy times to establish a railway preservation project. In the first place, raising money was an uphill struggle. Almost the only source of large-scale funding until the mid-1970s was a benefactor with deep pockets. There were some – businessmen, mainly – who put money into new railways, but most preservation groups had to accumulate funds through all the usual means, such as sales stands and sponsored walks. Inflation, meanwhile, ate away the value of funds before the societies had a chance to spend them, and it also meant that the asking price for the trackbed might be raised while the funds were being painstakingly accumulated. There could be compensations, as the Keighley & Worth Valley Railway found when it agreed to buy its line by hire-purchase: inflation made the repayments easier.[52]

Gaining a lease for a base station on the railway to be preserved was a major achievement. It showed the group was gaining the confidence of British Railways, and maybe other authorities. The society could now hold open days, which attracted the public and boosted funds. More than a thousand people came to the seven events held by the nascent Dean Forest Railway Preservation Society in 1972, which put the group on the map.[53]

Preservation and prosperity undoubtedly go hand in hand, and many of the branch lines then being closed were in areas not at that time particularly prosperous. Many were then off the tourist map. That made it difficult to build up the core of local support, both financial and of voluntary workers, which was usually essential to get a preservation scheme off the ground. The small number of preserved railways in Scotland demonstrates this. Sparse population in rural areas and declining industries in many other districts meant that the progress made by the Scottish Railway Preservation Society in the early 1960s was a major achievement. From its foundation in 1961 the intention was to have a working railway on which the society's collections of locomotives and stock could run. However, with modest support compared with some railways in more affluent parts of England, the society had to concentrate on preserving historic locomotives and coaches before they were lost, deferring the acquisition of a railway until the late 1970s. The Welsh railways, in contrast, built support, partly because of their particular character as narrow-gauge lines, and partly because, although in the farther west of the country, they were not so inaccessible from the Midlands and north west of England, especially as roads were improved. For the society members certainly, making the extra effort to journey for volunteering weekends and holidays allowed them to build a close camaraderie.

Officialdom was not always kind to railway preservationists. Despite the example of the Talyllyn Railway's success as a voluntary organisation, there remained a persistent view among BR management and officials in councils and Whitehall that railway preservation groups were just grown men wanting to play trains. Or not so grown men, for youth and enthusiasm for new projects often went hand in hand. Their view was understandable. In particular, they worried that a preserved railway might fail, and they would be left to pick up the pieces.[54] However, BR's lack of enthusiasm did thwart a number of preservation schemes, and a further frustration was a lack of consistency, with differences of approach between local and regional management.

In 1959 R.J. Cottrell wrote to the railway press announcing plans, through a newly formed South Devon Railway Preservation Society, to operate the recently closed branch from Newton Abbot to Moretonhampstead, and, 'if finances and circumstances permit', the neighbouring Teign valley line. Nothing further was heard of these plans, however, as BR didn't offer support. Many from the South Devon society next turned their attention to the Kingsbridge branch. Here, T.W.E. Roche, a writer on railways, was leading efforts to preserve the railway, which was closed in September 1963. With the backing of both Kingsbridge and Salcombe urban district councils, and a willingness to negotiate terms from the Western Region's divisional management in Plymouth, there looked to be a future for the 'Primrose Line', under which name it was already being promoted. The Western Region's central management in Paddington were not party to any of this, and while Roche was building local support, they had already appointed demolition contractors, who set to work in November 1963, only two months after the line closed. That dealt a body blow to the local preservationists. Many went on to join the association supporting the Dart Valley Railway on the Buckfastleigh line, continuing later with the independent South Devon Railway.[55]

British Railways was not always a willing seller, but even when it was co-operative, it was in all cases obliged to seek the highest price for any land it disposed of. That highest price was often determined by development potential beyond its use as a railway. Many a preservation group was thus faced with a price for the trackbed far higher than a small number of mainly local people could raise in the time demanded. This happened to the group attempting to buy the Chasewater branch in the 1960s.[56]

This was a period when the popular tide, both inside and outside of government, was flowing strongly in favour of road transport, and railway preservationists suffered from the effects of this as much as the management of the national network. Private car ownership was growing rapidly – forty-five per cent of British households had a car by 1969; so, too, was freight traffic on the roads. There was a strong lobby advocating the closure of railways, even main lines, and converting them to roads. Politicians were not prepared to go as far as that, but certainly were keen on modernisation; they were inclined to pander to a 'car-owning democracy', and there was a consensus on the need for new roads to meet growth in traffic. State expenditure on road-building increased, resulting most prominently in the nearly 700 miles of motorway built during the decade following the opening of the first one in 1959. Trunk roads were rebuilt and widened into dual carriageways, towns bypassed and new routeways developed. Railways, with their bridges and crossings, were seen as an obstacle to road improvement. Officials in the Ministry of Transport and local authorities were likely to view a closed railway more for its potential as a new road than for any value it might have if it was reopened as a local transport link, or as a tourist business. Local economic benefits, such as employment, were reckoned to favour the road more than the railway.

This did not necessarily amount to an anti-rail bias in government, as was often alleged at the time and later, but the Treasury was consistent in keeping deficits and costs of investment in nationalised industries under control. The closure of unprofitable railway lines was a major part of that. This did not work to the advantage of railway preservation, as the revival of a closed branch line went against the modernisation and deficit-reducing policies. The Westerham Valley Railway Association was one group that came up against these policy preferences. This branch line in Kent had been seriously losing money, and closed in 1961 after a bruising fight between ministry and locals. The association's proposals to revive the line did not convince BR, which was unwilling to lease the line, nor government. Officials did not actively force the preservationists out, but Kent County Council's demand for £26,215 for a bridge to accommodate the preserved railway put paid to preservationists' hopes, 'finally destroying all hope of operating a viable scheme', as the Vice-Chairman of the Westerham Valley Railway Association subsequently claimed.[57] Hopes of preserving the Hayling Island line were also scuppered by road improvements, and the Dart Valley and the Lakeside & Haverthwaite had their ambitions cut short by priority given to road schemes. The prospect of finding £200,000 to bridge the new bypass road was beyond the Lakeside & Haverthwaite, and the railway had to settle for being cut off from the main network. The effect that reopening the Kent & East Sussex might have on local roads was a major factor in the refusal of the first application for a Light Railway Order. Officials at the Ministry of Transport had early on raised concerns about the level crossings on the route, and their attitude, as much as any political bias on the part of the Minister, probably influenced the outcome.

Central government was unlikely to encourage or promote railway preservation. Labour governments were not naturally sympathetic towards private enterprise enthusiasts taking on a line cast off by the state enterprise. That might appeal more to the Conservatives, but in government the party on the whole leaned towards road transport. Government was, however, going to accept the rules as they stood then. Lord Lindgren, Joint Parliamentary Secretary, Ministry of Transport, told the House of Lords in 1965, 'I can give an unequivocal assurance that he [the Minister of Transport] is very ready to consider applications for Light Railway Orders.'[58] Supporters of the Kent & East Sussex Railway found that unconvincing. In 1968 a group of businessmen, led by John Snell, Patrick Whitehouse and others, made an offer to buy the Vale of Rheidol narrow-gauge railway. The line arguably did not fit into a steam-free British Railways, but ideologically this was not a time to transfer a going concern from the state business. Another approach to BR in 1976 was likewise unsuccessful.[59] It was a time, too, of trade union opposition to anything that smacked of private enterprise at the expense of a nationalised undertaking. The National Union of Railwaymen's antagonism towards the attempts of the West Somerset Railway to reach Taunton was the most high-profile example of that. It was a longstanding attitude. When the Royal Engineers undertook some tracklaying on the Talyllyn in 1953 as a training exercise, Vic Feather of the TUC cried 'unfair to railway workers', even though there were none to be displaced on the TR. It needed representations from the railway society's president, the Earl of Northesk, to persuade the TUC to calm down.[60]

It might appear that dealing with public authorities was an uphill struggle, but railways did achieve some successes, and there were areas of positive and fruitful contact. The Middleton Railway in 1970 was threatened by a new M621 road, which would cut across the railway. Dr Youell forcefully reminded the civil servants that the Middleton had a right of way guaranteed by its 1758 Act of Parliament, and a bridge had to be built to accommodate the railway. Pressure on the sites occupied by some of the stations was a problem for many railways; again local authorities did not really understand what the railway preservation groups were about, and thus were not always on

It might have been a car park: Minehead station of the West Somerset Railway. Much has happened since 2000 when this photograph was taken, with new catering facilities and a locomotive turntable installed.
(Chris Marsh)

their side. Somerset County Council proposed to buy Minehead station for a car park, even though it was officially a supporter of the West Somerset Railway. A lease agreement between railway and council saved the site as a station. At Pickering the UDC wanted to turn the town's station into a car park, even issuing the compulsory purchase order. The North Yorkshire Moors Railway was supported with objections from the county council, the Council for the Protection of Rural England, and others, and this forced a public inquiry that favoured retaining the station. Reorganisation of local government in 1974 came to the rescue, for the new Ryedale District Council that succeeded Pickering UDC was more supportive of the railway coming to the town. Permission to use the station was granted later that year.[61]

The Severn Valley Railway faced objections to its application for a Light Railway Order from Shropshire County Council on the grounds that keeping the line open with its bridges would stop the council improving the roads in the area. In particular they had plans for a bypass at Bridgnorth. Solicitors for the British Railways Board, making the application for the Order, took a strong line against the council, describing their objection as 'premature as well as irrelevant and inappropriate'. The Ministry of Transport deferred granting the Light Railway Order, despite the recommendation from the inspector holding the public inquiry, citing the potential conflict between railway and improvements to the bypass road. The Minister this time was well-disposed towards the railway and referred the matter back to the railways and local authorities to resolve.[62]

Some public authorities gave greater support to railway preservationists. In mid-Wales, the success of the narrow-gauge railways and their contribution to tourism won over the local authorities so much that Merionethshire County Council initiated moves to create a new railway. Having bought the trackbed of the Bala to Morfa Mawddach line, the county proposed building a narrow-gauge railway along part of it.[63] The Isle of Wight County Council was similarly supportive of preserving parts of the Cowes line. The Peterborough Development Corporation became an active partner with Peterborough Locomotive Society's proposals for preserving the branch line to Wansford as what became the Nene Valley Railway. In another local-authority initiative, Derby Corporation museum set up the Midland Railway Project Group to preserve material connected with that railway. Alongside that was the aim of developing a short working museum railway, and attention focused on the Ambergate to Pye Bridge line. This project developed over the years into the Midland Railway at Butterley.[64]

For the railways already running, the 1960s were promising. Traffic was growing strongly, for many by twofold or threefold. The Bluebell Railway had reached 200,000 passengers by 1965; ten years later the figure was more than 273,000. The narrow-gauge railways were breaking records almost every year, as the Talyllyn's results [Figure 1] demonstrate. The Ffestiniog's traffic doubled between 1961 and 1967, rising from 109,000 passengers to 220,000, this before the extension to Dduallt opened. From 10,000 passengers in its first year, 1963, the Welshpool & Llanfair was carrying 37,600 by 1970. All of these railways were planning for expansion to cope with the demand. New coaches and locomotives were built for the Ravenglass & Eskdale. The Ffestiniog and Talyllyn both had extensive programmes for building new bogie coaches that could carry the increasing numbers of passengers in greater comfort and would help preserve their original stock by using it less often. Shortages of motive power led the Talyllyn to consider ordering a new locomotive before finding a second-hand one that could be converted to their needs. The Ffestiniog found some relief in the

FIGURE 1

Talyllyn Railway traffic figures, 1960-1970

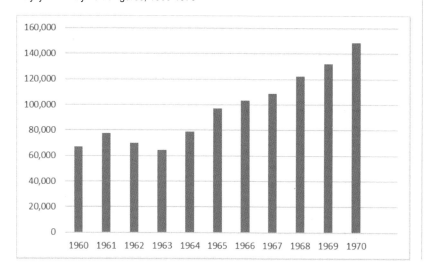

locomotives acquired from the Penrhyn quarry railway and *Mountaineer*, bought from a society member. Even with these, by the end of the decade the railway's board was considering reports on the need for new locomotives, and recommendations that searches should be made overseas. The Welshpool & Llanfair had already imported additional stock and motive power from Austria, a result of a fruitful relationship with the Zillertalbahn. They also brought locomotives and stock from Sierra Leone. New timetables allowed more trains to be run. Alongside these developments the railways were making improvements to their stations, shops and cafés to cope with increasing traffic.[65]

An editorial in the *Railway Magazine* for June 1973 gave an upbeat assessment of 'the remarkable and continuing growth of railway preservation in its various forms'.[66] Three new railways had opened that year: the Lakeside & Haverthwaite, the North Yorkshire Moors Railway and the Paignton to Kingswear line. However, things were not quite so rosy. The growth of traffic on operating railways slowed: from more than ten per cent a year in the late 1960s, 1971 saw growth of only five per cent. By 1973–74 slower growth had turned into decline as inflation, economic crises – such as the miners' strikes and the oil crisis of 1973 – and the advent of cheap package holidays overseas, all worked to the disadvantage of the preserved railways. Decline set in on the Talyllyn from 1973, and on the Ffestiniog traffic peaked in 1974 at about 400,000 passengers. It was not perhaps the best time for new railways to open: 'in these difficult economic times the directors will obviously be watching the situation with concern', it was observed as the West Somerset opened in 1976. Traffic figures of more than 50,000 passengers for 1976 and 1977 were encouraging, but covering the running costs was more difficult. The Severn Valley had a similarly shaky start, with fluctuating traffic and financial returns in the late 1970s, and the NYMR had difficulty meeting its bills in the first years. The Keighley & Worth Valley Railway was more fortunate: with the boost provided by its role in *The Railway Children* film, it welcomed its one-millionth passenger in 1977.[67]

Recession in the early 1980s resulted in further decline in both traffic and revenue. Not even the opening of the extension to Blaenau Ffestiniog could stop traffic on the Ffestiniog from going gradually downwards during these years. Expansion plans were deferred, even abandoned. The Talyllyn cancelled the order for its next new coach, No.24, and its recently acquired locomotive languished for several years before its rebuilding was completed. The rate of increase in the numbers of paid staff was held back, at least for a while, as the boards of the companies critically examined their finances. Even with large amounts of voluntary labour, salaries for staff could take up to half of the expenditure on the revenue account.

Inflation in the 1970s was high, at an annual rate in double figures in many years. Costs as a result rose rapidly, especially the cost of staff. In 1973 the staff on the Ffestiniog Railway claimed an increase of wages of twenty-five per cent. The settlement was nearer fifteen per cent, but regular increases on this scale, and the management's effort taken up in reaching agreements, necessarily strained finances.[68] Fares were increased annually, and often these counterbalanced the decline in traffic so that in most years net receipts from ticket sales rose. That was not always enough to match the increase in costs, however. Deficits and borrowings were likely to increase.[69]

Despite the poor economic prospects, the railway preservation movement pressed on. The writer of the editorial in June 1973's *Railway Magazine* could feel justified in looking forward to the existing lines flourishing. 'They should consolidate,' he wrote, 'and at the same time maintain a pioneering spirit and work towards fresh goals.' He could even look forward to new groups setting up when many people argued that there was no room for any more. There was good reason for such an optimistic view, for railway preservation was making considerable progress. Operating railways were consolidating, by improving the track and facilities. Relaying of track and improvements to stations meant that by the end of the 1970s the lines that had been taken over by the Ffestiniog and Talyllyn in the 1950s had been almost rebuilt. On all railways new buildings were needed. The Bluebell showed the way many followed when in 1972 it launched a project to build a new workshop and running shed at Sheffield Park. This would be a works capable of handling major overhaul and restoration work. Building started in 1975, and the first locomotive overhauled there was completed at the end of the following year. The pioneering spirit was still there as the Ffestiniog opened its extension to Dduallt in 1968 and planned

The first locomotive David Shepherd bought for preservation, No.92203 *Black Prince* at the Gloucestershire Warwickshire Railway in 2005.

for progress to Blaenau Ffestiniog, and the Talyllyn extended to Nant Gwernol.[70]

At the same time as the railway projects were being developed, there was a parallel effort to save large numbers of locomotives, coaches and wagons, withdrawn by the modernising British Railways and industrial users. The railway preservation groups were involved in buying locomotives for their own lines, but many were bought by other individuals and preservation groups. The interactions between preservation schemes for locomotives and railways could be complex, sometimes confused, at times difficult, but most often fruitful. Most locomotive preservation was not directly connected with a railway project. The individuals, syndicates and preservation societies involved usually first targeted the locomotives they thought worthy of saving. Finding a home for them came second. However, the need for somewhere for preserved locomotives to run was the genesis of at least two railways.

The Nene Valley Railway was one. In the first place there was the purchase by Reverend Richard Paten of standard 4-6-0 No.73050 in 1968. He brought this locomotive to his home town of Peterborough, and a group of enthusiasts helped restore it. At the same time the East Anglian Locomotive Preservation Society, to which many of Paten's supporters belonged, was raising money to buy a Britannia class engine. Differences of opinion arose between those working on the locomotive already bought and those fundraising for *Britannia*, and the Peterborough group split off into the Peterborough Railway Society (PRS). Thoughts turned to where they might run No.73050, now that British Railways would not allow steam on its tracks. The line from Peterborough towards Rugby and Northampton had recently closed, and the PRS eventually persuaded the Peterborough Development Corporation to support it in buying a small section, between Longueville Junction and Wansford.[71]

David Shepherd, a well-known wildlife artist, bought Cranmore station, Somerset, in 1972 as a working base for the two BR standard steam locomotives that he had already bought. By the end of the following year, Shepherd's collection of locomotives and stock was moved to Cranmore, and plans were being developed to open the site to the public as a steam centre in 1975, and even to run trains over the branch line towards

The driver looks back from Great Western 0-6-2T No.5637 as it leaves Cranmore station with the 2.00 pm train on 8 July 2015.

A diesel shunter at work: D3018 at Chinnor coming to draw coaches from the station.

Shepton Mallet then operated by the quarry owners, Foster Yeoman. The centre at Cranmore officially opened on 20 June 1975. The following year David Shepherd negotiated for the purchase of some of the route towards Shepton Mallett, securing three miles from Cranmore in 1977 for what would become the East Somerset Railway. The first extension, of a mile, was authorised for works trains in 1979.[72]

There were differences of opinion about where the locomotive preservation effort should be directed, especially when people seemed to go for quantity rather than quality in rescuing engines from the large store at Barry scrapyard. In the longer term, the preserved railways benefited from the large numbers of good, workaday locomotives that still provide the mainstay for many of their services.

The first moves into the preservation of modern traction also came during this time, as some diesel locomotives from industry and a few non-standard locomotives and railcars from British Railways became available. Many of these found homes on the preserved railways. The Middleton Railway's pioneering diesel locomotive *John Alcock* was one of the first to be preserved as an object of historic value. The Kent & East Sussex Railway Association acquired a Great Western railcar in 1964, when it was still the intention to run local commuter services. That was followed by a shunting locomotive built in 1932, presented by Ford's Dagenham works in 1966.[73] The Keighley & Worth Valley was another early entrant into diesel preservation, with an English Electric shunter, No.D0226, and some early railbuses. However, diesels had secondary status on most railways. They were there to do jobs, such as shunting in the depot or running trains for local shoppers; steam handled the 'real' trains. That was the motive for Lakeside & Haverthwaite's acquisition of a class 03 shunter, No.2117, from British Railways in 1972, and most preserved railways soon had a diesel shunter or two. It took time before diesel and electric traction was recognised as having value for preservation, but once main-line diesel locomotives and railcars became available the situation changed quickly.[74] An early sign of changing times was the presence of the Diesel & Electric Preservation Group with their Hymek diesel-hydraulic locomotive on the West Somerset Railway when it opened in 1976. The following year this engine took its first passenger train on the line. The North Yorkshire Moors Railway was the first to operate a diesel multiple unit and the first to operate a main-line diesel on scheduled services. That was in 1976, when increased fire risk during the summer

A diesel locomotive on a scheduled service: D7628 at Grosmont, North Yorkshire Moors Railway, September 2014.

drought restricted the use of steam; the railway obtained a class 24 locomotive, No.24032, from a scrapyard to maintain services. Among the early arrivals on the Nene Valley Railway were southern electric coaches from a 4COR set saved by the Southern Electric Group.[75]

With all this activity, preserved railways were taking on a more varied character. Some emphasised the museum aspects more than others, and some were commercial enterprises rather than being founded by amateur societies. Some had ambitions, largely thwarted at this time, to operate community services alongside the tourist and leisure services.

The frustrations of preservation

Nowhere were the problems of getting a preservation project off the ground more pronounced than in the experiences of the Kent & East Sussex Railway. This railway was almost as natural a candidate for preservation as the Welsh narrow-gauge railways. Built as the Rother Valley Railway under the Light Railways Act 1896, to serve the agricultural district of the Weald between Robertsbridge and Tenterden, the line had gained a romantic aura through its management by Colonel Stephens. The Colonel Stephens light railways were all run on a shoestring, resulting in an odd collection of locomotives and rolling stock and somewhat idiosyncratic operating practices. Nationalisation had done little to diminish that, and when it was announced that the last goods services were to be withdrawn from 12 June 1961, it was little surprise that a preservation scheme should soon be promoted. It was not the first time the idea had surfaced: in 1954, when passenger trains were withdrawn, someone wrote to the Southern Region management to suggest that the line should be retained as a museum railway and hired as a film location.[76] British Railways were not interested.

In common with several other preservation schemes of the time, a group of teenagers made the initial running in 1961. A letter from one Maidstone Grammar School boy, Tony Hocking, to the *Kent Messenger* started a ball rolling that attracted a lot of local support, including some businesses. The Kent & East Sussex Railway Preservation Society was founded in March 1961. Its aims were ambitious: to operate the whole of the 13½

miles from Tenterden to Robertsbridge, including regular services for commuters, and freight services. Among early committee members was Leonard Heath-Humphrys, who had been instrumental in preserving the Ffestiniog Railway.[77]

Although British Railways were not particularly sympathetic towards preservationists at this time – understandably, perhaps, in view of the trouble that the attempt to close the Bluebell Railway had caused them – the new society was allowed to establish a base at Tenterden Town station by the end of 1961. Here they assembled engines and stock, and carried out maintenance work on the track. Full of optimism at this point, membership of the society was growing, reaching 700 by 1966. At this time the Westerham Valley Railway Association merged with the Kent & East Sussex following the demise of its own project.[78]

Meanwhile, serious problems were mounting. First was the capital required to buy the line. British Railways set a price of £40,000, a considerable sum for a small society. This resulted in the society making an unfortunate agreement with Mr Pickin of Dublin, who offered to buy a controlling interest in the Kent &

When the Kent & East Sussex Railway was expecting to reopen the whole of the line in the mid-1960s, some stock was stored at Robertsbridge, including H class No.263, originally bought by the Westerham Valley Railway Association. It is now owned by the Bluebell Railway.

East Sussex Railway Company, the body set up by the society as the operating company for the line. Mr Pickin then made a public announcement inviting support from other investors. The Kent & East Sussex society soon found that Mr Pickin's plans for the future of the railway differed from theirs. Dissension ensued between the society and Mr Pickin, and within the volunteer body itself. Fortunately for the society, Pickin failed to come up with the money to buy the line, and British Railways negotiated again with the society through a new company they had set up. The asking price was reduced to £36,000, and the contract was signed in early 1966.[79] Raising such a sum was daunting, and the society had to rein in their ambitions and restrict themselves to running initially only on the Robertsbridge to Northiam section of the line.[80]

Second, the application for a Light Railway Order ran into difficulty. The application was made on 30 November 1966 in the name of the Rother Valley Railway Company, the body set up by the society to operate the line. Objections were made by the Rother Drainage Board and the Kent River Authority, and a public inquiry was held. The inspector recommended that the Order should be granted, but on 4 September 1967 the Minister of Transport, Barbara Castle, ruled against the company. She upheld the objections of the river authorities, and added causes of her own. The number of level crossings on the line would hinder road traffic, she said, and future growth in road traffic might need public expenditure on bridges in ten or twenty years' time. Although the Ministry of Transport had indicated concern at the number of level crossings when the preservation scheme was first launched, this was a question that had not been raised in the public inquiry; nor had the local authorities objected on these grounds. The Minister was, therefore, perceived by many as being swayed more by political antipathy to the preservationists than by reasoned objection. Nick Pallant argues that this was to ignore the traditional practice of ministers to act very closely on the advice of their senior officials, who, in the Ministry of Transport in the 1960s, were more in favour of road transport than rail. Nevertheless, there was sufficient strength of feeling among the KESR's supporters for the local MPs to be drawn in and the matter raised in Parliament. W.F. Deedes, member for Ashford, asked the

Minister to think again, but John Morris, Joint Parliamentary Secretary, Ministry of Transport, refused, claiming that the KESR Association had been warned in writing during 1966 that any proposal that involved reopening level crossings over major roads would raise grave objections.[81]

Support even from Edward Heath, the leader of the opposition and local MP, did not secure a reversal of the decision on this Light Railway Order. The Association appealed unsuccessfully in the High Court against the Minister's decision.[82] Deedes used his good offices to bring the society and Ministry of Transport together to restart negotiations. By this time there was a new Minister and a willingness to reach agreement. The upshot of lengthy discussions was that the ministry indicated that there would be no objection to reopening the section of the railway between Tenterden and Bodiam. The society, therefore, had to rethink, to abandon its aims of running commuter and freight services, and to concentrate on being a steam heritage line. It also had to considerably reorganise to convince officials and ministers that it was fit to run a railway. A new chairman of the Kent & East Sussex Railway Association was elected in 1968, Mr P. Benge-Abbott.[83] A new company, the Tenterden Railway Company, limited by guarantee, was formed in 1971 to carry the project forward. The company gained charitable status for its historical and educational work, the first railway preservation organisation to achieve this. With this new organisational structure in place, negotiations could recommence with British Railways. New terms for the purchase of the line from Tenterden to Bodiam were agreed in 1972: £60,000 for the freehold, of which £20,000 was to be paid on obtaining the Light Railway Order, the remainder, plus interest, over a period of 25 years. After many a stay of execution, the demolition contractors Thomas Ward lifted the track on the remainder of the line from Bodiam to Robertsbridge.

The Light Railway Order was granted on 8 November 1973. A train for society members was run on Boxing Day that year, but public services did not start until 3 February 1974, operating between Tenterden and Rolvenden. The new railway opened at the height of a miners' strike, when coal was in short supply, so many of the first services were operated by the Great Western diesel railcar, No.20, which the society had acquired during the

Bodiam station stands amid wild flowers on a hot day in May 1984 awaiting the revival of the railway.

years of waiting. Despite such inauspicious conditions for reopening, by Easter the railway had carried more than 10,000 passengers. The full season brought the total up to nearly 38,000.[84]

The experience of those last few years had taught the preservationists of the KESR a great deal about responsible management. A new attitude was soon evident when they talked about a 'staged approach' to extending towards Bodiam 'in a time of national economic uncertainty'. There was as much economic uncertainty for the railway, of course, for the heavy mortgage on the line remained a weight around the railway's neck, and, with three bridges needing to be rebuilt, the costs of extension were formidable. There were the almost inevitable over-optimistic predictions of when the line might be extended – Bodiam was going to be reached by the early 1980s – but progress was slow. Like its Colonel Stephens predecessor, this preserved railway was not fashionable, and traffic grew at a modest rate, insufficient to generate funds to service the debt and pay for extensions. Nevertheless, the first extension, to Wittersham Road, opened in March 1977. The bridges had to be dealt with before Northiam was reached, and the railway had to wait until 1990 to achieve that. Bodiam was finally reached in 2000, by which time a millennium grant had aided the finances.[85]

Co-ordination and co-operation

Railway preservation was born of conviction, usually of one person or a very small group, and carried along by enthusiasm, often in the face of opposition. This type of approach did not lend itself to co-ordination. The group convinced of the need and the case for preserving a particular railway or locomotive was unlikely to be swayed by arguments that there should be co-operation to make sure that fundraising and volunteer efforts were not spread too thinly.

There were, however, many who were convinced that co-ordination was needed, and in various ways they kept pressing the case for a targeted approach to railway preservation. That was one of the founding aims of the Railway Preservation Society, founded in 1959 by Noel Draycott, who envisaged a national society dedicated to the preservation of Britain's steam heritage. The priority as he saw it was the preservation of historic artefacts, and the society began with the acquisition of a coach built for the Manchester, Sheffield & Lincolnshire Railway. This was to be a national society with a broadly federal structure, having a number of district groups responsible for collecting historical material from their regions. The broader national society was intended to encourage co-operation and to defend against fragmentation of the preservation movement. The West Midlands District was the first section of this Railway Preservation Society to be established, in the summer of 1959. This group immediately added as an aim the possibility of leasing a branch line on which some of the locomotives and rolling stock that had been saved might be operated.[86] Draycott's vision was not to be realised fully, as only two more groups of the Railway Preservation Society were established. Eventually the federal structure fell apart, but each of the three groups became successful independent societies. One became the Quainton Railway Society, which stuck closely to the original ideals in building up a good museum collection. The second was the Scottish Railway Preservation Society. It too had a first-class collection of artefacts, but also set out to find an operational railway on which to base its collections, eventually establishing the Bo'ness & Kinneil Railway. The West Midlands District, with a base at Hednesford, considered the Coalport branch, the Stafford to Uttoxeter line and the line from Aldridge to Brownhills as candidates for operational lines. Support from Aldridge-Brownhills Urban District Council, which saw the value of a steam railway in conjunction with a leisure park then being developed, shifted the focus from 1965 onwards to a former colliery railway at Chasewater. Development by the small society proceeded slowly, until they held their first open days in 1968. The Chasewater Light Railway Company was formed to operate the line in 1973.

For all his vision, however, Draycott's RPS was not felt to be effective by many preservationists. Something more was needed, it was thought, and the first attempt to meet that need came in 1962 with the foundation of the Railway Preservation Association. Its chairman was Captain W.G. Smith, owner of one of the first preserved locomotives to have been bought privately from British Railways. This new organisation was to co-ordinate locomotive and railway preservation schemes, working with the Consultative Panel for the Preservation of British Transport Relics. It would encourage the worthwhile projects, and give 'sound reasons for discouraging proposals with little chance of success'. The *Railway Magazine* was supportive: 'In view of the recent upsurge of preservation schemes all over the country, some such co-ordination of effort, or at least exchange of experience, would seem to be highly desirable, lest irresponsible action bring all preservation into disrepute.'[87] This association never got going. The Kent & East Sussex Railway Preservation Society was one of those groups that joined, but, after hearing nothing for more than six months, decided in June 1963 not to maintain its membership.

Another approach suggested was the formation of a railway equivalent to the National Trust, the object of which should be to run some of the lines, such as the Cambrian Coast, which were being threatened with closure. This was never taken up, and, as it happens, most of the lines that this railway trust might take over have so far not closed.[88]

Meanwhile, Draycott and the Railway Preservation Society persevered with their message of co-operation. The drive to create a new co-ordinating body was now coming from Captain Peter Manisty, who was a leading light on the Bluebell Railway. It was largely through his efforts, along with John Snell and others, that early in 1965 the National Council of the RPS decided that those aims would best be served if it was reconstituted to make it 'completely impartial and non-partisan', as the secretary wrote to the *Railway Magazine*. The group was now to be known as the Association of Railway

Preservation Societies (ARPS). The original constituents of the RPS, the London, West Midlands and Scottish railway preservation societies, were naturally among the first members of the new association. They were joined by three locomotive-owning societies, one museum trust, and the Keighley & Worth Valley and Middleton railways.[89] The solid foundations of the association gradually attracted other member societies from across the spectrum of railway preservation. By 1969 there were more than sixty members. Among the early successes of the ARPS was a 'package deal' with BR for the purchase of half a dozen locomotives and several coaches at a discount price in 1968. They have all proved their worth in operation on preserved railways. Another co-ordinating activity was the creation of a register of facilities for film-makers as a means of attracting more filming work.[90] Manisty was chairman of the new body from the outset, and under his leadership the ARPS became very effective as a trade association for preservation groups. The objectives, as he explained in a letter to the railway press, were to 'promote the welfare and co-operation of railway preservation societies in the British Isles'. It was not to act as a fundraising organisation. Instead, Manisty built good relationships with the railway inspectorate, encouraged the government to take preservation seriously, and persuaded Dai Woodham, a scrap merchant who had bought large numbers of locomotives from BR, to allow preservationists to save some of them. Manisty was, wrote David Morgan, 'the true father of railway preservation'.[91] The tendency of the ARPS was to channel efforts towards existing groups. It could not stop new societies being established, however, and was usually happy to welcome new groups into the fold provided they conformed to the association's code of practice.[92]

The Association of Minor Railways had been founded in 1938, but had been largely neglected since 1952. Nationalisation and closures had left it with the Derwent Valley Railway, the freight-only line near York, as one of very few members. During the 1970s, however, led by Allan Garraway, some of the preserved railways decided the Association was worth reviving as a forum for operating lines. The Derwent Valley emulated the preserved railways by introducing steam passenger trains in 1977, although they were not an unqualified success.[93]

Chapter 5

STANDARD-GAUGE PRESERVATION OF THE 1960s AND 1970s

In April 1967 Mr H.I. Quayle wrote to the *Barrow News* to say that the railway from Ulverston to Lakeside on Windermere, which had closed to passengers two years previously, would be a strong candidate for preservation. This was typical of the way many railway preservation schemes started in the 1960s – local response to the closure of a branch line. Its subsequent development exhibited many common features, as dealing with the authorities, raising finance and changes among the people involved all played a part.

Mr Quayle received an encouraging response, enough for a company called Lakeside Railway Estates Co. Ltd to be formed by local businessmen Austin Maher, John Parkin and Peter Beet. Their objective was the reopening of the whole branch line to passenger and goods services. At the same time the Lakeside Railway Society was formed – or more strictly, perhaps, reformed, from the Lancaster Railway Circle – and agreed to work as the voluntary support for the company. Negotiations seemed to be proceeding satisfactorily with British Railways until the local authorities intervened. First, in 1968, came the Lake District Planning Board, which wanted to use the stretch of line from Lakeside to Haverthwaite for footpaths and car parks. The Board could claim prior purchasing rights, and BR had to return the railway company's deposit. The railway society organised protests: 'the more rebukes we get the more we will fight,' wrote one of its supporters. A petition attracted 5,000 signatures, most of them locals, and the company sought legal advice.

Even the Ministry of Housing and Local Government advised the Lake District Planning Board to reconsider its plans on footpaths. These pressures were enough for the Board to accept an agreement whereby it would buy the trackbed, and accommodation was to be made for both railway and footpath. The preservationists' relief was short-lived, for in the summer of 1969 Lancashire County Council came along with improvements to the A590 trunk road, for which they wanted sections of the trackbed at Greenodd and at Haverthwaite. After this setback, the railway company and society concentrated on the section from Lakeside to Haverthwaite. At the end of 1970 and 1971 the preservation group took the final opportunity to arrange with British Railways the movement of stock over the branch to Haverthwaite before the last section was cut off from the national network. Meanwhile, there had been a division of interests among the preservation groups. The original Lakeside Railway Estates Company led by Peter Beet was to concentrate its activities on the steam depot and works at Carnforth. This became Steamtown Carnforth, and the company changed its name to that in 1971. Austin Maher formed a new Lakeside & Haverthwaite Railway Company in 1970, in which the Lakeside Railway Society was a major shareholder, to continue with the branch-line project. The application for the Light Railway Order was submitted in 1971, and on 2 May 1973 the first train ran on the restored line.[94]

Like the Lakeside branch, most of the effort put into new standard-gauge preservation schemes in the 1960s and 1970s concentrated on railway lines cast off by British Railways. Campaigns against closure often prompted proposals to save the line. Although most failed, out of the endeavour some schemes did come to fruition: the Swanage Railway, the Severn Valley Railway and West Somerset Railway, each of which developed into a major heritage railway. However, saving branch lines was not the only form of railway preservation. Some were on industrial sites, and by the end of the 1970s railway preservation was embracing different forms. There were some lines with strong community involvement, especially in their initial stages; others might be called enthusiasts' preservation schemes. Some had a very commercial, tourist-based outlook, whereas others had a strong museum basis. Most, it is fair to say, were a mixture.

Local spirit

The Keighley & Worth Valley Railway was a prime example of a successful campaign to save a branch line resulting from a strong body of local support. It was one of two standard-gauge preservation projects to open during the 1960s. There was an outcry when the branch line of 4½ miles from Keighley to Oxenhope was scheduled to close at the end of 1961. Owners of mills wanted to keep the railway to transport their workers; residents of the valley wanted it for getting into Keighley for the shops. Ralph Povey of Oakworth wrote a letter to the *Bradford Telegraph and Argus* in November 1961 suggesting the formation of a preservation society, as had been done for the Bluebell and the Welsh railways. Shortly after the line had closed, Povey and Bob Cryer, a local college lecturer and later Member of Parliament, called a public meeting at Keighley to draw on local support. From that the Keighley & Worth Valley Railway Preservation Society was formed in January 1962. The line was bought from British Railways in 1964, but it took four years of delay and frustration before the Light Railway Orders were obtained. The railway reopened on 29 June 1968, a day when the British Railways network was closed as a result of industrial action.[95]

The community spirit behind the Keighley & Worth Valley was expressed in a desire to proclaim its new identity as an independent railway – it was not preserved so much as entering a new phase of life. Hence two of its locomotives, Ivatt 2-6-2 tank No.41241 and USA tank No.72, were painted in the company's own new livery. This horrified the authenticists among railway enthusiasts, who would object in the railway press to 'the painting of locomotives and rolling stock in fictitious and ridiculous colour schemes'. Other railways did the same. The Bluebell Railway's P class locomotive No.323 had been 'outrageously repainted' blue and named *Bluebell* and another engine bore the name *Primrose*. The railway enthusiasts might not have been happy, but the general public liked these engines.[96] The appearance of 2-6-4 tank engine No.2085 on the Lakeside & Haverthwaite Railway in Caledonian Railway blue, a colour it had never carried in its main-line existence, aroused particular ire among enthusiasts. This railway also compiled its own numbering sequence both for locomotives and coaches. The Kent & East Sussex gave the locomotives they acquired numbers to continue the series from the railway's days of independence under Colonel Stephens, and adopted blue or apple green as standard liveries.[97] The Dart Valley applied the

A Keighley & Worth Valley Railway train at Keighley on 22 June 1974. The locomotive is No.45212.

new company's name to its locomotives that otherwise maintained a Great Western theme. Coaches were similarly given liveries devised for their new operators. When the Strathspey Railway opened in 1978, some of its smaller locomotives were running in a company livery of Highland Railway olive green. By this time, however, the tide had turned, and owners of locomotives were more likely to choose a livery that was more or less historically accurate. The enthusiasts argued the merits of the different liveries, and at the same time were happy to change a locomotive's appearance to 'recreate' an engine that had been scrapped. Meanwhile, the operators of the railways had to establish their corporate identities in other ways than the liveries of locomotives and rolling stock.

Another strong local campaign was built up in support of the line from Alton to Winchester, which was among those listed for closure in the Beeching Report. The formal announcements

With some 'railway children' watching, USA class tank locomotive No.72 takes its train between Ingrow and Keighley, bearing the Keighley & Worth Valley Railway's homegrown livery. 11 August 1968.

(John Worley/Online Transport Archive) (JW22-83)

made in 1967 prompted one of the most bitterly fought contests, which held off closure until 1973. A natural consequence was that the line became the focus of preservation activity. Two serious and rival proposals were put forward. One, led by John Taylor, clerk to Winchester Rural District Council, planned to restore services over the whole line. The second group, the Mid-Hants Railway Ltd, concentrated on the section from Alton to Alresford, and gained a lease of Alresford station from the beginning of 1973. The two groups came together during 1973 to form the Winchester & Alton Railway Ltd, with the aim of reopening the whole line. It attracted the support of Miss Joan Quennell MP and John Arlott, the well-known radio cricket commentator, as directors. The county council at this time was not prepared to buy the freehold of the line to lease to the preservationists. The company failed to raise the capital now needed through a public share issue, which forced it to concentrate on the shorter line, on which steam tourist trains would be run, rather than a service for commuters. After that

Medstead station on the Mid-Hants Railway is kept in pristine condition. A diesel multiple unit arrives on 21 September 2011.

decision had been made, the council changed course and bought the trackbed in 1974, paying also for the track to be left in place. The first trains ran on the three-mile section between Alresford and Ropley from 30 April 1977, just over two years after the closure of the line. Operating on twenty-five weekends, the railway attracted 50,000 passengers in its first season. Extensions reopened the line first to Medstead & Four Marks in 1983, and in 1985 to Alton.[98]

The birth of the premier lines

The heritage railway scene in the twenty-first century has a few railways generally acknowledged as leaders in the field – a premier league. Most are long lines, usually with a mainline connection, and can handle big locomotives. As businesses they return impressive passenger numbers and turnovers, they have long running seasons and put on big events. Most were founded during this period, with early years that were distinctly shaky.

The North Yorkshire Moors Railway is one. The Beeching Report recommended the closure of all railways to Whitby. The Esk Valley route from Middlesbrough was reprieved, but the coastal route from Scarborough and the line from Malton and Pickering both closed. An attempt to establish a preservation society for the coast line failed, but a later scheme to preserve the line from Pickering to Grosmont, where there was a junction

The first section of the North Yorkshire Moors Railway to be opened includes one of the steepest gradients on the line, between Grosmont and Goathland. Class 5 No.44806 tackles the bank through Esk Valley in September 2014.

with the Esk Valley route to Whitby, did get off the ground. The North Yorkshire Moors Railway Society was formed in 1967, two years after passenger services were withdrawn, and by the end of 1969 had 2,300 members. The strength of support meant it was already in a position to sign the contract for the £42,500 purchase price of the line. Local authorities gave support, encouraging the society to reopen the full eighteen miles of line to Pickering. The authorities' advocacy and financial support was important, for some of the leaders of the preservation group were inclined to concentrate on a line of only six miles, from Grosmont to Ellerbeck, as being more manageable for a volunteer-run railway. The cautious were concerned that the longer line would require more paid staff, and more working capital, overstretching the organisation. On the other hand, the full line to Pickering was a far more attractive tourist proposition. Trains on the first section to be reopened started running on Easter Sunday, 22 April 1973, with a formal opening on 1 May. It quickly became a major tourist railway, claiming more than 200,000 passengers by 1975.[99]

A prospectus for the West Somerset Railway Ltd was issued at a public meeting held on 22 May 1971. This meeting followed the growth of interest locally in reopening the branch line from Taunton to Minehead, sufficient for the West Somerset Railway Association to gain pledges for the £25,000 deposit on the line within a few months. The movement for reopening prompted the county council to commission a feasibility study into the prospects for the line. A sale price was agreed between British Railways and the Association of £200,000, with running powers into Taunton station. The deposit of £50,000 was paid in 1972. Progress was frustratingly slow for the preservationists. The application for a Light Railway Order had to go before a public enquiry, when objections were received. There were three individual objectors, including a retired army officer, who claimed the return of trains would disturb wildlife along the route, and the Western National bus company, concerned at what they saw as a potentially unfair subsidy made to the railway by the local authority. When the public enquiry resumed in 1974, the bus company withdrew its objection, but others remained, including a Mr Somerset, whose grounds for objection were that the railway could become a heavy liability to the county's ratepayers. The involvement of Somerset County Council certainly looked extensive. They were buying the freehold of the line, paying £250,000, and were to lease it to the West Somerset Railway Company at a rate that was to include an initial period at a peppercorn, and thereafter would be lower if the diesel commuter service was run. The county was also making a loan of £60,000 to the company at ten per cent, a rate lower than the then current commercial rate of interest. The railway opened its first section of three miles from Minehead to Blue Anchor in March 1976. Hopes then were high that the rest of the line into Taunton would be reopened during that year, with the local commuter service in operation. In the event, the extension got as far as Williton, from 28 August. In September the local branch of the National Union of Railwaymen (NUR) declared that they would not co-operate with an independent operator of trains into Taunton over BR tracks. This stalled the Taunton project, meaning that the West Somerset would be unable to meet its obligations under the agreement with the county council. The council withheld further payments under the loan agreement, contributing to a financial crisis on the railway in 1976–77. Staff redundancies and the voting out of the company chairman ensued. Although the railway extended the line to Stogumber in 1978 and Bishops Lydeard in 1979, the prospects of getting to Taunton were not promising. The NUR remained intransigent, and financing the extension was going to be difficult. British Rail wanted £20,000 towards alterations at Taunton to accommodate the West Somerset, together with an annual rent of £13,000. It needed a lot of commuters to make that pay, and the WSR's finances were still fragile at the end of the 1970s. A change of government in 1979 brought helpful statements from the new environment minister and local MP, Tom King, who said that he would try to bring down the costs of restoring the link at Taunton. But it was hardly a priority for government, and both serious political will, and the West Somerset's finances, were lacking. It was some years before the railway achieved a measure of stability, by which time thoughts of commuter services into Taunton had been deferred indefinitely, and the railway was transformed into a tourist railway with a strong Great Western character.[100]

A third major railway is the Severn Valley Railway, which now runs from Kidderminster to Bridgnorth, a distance of sixteen miles. The railway north of Bewdley closed in 1963. The Severn Valley Railway Association was formed in 1965, and a few months later made a formal offer to British Railways to buy the line between Bridgnorth and Hampton Loade for £25,000. That was accepted and the deposit paid on 23 September 1966. Not everything ran smoothly, of course. Shropshire County Council were reported to be opposed to the railway's reopening, as it would involve them in added expenditure for a bridge over the line for the proposed Bridgnorth bypass. Nevertheless, trains began running on this section on 23 May 1970. By 12 July 10,000 passengers had been carried, despite a temporary suspension of services for two weeks in June, when British Railways imposed its ban on steam motive power on Bridgnorth station, which was still its property. With the resolve that was to characterise this railway, the society quickly raised the £20,500 balance of the purchase price to release it from this ban. Plans for the next steps in expansion were in hand by then: the extension towards Bewdley, which it was hoped would open in 1973, thence further to Foley Park, the junction with the mainline network outside Kidderminster, and the construction

of a four-road engine shed. Severn Valley (Holdings) Ltd, a company formed to facilitate the southward extension, attracted Sir Gerald Nabarro, the flamboyant local MP, to act as chairman. This was a time of some turmoil in the affairs of the railway, with tensions between the voluntary society and the companies formed to operate the railway and extend it. Some of these focused on Sir Gerald, whose tenure in office lasted little more than a year. The extension to Bewdley, which Sir Gerald had championed, was opened in May 1974. Meanwhile, the county council had not taken up the option available to it under the Transport Act of buying the trackbed of the rest of the route to Foley Park, leaving the Severn Valley free to contemplate raising the £74,000 then quoted as the purchase price. Extending the line through to Kidderminster, with a connection to the national network, was completed in 1984.[101]

The line from Wareham to Swanage was one of many railways in which there was interest from preservationists before it was closed by British Railways. The Isle of Purbeck Railway Preservation Society had been formed in the 1960s, with one of its aims the preservation of the Swanage branch.

LMS class 5 4-6-0 No.45110 receiving the attention of many hands at Bridgnorth. 7 March 1971.

The merits of the branch as a preservation project were being widely canvassed by the late 1960s: there was an element of rivalry between supporters of Swanage and the proposed Longmoor scheme as a centre for southern steam preservation.[102] With such a build-up, it might have been expected that there would be a relatively easy transition into preservation once BR closed the line. That closure was vigorously opposed locally: a petition organised by Dr Ernest Rutland attracted 3,000 signatures. However, it was not enough to stop closure taking place on New Year's Day 1972. Nor were the efforts of the Isle of Purbeck society. Negotiations with BR were fruitless because BR still owned a short section of the branch line to Motala, half a mile east of Furzebrook Junction serving an oil depot, and controlled the route from Furzebrook to Wareham. At that time the plans of all preservationists were for services to be restored through-out from Swanage to Wareham, run as a year-round local amenity, and any support from local authorities was largely dependent on that restoration. On that rock the Isle of Purbeck RPS foundered.

A new Swanage Railway Society was formed in the summer of 1972, and embarked on the lengthy process of negotiation with BR and with the local authorities. The aims of the new group were the same – trains running through to Wareham – and there was some initial support from local authorities, but it took another three years before they put aside their alternative plans for roads on the railway land. British Rail were no more helpful than they had been with the Isle of Purbeck society, and their stump of branch line continued to be a stumbling block. Connection with the main line was not restored until 2007, and services are yet to run into Wareham. BR also were obliged to give priority to proposals the county council was considering for a bypass round Corfe to be built on the track. Of the local authorities, Swanage UDC were keen for the restoration of services, but Swanage Town Council bought the town station in March 1974, and promptly demolished the platform and filled in part of the trackbed – not quite what the railway society wanted to see. After some persuasion and protest, including a sit-in to prevent contractors dismantling the line, Dorset County Council in January 1973 rejected its planning committee's recommendation that railway land should be used for the Corfe

bypass. The council exercised its statutory right to buy the trackbed that the town council had not already bought, and completed that purchase in 1975.[103]

The county council's support had been won by 1973. It was, however, conditional upon the restoration of services through to Wareham. The railway society had been pursuing possibilities towards achieving that, including an ambition, in the longer term at least, to lay its own track from the junction into Wareham. With progress necessarily snail-paced, the council announced in 1977 that it would withdraw its support. Meanwhile the town council had been won round. In February 1976 they agreed to lease part of the station to the society, although with many restrictions. Locomotives and stock arrived, open days were held, but still another three years passed before agreement was reached with the local authorities to allow trains to run again. The body to operate the line, the Swanage Railway Company, was formed in February 1979, and in August 1979 trains ran under its management along the first few hundred yards out of Swanage station towards Herston. Although the track was relaid to Herston, a mile from Swanage,

In August 1983 the Swanage Railway still had only a mile of track. Swanage station was still a project in its early stages of development, in marked contrast to the scene in the cover photograph.
(Chris Marsh)

it was not until April 1982 that public services ran there. A further extension of half a mile to New Barn was added in 1987. Harman's Cross, three miles, was reached in 1988, and Corfe Castle and Norden welcomed their first trains in August 1995. That left only one target – reconnection to the main line at Furzebrook Junction. Relaying of the track to the connection at Motala was completed by 2002, but negotiations with Railtrack and then Network Rail to allow trains to run into Wareham have again been long-drawn-out.[104]

New-towns lines

The Nene Valley Railway had its origins in the decision by central government to close the transport museum at Clapham and create a new national railway museum. In 1970 the government invited proposals for a suitable site for this museum. Peterborough Locomotive Society suggested to the Peterborough Development Corporation that their city would be an ideal site, based on the Great Eastern Railway station, and with a section of the line towards Oundle used as a working museum. Peterborough was beaten by York in the competition for the national museum, but links having been established between society and development corporation, the prospect of a restored railway running through what was to be called Nene Park took positive form. Proposals concentrated on the line from Longville to Wansford, which had been part of a cross-country route that linked Peterborough with East Anglia, the Midlands and Euston station in London. It was thus a main line in character, well-engineered, with double track. The development corporation was agreeable to buying a section of this line five miles in length, from Wansford to just west of Woodston. That was less than the society hoped, for it stopped well to the west of Peterborough. Connection with the main-line network was retained through the Fletton branch, and this allowed the railway to bring in large engines and special trains.[105]

Peterborough Locomotive Society was already custodian of Standard class 4 locomotive No.73050, bought some years earlier by Reverend Richard Paten as a reminder for the town of its railway heritage, and as restoration progressed it was looking for somewhere to run the engine. After reaching agreement with the development corporation, the society gathered more locomotives and stock with a view to operating the railway. It changed its name from Locomotive to Railway and was registered as a charity in 1972. Two years later the society was raising £25,000 for further coaches. Among the first locomotives offered to the new railway was a Swedish tank engine. This led to the decision that the railway should adopt the Berne loading gauge in the rebuilding of stations and track so that additional continental engines and coaches could be accepted and operated. The first public trains were run on a short section of track that had not been bought by the development corporation. This was at the west end of the line, from Wansford to Yarwell Junction. The five miles of the Nene Valley 'proper' saw their first trains in June of 1977. More than 55,000 passengers had been carried when the first summer season closed in October. The short section of route on to Yarwell became a storage siding once the main service was opened.[106]

The Telford Development Corporation commissioned a study in 1973 into the possibility of opening a light railway on the former Coalport branch to serve Ironbridge, where an industrial museum was growing. Hills & Bailey, the engineers who produced the report, were not very encouraging. In the light of this no progress was made towards developing a preserved railway, but Telford Development Corporation did buy a Great Western tank locomotive, No.5619. The Telford (Horsehay) Steam Trust (later the Telford Railway Society) took on the job of restoring this engine, and almost immediately cast around for a line on which to run it.[108]

Societies in search of a railway

Some railway preservation projects changed considerably between their inception and opening to traffic. Sometimes the preservationists altered focus to establish their project on a line different from that originally envisaged.

The Midland & Great Northern Railway Society had been established in 1959 with a view to maintaining railway services over the M & GN system in East Anglia, which was rapidly being closed. Like a number of railway preservation schemes at this time, the ambitions of the society were to revive a public railway service using volunteer labour to contain costs, not to run a purely tourist railway. So it was that initial ambitions were for the whole of the M & GN main line of about a hundred miles running inland from Great Yarmouth. These were soon cut back to the section from Aylsham to Yarmouth Beach. That line was itself nearly fifty miles in length. Neither British Railways, which started lifting track the week after the major part of the M & GN system was closed, nor the county council, which announced plans to use some of the railway land for road schemes, took the society seriously. It was not long before another set of proposals emerged, this time to take over the twenty-one miles of line from Melton Constable to Norwich. They in turn failed. Eventually, in the mid-1960s, the society established a base on the line from Weybourne to Sheringham, one of the last parts of the M & GN network to remain open, until April 1964.[109] During the search for a railway to operate, the society had already made major contributions to preservation in securing two locomotives of types that had significance in East Anglian railway history, both of which were sole representatives of their class in preservation. These were the Great Eastern J15 0-6-0 and the B12 4-6-0 built by the LNER. With the move to Weybourne, and a much shorter branch line, the emphasis shifted towards the operation of a mainly steam-powered tourist railway. The idea of running public service trains was never abandoned, however: two railbuses were bought with that end in view. The operating company for the Sheringham line was established as the North Norfolk Railway, which effected the purchase of the line in 1969, with the exception of Sheringham station, which was subject to a lease agreement. This was another railway that needed great patience: it was not until 1973 that the Light Railway Order for the line was obtained.[110]

Closure of the Bury–Stubbins Junction line in Lancashire in 1966 prompted the formation of the Helmshore & District Railway Preservation Society in 1967. An encouraging amount of local support allowed it to start raising funds towards reopening the line, but they were not enough, and the society was wound up in 1968.[111] A new group, the East Lancashire Railway Preservation Society, was formed almost immediately, and set up a base at Helmshore station. Like its predecessor, the new society aimed to preserve the Accrington line, but demolition of a bridge truncated it to the three miles from

Stubbins Junction to Grane Road. The asking price of £28,000 for this line proved contentious, and for a while the society withdrew its interest. Nevertheless, the society formed the East Lancashire Light Railway Co. Ltd as the corporate vehicle to pursue the negotiations. By 1972 the society had a new base for its collection of stock in a former railway goods shed at Bury leased from the local authority. The strength of the scheme meant that a proposed preservation of the line from Rose Hill to Macclesfield, put forward in 1970, faded. The society's attention was now turning to the line from Bury to Rawtenstall. Passenger services were withdrawn from this route in 1972, but freight traffic continued. The society hoped to operate trains along the line at weekends when no goods trains ran, but BR was not prepared to allow any preserved stock on its land, and the society had to be content with a short stretch of track within its base at Bury. The withdrawal of the goods services on the Rawtenstall line in 1980 allowed negotiations to buy the line to restart. It was not until 1986 that the scheme came to fruition, allowing services to start on 25 July the following year, on the first section of the route, from Bury to Ramsbottom. Extension to Rawtenstall was achieved in 1991.[112]

The railway now known as the Embsay & Bolton Abbey Steam Railway in Yorkshire is one with a complicated preservation history. The Embsay & Grassington Railway Preservation Society was formed in 1968 to preserve the railway from Skipton to Grassington, then still in use for goods trains. The society changed its name to the Yorkshire Dales Railway Society in 1970 and formed the Yorkshire Dales Railway Company as the operating organisation for a steam centre being established at Embsay station. Here a collection of material relating to the history of railways in Yorkshire was put together that was to achieve registered museum status. With goods trains still running on the Grassington branch, attention shifted to the route from Skipton to Ilkley. Operation began between Embsay and Embsay Junction in 1979, and extension towards Bolton Abbey proceeded in the years following.[113]

The Flint & Deeside Railway Preservation Society was formed in 1972 with a view to running a standard-gauge line in north Wales. It was interested initially in the branch from Prestatyn to Dyserth, but switched to the Ruabon–Barmouth

The Llangollen
Railway was still a
small project in May
1979, when this
collection of stock
was seen at
Llangollen station.

line. It took a lease on Llangollen station in 1976, and became
the Llangollen Railway Society the following year. The aim was
to rebuild the railway to the east and west. Ruabon, with its
network connection, remained an objective for some years – a
lease was taken out for Ruabon goods yard in 1988. Effort has
concentrated, however, on the route west: the first section was
opened in 1981, and extensions in following years brought the
line to Carrog in 1996.[114]

The Midland Railway Society in 1969 opened negotiations
with BR with a view to acquiring part of the branch from
Nuneaton Trent Valley to Measham, but this failed to progress.
Instead, the society turned its attention the following year to a
section of the former Ashby & Nuneaton line between

Shackerstone and Market Bosworth. The society subsequently became the Shackerstone Railway Society, rapidly building up a collection of small locomotives and rolling stock for the line.[115] Trains began running on 28 May 1978, with a Sunday service for the rest of the summer. The Market Bosworth Light Railway Ltd, a subsidiary of Barton Hover Engineering Ltd, were operators of the service, in conjunction with the Shackerstone Railway Society, which had had a museum at the station since 1968.[116]

The Teifi Valley Railway Preservation Society, formed in 1972 with a view to taking over the Newcastle Emlyn branch, later became involved in the promotion of the Gwili Railway, which became the first standard-gauge preserved railway in Wales. When the local authority withdrew its subsidy for the local services on the branch from Abergwili Junction to Bronwydd Arms, the society proposed the preservation of part of it as a tourist railway. The Gwili Railway Company set up to take on such an operation should be financed by a share issue, it was suggested. The railway gained its Light Railway Order in 1977, and started passenger services over the first half mile from Bronwydd Arms on 25 March that year. Already by 1976 the Gwili Railway was ready to contemplate an extension of two miles northwards towards Llanpumpsaint.[117]

The Stour Valley Railway Preservation Society never did find a railway. It proposed in 1968 to buy the line in Essex from

Austerity tank locomotive *Welsh Guardsman* at the Gwili Railway, September 1996.
(Chris Marsh)

The Stour Valley Railway project was still expecting to result in a running railway when this open day was held at Chappel and Wakes Colne in September 1972. A former industrial saddle tank locomotive, *Jupiter*, was leading the trains on the line in the goods yard, with Great Eastern and Manchester Sheffield & Lincolnshire Railway coaches. This half mile of track now operates under a Light Railway Order as the Chappel and Wakes Colne Light Railway.

Sudbury to Haverhill; despite enlisting the public support of local MPs, this hope eventually faded. Next they proposed to take over the branch from Marks Tey to Sudbury, with local subsidy being paid to the preservation company instead of BR. The society established a steam centre and museum along the line at Chappel & Wakes Colne station. The Sudbury branch itself has remained open. Still hoping to run a railway, the society formed the Branch Line Preservation Co. Ltd in 1970 to finance 'any railway the society might take over', and hankered after the line beyond Sudbury for some while before settling for making the East Anglian Railway Museum a successful attraction.[118]

Projects launched in the 1970s
In 1975 Derbyshire County Council negotiated with BR for the purchase of part of the old railway from Matlock to Buxton, a stretch as far as Rowsley, at which point the Peak Park Planning Board was already completing the purchase of the route northwards. Neither body initially was interested in restoring this railway, which had closed in 1968. The county council was thinking of using the land for road improvements, and the national park authority had ideas of creating a walking trail. Paul Tomlinson, who worked for Derby City Council, along

with some work colleagues proposed to both authorities that the railway should be rebuilt. They were surprised that they were 'by no means laughed out of court'. This was sufficient encouragement to hold a public meeting. It was attended by 123 people and led to the formation of the Peak Park Railway Society. The society saw itself as a community organisation, gaining strong local support, including the patronage of the Duke of Devonshire and the local MP. With this local emphasis, plans were to restore the whole route, over which year-round community services would run, as well as tourist trains. The outlook in the early months seemed sufficiently good for the society to reserve five locomotives at Barry scrapyard with a view to their use on the line. Negotiations to acquire the line proved far more protracted, however, not least because of the number of public bodies involved, each with its own policy. It was not until 1991 that the first heritage trains ran on the short section of line from Matlock to Darley Dale. Many obstacles remain before the society's original ambitions are realised.[119]

The Bristol Suburban Railway Society opened negotiations in 1972 for the line from Bristol to Mangotsfield and Bath, including the loop to Yate. The society was established at Bitton, where it held open days from 1974. In 1979 the society was reconstituted as the Bitton Railway Company. Road developments restricted some ambitions, but tracklaying reached Oldland in 1988, when the line became the Avon Valley Railway.[120] Similar proposals to revive some Bristol suburban services along the route from St Philips station to Warmley, again with some steam working at weekends, came to nothing.[121]

The Cheshire and Staffordshire Railway Society submitted plans to Staffordshire County Council for the reopening of part of the North Staffordshire Railway in the Churnet Valley in early 1974. The society had changed its name to the North Staffordshire Railway Society by the time it received planning permission in 1977 to convert Cheddleton station to a museum in 1977.[122]

When the Dean Forest Railway Preservation Society launched its plans for a preserved railway from Lydney to Parkend in 1970, the line was still used by BR for freight traffic. The society considered alternatives, such as the line from Parkend to Cinderford, but opposition from the Forestry Commission forced it back to its original ideas. Instead, having received planning approval for its initial proposals from Gloucestershire County Council, the society settled for patiently working towards reviving the Lydney branch, from a base established at Norchard.[123]

Scotland and Channel Islands

Scotland had been the subject of few railway preservation schemes. The leading preservation group, the Scottish Railway Preservation Society, offspring of the national Railway Preservation Society, had built up an enviable collection of locomotives and rolling stock. Although the society harboured ambitions to have a railway of its own, it had concentrated on developing its collections. In 1967 the recently created Highlands and Islands Development Board invited the society to join in a scheme to preserve the branch line from Aviemore to Boat of Garten. The line had closed in 1965, but the Board, created in that same year to 'assist the economic and social development of the Scottish Highlands', decided there could be potential for encouraging tourism in the Strathspey area. After negotiations with the Board and British Railways, the SRPS made an offer for the line in 1970. With a ban on steam on the main line, and declining opportunities for the operation of its stock, the branch line had definite attractions for the society. But after barely a year the society decided at its annual general meeting in 1971 to pull out of the Aviemore project. The problems facing railway preservation in Scotland were encapsulated in this decision. The SRPS, with headquarters in Falkirk, drew most of its support from the Central Lowlands, and for many of its members Strathspey was remote, possibly more so than the Welsh lines were for their many English supporters. Attractive though the line was, and enticing though development board funding might be, the majority found the prospect of operating at Aviemore daunting, and decided the society should look for a line nearer to central Scotland. Not all were happy with the decision: six members formed the Strathspey Railway Company to continue with the Aviemore project.

The Scottish Railway Preservation Society still had thoughts of operating a preserved branch line, but the search for a suitable line within reasonable distance of their base in Falkirk took time. Plans for the line from Haddington to Longniddry

North British Railway 0-6-0 No.65243 runs through Birkhill, Bo'ness & Kinneil Railway. 22 June 1996.

(Les Folkard/Online Transport Archive) (LF697-34)

were opposed by the local authority, and were abandoned. Thoughts turned next to the branch from Alloa to Dollar, on the other side of the Forth from Falkirk.[124] In 1979 the society received planning permission to develop a railway museum at Bo'ness station, which became the first step towards achieving their aim of operating a railway.[125]

One of the furthest outposts of railway preservation in the British Isles is the Alderney Railway. A railway taking stone from a quarry inland on this small Channel Island to the harbour was still operating in the 1970s under the ownership of the UK Property Services Agency. The States of Alderney made the first moves towards the creation of a tourist railway when they suggested in 1976 that a Riduna Railway company should be formed to run trains on Sundays, when the quarry was not at work. Two years later a further proposal was put forward by the building inspector for the States. Negotiations for a lease of the line eventually allowed the first passenger trains to run in 1980.[126] Elsewhere in the Channel Islands members of the Jersey

Overlooked by one of the German Second World War defence batteries, the Alderney Railway's D100 *Elizabeth* stands at the Mannez terminus with its London Umderground coaches Nos.1044 and 1045 on 10 September 2006.

Transport Preservation Society hoped to restore some of the 3ft 6in railway, but had to settle for other ways of recording the island's heritage.

Commercial enterprises

The Dart Valley Railway caused a stir among railway enthusiasts when it opened in 1965, for it introduced a new element into preservation – a line bought as a business proposition. There was nothing new about running a tourist railway as a commercial enterprise. The Ravenglass & Eskdale was already managed in this way. When the railway had been saved from closure the Ravenglass & Eskdale Railway Preservation Society played an important part, but did not gain control of the line, remaining essentially a support organisation for a commercial enterprise, albeit with a seat on the board.[127] Nor was the Dart Valley the first to be promoted as a commercial undertaking. Vectrail on the Isle of Wight had stressed that its plans were commercial more than preservationist. George Pickin believed he could make the Kent & East Sussex Railway into a profitable enterprise, and there were others with similar ambitions to make a success of branch lines closed by Beeching.

The Dart Valley was, however, the first successful transfer of a standard-gauge railway to a commercial organisation to operate as a steam tourist railway. The Dart Valley Light Railway Co. Ltd was set up by a group of businessmen in 1965. They were railway enthusiasts, and experienced in railway preservation. Pat Whitehouse, Pat Garland and Bill Faulkner had worked together on the Talyllyn. Some of the others had been involved in the unsuccessful attempt to preserve the Kingsbridge branch. But it was as businessmen that they set up the railway company to buy the railway line from Totnes to Ashburton in Devon, which had been closed in 1962. Their business calculation was a simple one – that summer tourist services in this popular holiday area would be profitable.[128] The operating company was converted into a public limited company, although without a quotation on the stock exchange, in 1972, when the Kingswear branch was acquired.

The new owners took possession in October 1965. A Light Railway Order was granted early in 1966, and the company looked forward to reopening at least part of the line on 1 July. However, even for an organisation as strong commercially as this, hopes and ambitions were frustrated by lengthy negotiations over the transfer of the undertaking. A major sticking point was that the Ministry of Transport wanted to use at least some of the branch for improvements to the A38 trunk road. Eventually agreement was reached for the Dart Valley to take over the line from Totnes to Buckfastleigh, the section from there to Ashburton being lost to the road. It was not until 1969 that the line was reopened. In a nice touch, the company had Lord Beeching perform the official opening on 21 May, public passenger services having started on 5 April. It got off to a good start: in three weeks 22,398 journeys were made on the line, and by 1971 annual passenger figures had reached 125,000.

At Totnes there was no bay platform, making access difficult for the independent railway. An arrangement was made with British Railways that ran from 1985 to 1988, but it was never very satisfactory, and was costly. Eventually the Dart Valley built its independent station of Totnes Riverside, later renamed Littlehempston Riverside. At the other end of the line, Buck-

In August 1973 *Flying Scotsman* visited the Torbay Steam Railway. It is seen arriving at Kingswear double-heading No.7827 *Lydham Manor*.

(Les Folkard/Online Transport Archive) (LF285-10)

fastleigh had by 1979 developed into a servicing depot and workshops for locomotives and carriages, allowing the railway to undertake much of its own engineering work.

In 1972 the Dart Valley Light Railway Company bought another railway, paying more than £200,000 for the branch from Torquay along the coast to Kingswear, which was just being closed by BR. Transfer of this branch was seamless, with no period of closure. The DVR took possession from 1 November and services were operated under their name from 1 January 1973, the line soon being marketed as the Torbay Steam Railway, becoming in turn the Paignton & Dartmouth Railway in 1977. The new railway offered greater profit than the Buckfastleigh line, having one terminus at a major resort, and with a good connection to the main line. Plans on purchase of the line were to run a diesel service throughout the year, with steam in the summer months. These were not quite fulfilled, but very soon the Buckfastleigh line was relegated to secondary status, until in 1990 the DVLR declared that it was losing money and threatened to close it. The Dart Valley Railway Association stepped in to run the Buckfastleigh line, which became the South Devon Railway. Under the management of the South Devon Railway Trust, with an enthusiastic body of volunteers, the line became one of the great successes among preserved railways. A successful issue of shares in the operating company allowed the freehold of the railway to be bought, and separation from the Dart Valley was complete.[130]

The arrival of the Dart Valley aroused disquiet in enthusiast circles. In March 1969 the *Railway Magazine* carried an editorial headed 'Second Railway Mania' that commented on the number of commercial enterprises 'following on the heels of the dash of enthusiast-supported railway preservation societies'.[131] There were other lines being promoted by commercial undertakings at the time, notably the purchase by Modern Electric Tramways of part of the Seaton branch to convert into a 2ft gauge tramway. A similar plan by a company called Minirail to convert the Lyme Regis branch failed, as did a later proposal by the Axe & Lyme Valley Light Railway Co. Ltd for a 15in gauge railway on the line. Loan notes for this last were issued, and locomotives, rolling stock and track were acquired in 1974–75, but that was as far as it went.[132]

What concerned the *Railway Magazine* was the control and long-term security of preserved railways: 'Enthusiast-backed schemes have a certain resilience in that the members will be prepared to make special efforts to overcome difficulties and dangers to their lines, whereas the commercial enterprises

Now painted black, *Lydham Manor* runs round its train at Kingswear on the line now called Dartmouth Steam Railway. 8 April 2016.

would be largely dependent on the goodwill of shareholders expecting a financial return, and this is where the enthusiasts may have the edge over them.'[133]

Whatever the fears of enthusiasts, the purchase and operation of railways by businessmen rather than preservation societies became an established part of the preservation scene. The Bala Lake Railway, which opened to traffic on 13 August 1972, was described by its operators as a 'purely tourist' railway rather than a preserved railway. It was essentially a new construction; it had new coaches built by Severn-Lamb Ltd, although it used preserved steam locomotives as motive power.[134] In 1974 Hills & Bailey Ltd launched a project to build a narrow-gauge line on 5½ miles of the Brecon & Merthyr railway from Pant to Torpantau. Planning permission for what was to become the Brecon Mountain Railway was granted in 1976.

The Strathspey Railway Company was established by six members of the Scottish Railway Preservation Society who were disappointed at the society's decision not to pursue the project to reopen the branch line from Aviemore to Boat of Garten. These six owned locomotives, such as LMS class 5 No.5025 and Standard class 2 No.46464, and were the major shareholders in the new company, with additional backing from the Highlands and Islands Development Board, which made a grant of £10,000 and a loan of £22,000. The company agreed terms with BR for the purchase of the line in 1972. The Strathspey Railway Association was formed shortly afterwards as a supporting group, though it, too, contributed to the finances, becoming a shareholder in the company. The railway opened on 22 July 1978, although some of the facilities on the line, such as Aviemore station, were 'works in progress'. Operations for that first summer season were at weekends only.[135]

In 1974 there were reports in the railway press about two tank engines that had appeared near Castle Hedingham in Essex. 'We understand', wrote the *Railway Magazine*, 'that these locomotives belong to a Mr Hymas, who has plans for reopening a short stretch of the Colne Valley & Halstead Railway.' This was Dick Hymas, who, with Gordon Warren, founded the Colne Valley Railway Preservation Society, having previously been involved with the Stour Valley society. Hymas purchased three-quarters of a mile of track between Castle

Hedingham and Yeldham, and opened the stretch in 1974. The preservation society was an active supporting organisation, but it had no control. The railway was owned and run by Hymas and his wife as a commercial undertaking.[136]

Enthusiasts were involved with these railways in supporting roles only. Acknowledging that enthusiasts 'will be interested in the project', a Dart Valley Railway Association was formed, but its members would have to 'work in the wings' of the company. For a while at the beginning of the Dart Valley's operation, the Great Western Railway Society had an agreement to store much of its collection of stock on the line.[137] Similar developments took place at the independent narrow-gauge railways, such as the Romney Hythe & Dymchurch and the Fairbourne Railway. These had always been independent commercial operations, but during the 1970s they added supporters' associations, which provided financial support and volunteer labour. They were only a small part of the operation, however: the Romney Hythe & Dymchurch Railway Supporters Association was providing just three per cent of the labour for the railway in the mid-1970s. Financial restructuring sometimes went along with these moves. After some years of declining profits, following the death in 1963 of Captain Howey, the founder-owner of the railway, the RHDR was in danger of closing in 1971. A group of enthusiasts led by William McAlpine stepped in to buy it and announced that the railway would be run as a social amenity, with profits being ploughed back into the business. The new owners were faced with a backlog of maintenance. Between 1972 and 1976 £40,000 was spent on an extensive programme of investment in relaid track, signalling renewals and new rolling stock. In 1976 additional capital was sought through a public share issue, which raised £79,000, which was held to be disappointing in comparison with the results of issues elsewhere. On the operating side, the season was to be extended from 1 April to 11 November, with a view to increasing traffic to 400,000 passenger journeys from the 305,000 in 1973, and a contract to carry schools traffic in 1977 proved a boon.[138]

The involvement of volunteer societies perhaps disguised the extent to which individuals with deep pockets were financing railway preservation in the 1970s. They provided the large

Vale of Rheidol locomotive No.9 at Devil's Bridge in 2010. (Peter Bosley)

capital sums needed to get a project off the ground. The West Somerset Railway was one example. When plans for reinstating services on the Taunton–Minehead route took shape, two groups emerged: the West Somerset Railway Company and the West Somerset Railway Association. They were interconnected, but the association did not have financial control of the company. For many years it held no shares and had no representative on the company's board, thus realising the fears perhaps of the *Railway Magazine*. The association's lack of control was a cause of friction between it and the company. The railway was still young when the association first complained of lack of representation on the company's board. From time to time a dispute has surfaced, most recently in 2013 when association and company each prepared competing proposals for the purchase of the freehold of the railway from Somerset County Council.[139]

The Lavender Line in Sussex was founded by David Millham, who bought the station at Isfield in 1983. In 1992 he sold the line to the volunteers in the Lavender Line Preservation

Society. Many preserved railways changed structure during later years, transferring assets to a trust to take advantage of charitable status. This happened to the Vale of Rheidol Railway, sold in 1989 to Tony Hills and Peter Rampton, the owners of the Brecon Mountain Railway. After Tony Hills withdrew from the line's management, it passed into the ownership of the Phyllis Rampton Narrow Gauge Railway Trust in the mid-1990s.[140]

Isle of Wight lines: commerce or preservation

The fate of railways on the Isle of Wight was one of the many *causes célèbres* in the annals of the Beeching rationalisation. Proposals to close all the railways on the island provoked furious protest. Campaigns in the local press, public meetings and lobbying of politicians all played their part. In July 1965 the Minister of Transport announced his decision following the inquiry into the closure proposals: the route between Ryde and Shanklin must be kept open, but the rest could go.[141]

With such a background, it is hardly surprising that the Isle of Wight should attract proposals for the revival of its railways under new management. Ambition ran ahead of reality in several. Among the earliest, the Altrincham Railway Society announced to the railway press its intention to rent all the lines from Ryde to Cowes, Ventnor and Shanklin. This scheme was short-lived.[142] The Vectrail Society had a longer run. It proposed to revive the island's railways as modern light railways. Evidence presented to the public inquiry into the closure of the railways by Professor Hondelink, of the European Central Inland Transport Organisation, that such an operation should be profitable seems to have encouraged these proposals. Vectrail initially planned electrification, but subsequently opted instead for new diesel railcars then being developed by the Sadler Rail Coach Company. The society and Sadler-Vectrail Ltd, its operating company, negotiated with British Railways for the purchase of the Newport and Cowes line, with a view to operating services along that route into Ryde. There was talk then of Vectrail building its own line from Smallbrook Junction to Ryde. In 1969 the Isle of Wight County Council became a party to these negotiations, as it exercised its right under the Transport Act to buy the line from BR. The council was planning to lease the line to Sadler-Vectrail once negotiations with BR had been

One of the glories of the Isle of Wight Steam Railway is its collection of vintage carriages. No.24 *Calbourne* leads a train out of Havenstreet, with four-wheeled coaches at the front.

completed.[143] It all came to nothing, however: ambitions became too great, and Sadler-Vectrail and its plans folded in 1970.

The Wight Locomotive Society, meanwhile, launched a fund in 1966 to preserve some of the locomotives and rolling stock from the island's railways. The intention was to establish a museum where these could be housed, with perhaps a short demonstration line. The society had 'no illusions of being able to purchase, lease or rent any section, or of competing with other bodies in the running of a railway', its secretary declared.[144] The fund got off to a slow start: after two months only £36 had been raised, a clear example of the difficulties that preservation schemes faced.[145] However, the society built support, succeeded in buying the last survivor of the O2 class locomotives that had operated the island's trains, No.W24 *Calbourne*, several coaches and a number of other objects, which were housed in a base at Newport.[146] By 1969 the society was looking to operate some of the stock that had been collected and use it on the Cowes line after Sadler-Vectrail took over. A year later everything had changed. The collapse of Sadler-Vectrail

Ready to clean the coaches at Havenstreet.

presented the society with the opportunity of having a line of its own. The Isle of Wight County Council, now possessors of the trackbed, were still willing to see a railway scheme developed. The society negotiated initially to buy Haven Street station to act as a base, but had the view of taking on the section of railway from there to Wootton. The first trains ran in 1971, and the railway has since extended to five miles, operating tourist services with strong museum authenticity, a far cry from some of the earlier ideas for the island.[147]

Museum railways

The biggest contrast with the commercial undertakings was those railways that concentrated on the museum aspect. Although preservation is a core component of most heritage railways, and in more recent years most have gone through official accreditation as registered museums, there are some railways for which a museum project has been the heart.

The Midland Railway project was launched by Derby corporation's museums department in 1970 to preserve and record material relating to the Midland Railway, and in particular to Derby and its railway works (see p. 54-5). Having started the project, Derby Borough Council lobbied other local authorities for their support, securing first the backing of

Sir Berkeley was built by Manning Wardle in Leeds in 1890. It was one of the stars of the film *The Railway Children*. Here it is working with two vintage carriages at the Midland Railway – Butterley on 21 June 1994.

(Les Folkard/Online Transport Archive) (LF640-33)

Derbyshire county planning committee early in 1971. Derby corporation built up a collection of material for this museum project. As well as a large collection of small objects, wagons and coaches were acquired, including an inspection saloon built for the LMS in 1930. Locomotives were also bought. One was a BR Standard Class 5 locomotive with Caprotti valve gear, bought from the Barry scrapyard, which became the sole surviving example of this type of engine. As the collection grew, a new working site was sought and a centre was eventually established at Butterley on the route from Pye Bridge to Ambergate. Derby council withdrew its funding in 1973, although the stock acquired by the authority continued to be kept at the project, which was now reconstituted as the voluntary Midland Railway Trust. The project's collection of stock was moved to Butterley during 1975, and the first public open days were held. The museum's collection was soon joined by the Stanier Pacific locomotive *Princess Margaret Rose*, one of the engines that had been bought by Butlin's. A Light Railway

Order was obtained in 1981 for trains to run over the first mile of track towards Swanwick.[148]

Some museum railways were developed on industrial sites. Theirs has been a distinctive contribution to the railway preservation movement, with their tank locomotives, industrial surroundings and small-scale, intimate atmosphere. Two of these railways are in the north east. The Bowes Railway was formally inaugurated by the Queen Mother in July 1976. The National Coal Board closed the last surviving part of this railway, part of what had been until 1932 the Pontop & Jarrow Railway, on 4 October 1974. Tyne and Wear County Council bought the land from Black Fell to Bank Head, appointing the Bowes Railway Project Committee to manage it as a museum project to preserve this line, which is a scheduled ancient monument. It is unique in having operational rope-worked inclines, and most of the workshops survive. The local authorities – now Sunderland City Council and Gateshead Council – have retained ownership of the railway, and operation has been in the hands of the voluntary Tyne & Wear Industrial Monuments Trust (now the Bowes Railway Company).[149]

Marley Hill was linked to the Bowes Railway. So, too, was the Tanfield Railway, another line along an old wagon-way, the origins of which go back to the seventeenth century. What survived into the twentieth century had become part of a British Railways branch line, partly occupying the site of a wagon-way built in 1725, giving the restored railway its marketing slogan

An important aspect of the museum side of preserved railways is the collection and restoration of historic coaches, such as Taff Vale Railway coach No.220, built in the 1890s, restored at the Gwili Railway.

(Chris Marsh)

Among the fine collection of coaches at the Severn Valley Railway is Great Western third class No.3930, built in 1915.

as the 'World's Oldest Railway'. When Marley Hill colliery closed, the Stephenson & Hawthorns Locomotive Trust, founded in 1970 to preserve representative examples from Tyneside's railway building history, sought to take over the engine shed as a base, with the prospect of rebuilding three miles of railway between Sunniside and East Tanfield. The aim of the new Tanfield Railway was to retain the character of the independent industrial railways of the region. Locomotives would be small. There would be no bogie or corridor coaches on the passenger trains. The first trains ran on a short stretch of line at Marley Hill in 1975. An extension north to Sunniside opened in July 1981; going south, the route was extended to Causey in July 1981 and East Tanfield in October 1982.[150]

The Foxfield Railway was established on a former colliery line that ran from the Foxfield colliery at Dilhorne, Staffordshire, to the main network at Blyth Bridge four miles away. The closure of the colliery in 1965 prompted the foundation of a preservation society, which has built up one of the best collections of industrial steam locomotives in the country. The railway began operations on open days in 1967. It bought the whole line in 1978, but that did not include all the land needed for full public access. It was not until 1982 that a new station at Caverswall Road was opened and a fuller service brought into operation.[151]

Chapter 6

MAIN-LINE AMBITIONS

Most preserved railway projects were based on branch lines, but during the mid-1960s thoughts turned to the preservation of longer lines, to recreate and preserve the express steam railway. By 1966–67 the end of steam on British Railways was in sight, and enthusiasts were concerned about the prospects for the continuance of steam-hauled excursion trains on the main line. Many were not hopeful.[152] Meanwhile, since Alan Pegler's purchase of *Flying Scotsman* in 1963, many large and powerful steam locomotives had been saved. The groups owning these locomotives needed bases from which they could operate, capable of handling main-line power. This led to the establishment of steam centres with engineering capacity. Some were on preserved railways, whereas others, such as Didcot, Carnforth and Tyseley, were independent of operating railways. At the same time, owners wanted to see their locomotives do more than potter up and down a five-mile branch line at 25mph. The logic pointed towards the preservation of main-line railways that could offer longer stretches of line with double track on which trains could be run at higher speeds. When British Railways announced that no steam locomotives would be permitted to run over their tracks after the final withdrawal of regular steam operation in August 1968, this logic seemed compelling.

Railways that might be suitable for main-line preservation schemes were becoming available with the closure of some much-loved routes, including the Waverley route between Edinburgh and Carlisle and the Great Central line to London. Both of these became the object of revival and preservation plans. Another celebrated railway closure was the Somerset and Dorset cross-country route, which also attracted hopes of revival. In the mid-1970s the Somerset & Dorset Museum Trust planned to buy half a mile of the route from Radstock to Writhlington, but was unable to realise such ambitions, although ideas of reviving the route of the S&D have never gone away.[153]

When the Stratford-upon-Avon Transport Action Committee proposed to save the route from Stratford to Cheltenham, there was much tut-tutting in the railway press, with talk of a 'second railway mania' and warnings of dire consequences of failure to co-ordinate and concentrate on the strongest scheme.[154] The doom-mongers could perhaps have felt justified, for of all the projects for long routes, only one got off the ground in the 1960s and 1970s. However, recent years have seen the revival of plans for some form of preservation of the others. Many thought the Stratford-upon-Avon to Cheltenham line was the most promising for preservation. It was in an area with good tourist potential and near major centres of population. The Stratford-upon-Avon Transport Action Consultative Committee announced in 1968 that it was considering setting up a body to buy or lease the line. BR's response to initial approaches was that the line would be needed until 1974 at least as a diversionary route.[155] The action committee had to put its plans on hold. After the line was closed, the southern section, from Cheltenham to Broadway, became the focus for the Gloucestershire/Warwickshire Railway, established in 1979, and dreams of reopening the remainder through to Stratford remain alive.

The closure of the Waverley route in 1969 in the face of considerable protest immediately inspired proposals for its revival. R.A. Symes-Schutzmann, known also more simply as Bob Symes, was a television producer who had turned his hobby into work on occasion with documentaries on railways. He had cut his teeth in the world of railway preservation by working on the Talyllyn. Now he was the front man for the Border Union Railway Company, founded by him and others, to preserve the Waverley route as a main-line railway. The company proposed to buy about eighty miles of railway and negotiate for their trains to run over British Railways tracks at both ends of the route to reach Edinburgh and Carlisle. A feasibility study commissioned by the company proposed a number of lines of business: the operation of commuter services on the northern section into Edinburgh; freight traffic centred upon Hawick and Galashiels; the promotion of tourist traffic; railtours coming through from both ends of the line; using the line for film location work; and offering facilities to the railway manufacturing industry for testing new products. It was a hugely ambitious project, in many ways innovative, although perhaps it needed to be, for losses on the conventional services operated by British Railways had been considerable in later years. Something entrepreneurial was going to be needed to counter such problems on a line this length. Many ideas were being floated for operating the line, including importing German Pacific locomotives to run some of the tourist services and coaches from Austria for other uses. The Waverley Railway Association, formed in 1969, was to provide the volunteer input.

This, plainly, was not going to be a cheap scheme. The feasibility study estimated a capital cost of £1.75m to buy the line, locomotives and rolling stock, and provide initial working capital. Such a sum would be beyond the railway enthusiast pocket, and the plan was to raise the capital through normal business channels, including a public share issue in the North British Railway Co. Ltd, which would be formed to operate the railway. For this project was conceived as a business enterprise. Like the Vectrail group on the Isle of Wight, the promoters of Border Union were at pains to point out that theirs was not a preservation scheme. Others in the railway preservation world were very sceptical. The projected growth in tourist traffic to 500,000 a year by 1975 was held to be ambitious, likewise the financial proposals. Patrick Garland, with experience of financing the Talyllyn and Dart Valley, argued that a minimum income of £3,000 a week would be needed to meet interest charges alone. The Border Union did, though, attract local support from those who saw the revived railway as a means to 'restore a link essential for the sound economic development of the Scottish Borders'. Some local authorities, including Roxburgh County Council and Melrose Town Council, promised support, offering relief from the rates. British Railways, too, took the company seriously enough to be prepared to enter discussions about the running powers. It all came to nothing, however, being just too ambitious for the times. Private investors were not then prepared to put up the capital on this scale. The project lasted only a few months. British Railways set a deadline for payment of a deposit of £250,000 plus a non-returnable fee of £10,000, and the Border Union were unable to meet it. In consequence BR broke off negotiations on 23 December 1969. The company and its supporting Waverley Railway Association both attempted to salvage alternative schemes of buying at least part of the line. However, relations between the two broke down; the Association decided to dissolve in October 1970, complaining of a lack of information from the company. Lifting of track on the route started at about the same time. Shortly afterwards BR decided to sell the route after concluding that the Border Union had no hope of revival.[156]

Twenty-five years later, interest in this line revived in the wake of privatisation. Some commercial businesses expressed interest in its possibilities for carrying timber from Kielder Forest. In March 2005 the Scottish Executive later gave its backing, and £115m of funding, to proposals for a revived passenger service at the Edinburgh end of the line. Meanwhile preservation groups at Riccarton (Friends of Riccarton Junction) and Whitrope (Waverley Route Heritage Association, founded 2001) developed heritage projects further south along the route. Track was relaid at Whitrope in July 2005, and on 1 July 2012 operation of the new, short Border Union Railway began.[157]

In 1968 news appeared in the railway press of the formation of a Main Line Preservation Group, the aim of which was to acquire a suitable line for the running of preserved steam-hauled trains at higher speeds than on the branch lines that so far had been preserved. The group soon decided to preserve part of the

The atmosphere of the main line captured at Loughborough Central. 2-8-0 No.48624 is about to take the 1.15 pm dining train out on 7 May 2016. The signs for the museum are accoutrements of the modern heritage railway.

A fresh coat of green paint gleams on 2-6-0 No.46521 at Quorn and Woodhouse, which is maintained as a 1940s station.

Great Central main line, basing itself in Leicester, with a local notable, the Earl of Lanesborough, accepting the post of society president.[158] It was not the first time that the Great Central line had attracted thoughts of preservation. Several letters supporting the operation of large preserved steam locomotives had appeared in the railway press during 1966.[159] Many hopes then were based upon the purchase of the forty-five miles of the route from Aylesbury to Rugby. The Main Line Preservation Group in 1969 moved its focus further north, to the section of the Great Central Railway from Rugby to Nottingham, another long stretch of forty-three miles. The large population of the east Midlands, for which there was then no other preservation scheme, and the tourist potential of Charnwood Forest were thought to give a good foundation to the scheme. It was decided to concentrate first on the northern section, from Leicester to Ruddington, a few miles south of Nottingham; soon it was accepted that it would be necessary to drop the section south of Leicester to Rugby from the proposals as being beyond the financial resources of the group. Further retrenchment, out of financial necessity, brought the group to concentrate on the section from Loughborough to Leicester, although the longer-term aim to reach Nottingham remained.

Firm negotiations with British Rail for the purchase of this line started in 1970, and a lease of Loughborough station was secured in that year.[160] The preservation group was reformed as the Main Line Steam Trust, and the launch of an appeal to buy the line was announced in January 1972, with an initial target of £75,000. The first open days were held at Loughborough, and in 1973 British Rail allowed the Trust to run a few trains to Quorn, a distance of two miles. The Trust succeeded in gaining charitable status in 1973, a useful fiscal aid for the difficult task of raising the money. A share issue launched by the Great Central Railway (1976) Ltd, the body formed to take on the purchase of the line, was successful, but did not bring in the funds quickly enough for British Railways, which proceeded with lifting the track. By the time the GCR was able to buy the line from Loughborough to Quorn & Rothley, it found itself in possession not of a lengthy double-track main line, but of a railway that was going to have to be built up again almost from scratch. Operations had to begin, not with the stirring sight of a main-line train, but, in common with most preserved railways, on a small scale using small tank engines on a short stretch of line, 2¼ miles, between Loughborough and Quorn. These first services actually began shortly before ownership of the line had passed to the GCR, British Rail agreeing to provide pilotmen until purchase was completed. The running line was doubled in length in January 1976, when services were extended to Rothley. Further extension took the railway south to Birstall, now renamed Leicester North, over trackbed that Charnwood Borough Council had bought in 1976–77. A share issue in 1977 raised more than £200,000 to fund purchase of the track between Loughborough and Rothley. The Great Central Railway was still single-track at this stage. It needed several years of rebuilding, first to take larger main-line locomotives, then to relay double track and install extensive signalling at Quorn and at Swithland. Ambitions were realised when 5½ miles of double track between Loughborough and Rothley were brought into operation in June 2000.[161]

Chapter 7

GREAT LITTLE TRAINS

W hile new preservation projects on the standard gauge were gaining prominence, the Welsh narrow-gauge railways, where it all began, were making progress that was steady, if beset by problems. The Talyllyn celebrated the centenary of its foundation in style in 1965, with a railway that had already been transformed since 1950, through relaying of the track and work on the stations and rolling stock. However, the long-planned extension to Nant Gwernol continued to be delayed. This had been projected in 1957, with the intention of having it open in time for the centenary. It was not until 1970, however, that work on the extension started. With too many other demands on labour and finance, the

The Talyllyn Railway's extension to Nant Gwernol was opened on 22 May 1976. Locomotive No. 2 *Dolgoch* was suitably decorated for a return to Tywyn.
(Gordon Brown)

railway could not afford to embark on a major new project before then. The new length of railway was opened in 1976.[162]

At the Ffestiniog Railway financial pressures were just as great. Allan Garraway's reports to the Board in the early 1960s continually stressed the parlous state of the locomotives and rolling stock, and the need for considerable expenditure to maintain a decent public service. When Beyer Peacock offered the railway their first Garrett locomotive, K1, in 1966, the Board deferred purchase because they could not find the £1,000 asking price.[163] Despite these difficulties the railway decided it could not hold back on embarking on one of the most ambitious projects in railway preservation of the 1960s and 1970s – the rebuilding of the line to Blaenau Ffestiniog.

Before the Festiniog Railway Company was bought by Alan Pegler and his associates, the eastern end of the line was already threatened with being submerged under the reservoir for the new Trawsfynedd hydroelectric power station, the plans for which were still to receive parliamentary approval. Compensation would be paid, but the new owners were determined to reopen the whole of the railway. It would be a major exercise, involving the building of a new railway on a deviation around the flooded section, and including a spiral to take the line to its new higher level, the building of a new tunnel and other substantial works. One who inspired the project was civil engineer Gerald Fox, whose initial survey showed that the engineering work did not have to be as extensive as feared. The reconstruction could be undertaken mainly by volunteers, 'with teaspoons, if necessary'.[164]

Negotiations with the British Electricity Authority (later the Central Electricity Generating Board) about compensation and possible routes for the deviation were protracted and sometimes difficult, involving a court case the second longest in British legal history. Both company and railway society had petitioned parliament against the North Wales Hydro Electric Power Bill in 1955. After the power station was approved, negotiations over compensation began but were not settled until 1971. Alongside that, plans for the deviation and applications for the Light Railway Orders were put in hand.[165]

Having paused at Tanybwlch for some years to allow for consolidation, work on the next stage, to Dduallt, began in 1965

Passengers mill around *Merddyn Emrys* at Tanybwlch, Ffestiniog Railway, 22 August 1961.

(Gordon Brown)

while arguments over the course of the deviation continued. Supplies of rail were bought from the closed Penrhyn quarries, and, with the help of the army on an exercise, track was quickly relaid up to Garnedd tunnel. An outbreak of foot and mouth disease in 1967, which restricted movement in the area for some time, slowed progress. However, work resumed, attracting large numbers of volunteers from a variety of interests besides members of the railway society, who gained the appellation 'Deviationists'. People who wanted an outdoor activity holiday came; there were groups from such organisations as the Crusaders, Westminster School and the Borstal. The extension's project management organised the volunteer labour into four teams, known as London A, London B, Northern and Gloucester. The line to Dduallt opened in 1968. This was the furthest point on the old route before the new deviation round the power station would have to be built. The deviation would take much

Fairlie locomotive *Merddyn Emrys* rounds the curve near Dduallt on the Ffestiniog Railway in the 1970s.

(Peter N. Williams/Online Transport Archive) (PNW2-28)

longer. The new Moelwyn tunnel was not completed until 1977, the same year that planning approval was secured for a new joint station for FR and BR at Blaenau Ffestiniog. In 1982 what had been the biggest civil engineering project so far undertaken by the railway preservation movement was completed, and the line through to Blaenau Ffestiniog was finally opened.[166]

The Welshpool & Llanfair Light Railway, having successfully opened in 1963, was almost washed away by floods in December 1964. The bridge at Sylfaen was severely damaged; the cost of rebuilding could have finished off the project, for it had a very hand-to-mouth existence. Courageously the society launched a national appeal for reconstruction funds, and Sir Thomas Salt persuaded the army to provide labour. With such support the railway was rescued again, and by 1967 the line was carrying 22,461 passengers. A further 1¼ miles to Sylfaen were opened in 1972, and the following year the society's offer of £8,000 to buy the freehold of the line was accepted by BR. In 1977 a fund was launched to raise £63,000 for the extension back to Welshpool at a new station to be built at Raven Square.[167]

The success of the Welsh narrow-gauge railways was being recognised by local organisations for their encouragement to tourism in the area. As early as 1961 the Wales Tourist Board proposed joint marketing leaflets for the railways featuring the Talyllyn, Ffestiniog and the Welshpool & Llanfair, even though the last was not yet open. There was a suggestion that the nascent Welsh Highland might be included in this marketing, but that was not pursued as the project was too little advanced, and the Ffestiniog was opposed to promoting that line.[168] Further development of joint marketing led in 1970 to the launching of the 'Great Little Trains of Wales' marketing panel to promote all the narrow-gauge lines in the principality. As well as the three preserved railways, the Snowdon Mountain Railway, the Fairbourne, and the Vale of Rheidol, operated by British Railways, were represented on this panel.[169] In 1964 the Welsh Tourist Board awarded the Ffestiniog a certificate of merit, which Pegler received at a ceremony at Cardiff, arriving there in a special train hauled by his own locomotive *Flying Scotsman*.[170]

By the early 1970s the strong appeal of the Welsh narrow gauge, based upon the success of the first three preserved railways, meant that many wanted to capitalise on it. As well as bringing such lines as the commercial–tourist Snowdon Mountain Railway into the marketing net, several new lines were promoted. Preservation groups and businessmen launched new projects, often constructing a narrow-gauge railway where a standard-gauge branch once ran. Local authorities keen to attract more tourists to their areas encouraged the developments.

The Llanberis Lake Railway was the first of this breed of more commercial ventures. Unlike its predecessors among the Welsh narrow gauge, this line did not rely on a preservation society but was promoted by a group led by Alan Porter. In operation, little volunteer labour was involved. The company stated that its aim was to provide as many jobs as possible to local people. The new line was built along the trackbed of the old 4ft gauge Padarn Railway that had served the Dinorwic slate quarries. The quarries closed in 1969, and at the auction of some of the assets that December the promoters of the new railway bought three of the small locomotives built by Hunslet for the 1ft 11in gauge internal system of Dinorwic quarries. Construction of the first section of the new railway began in autumn 1970. The three locomotives, *Red Damsel, Dolbadarn* and *Wild Aster*, were overhauled in early 1971, and six coaches were

From across the lake a Llanberis Lake Railway train is a small splash of bright colour against the forested hills behind. 4 April 2002.

built. The official opening of the first half-mile section was on 28 May. Clearance of the final hurdles of inspection delayed the start of regular passenger services from Gilfach Ddu to Cei Llydan until July. When trains did run they attracted plenty of attention, with 6,000 tickets sold in the first fortnight. An extension to Penllyn was opened the following year. By 1977 the railway was achieving passenger carryings of 80,000 a year. In 2003 the railway was brought into Llanberis village.[171]

The Bala Lake Railway, the Brecon Mountain Railway and the Teifi Valley Railway were further narrow-gauge lines in Wales, each built on the trackbed of former standard-gauge lines. The first of these arose out of an initiative by the Merionethshire County Council. Having bought the trackbed of the railway from Bala to Morfa Mawdacch after it was closed, the council proposed the building of a narrow-gauge line between Bala and Llanuwchllyn, a distance of 4¼ miles. After considering setting up a council-owned operation, they decided to seek a suitable independent organisation to run it.[172] The Brecon Mountain Railway was promoted by the engineers Hills & Bailey Ltd of Llanberis, which in 1974 launched plans to build a line of eight miles to 2ft gauge between Pontsarn and Torpantau on the former Brecon & Merthyr Railway. The capital cost of building the first three miles was estimated at £100,000.[173]

The Teifi Valley Railway was the work of a preservation society formed in 1972. Its initial aim was to take over the standard-gauge branch from Pencader to Newcastle Emlyn, the closure of which had been announced. When the line closed a year later, the society had already established a base at Henllan, with its first locomotive in residence.[174] The intention was to reopen the standard-gauge line, but eventually the line was rebuilt as a narrow-gauge railway.

On a smaller scale of ambition, at this time at least, was the Corris Railway Study Group. This was established in 1965 to 'carry out a full investigation of what remained of this historic 2ft 3in gauge line with a view to further preservation and perhaps restoration in some way'. Reconstituted two years later as the Corris Society, the group secured a lease on the old station at Machynlleth in which to gather its collection. Its efforts attracted criticism: one person wondered why the society bothered when the Talyllyn was successfully operating a few miles away. The society carried on, and opened its museum in 1970. The next year the society bought the stations at Llwyngwern and Esgairgeiliog.

Hunslet quarry locomotive *Holy War* comes out of the shed yard to take the first train out of Llanuwchllyn, Bala Lake Railway. 25 May 2016.

Kerr Stuart No.3117 *Sgt Murphy* on the Teifi Valley Railway, September 1996.

(Chris Marsh)

By 1973 the society was negotiating the purchase of land to allow a line of three quarters of a mile to be built between Corris and Maespoeth Junction. The Wales Tourist Board offered a grant of forty-nine per cent of the purchase price of £4,000. Later a short operational railway was developed.[175]

The Talyllyn and Ffestiniog soon prompted imitators in England. There was talk once again in 1960 of reviving the Southwold Railway, and there was an attempt to rebuild the Weston Clevedon & Portishead Light Railway in the 1950s from standard to 2ft 8in gauge. A North Somerset Light Railway Company was formed and a locomotive secured, but the project foundered. A successful rescue was of the Ravenglass & Eskdale Railway in Cumbria. Originally built as a mineral line at a gauge of 3 feet, the line had been converted to 15in gauge in 1915, and by the 1950s was owned by the Keswick Granite Company. The company closed its Eskdale quarries in the early 1950s, but operated the railway as a tourist line. In 1958 it was put up for sale as a going concern, but, with no takers, Keswick Granite kept it going. Two years later the company put the railway's assets up for auction, and at the sale on 7 September 1960 the winning bid was in the name of the recently formed Ravenglass & Eskdale Railway Preservation Society. The society in fact had nothing like enough money, and the bulk of the purchase price was found by Mr Colin Gilbert, a local businessman. Gilbert was given the ownership of the shares of the new Ravenglass & Eskdale Railway Company. The preservation society had representation on the board, as also did Sir Wavell Wakefield MP, a local landowner who had promised additional finance if required. When Gilbert died in 1968, the share ownership and control passed to Lord Wakefield, as he had now become. This railway was thus operated primarily as a commercial concern, with mainly professional staff. The new owners invested heavily in the line, introducing innovations such as radio signalling, and creating an efficient organisation. By 1967 passenger numbers had reached 185,000. The preservation society, to the disappointment of many members, had a supporting role rather than control. Its support was valuable none the less; it was the society that commissioned and paid

River Esk, built for the Ravenglass & Eskdale Railway in 1923, prepares to leave Ravenglass, June 1978.

for the first new locomotive of this era, the 2-8-2 *River Mite*, delivered in 1966.[176]

In 1970 the long-established Locomotive Club of Great Britain (LCGB) turned itself into a railway operator by taking on the industrial branch line of 2ft 6in gauge that linked the Bowater paper mills with the main railway network at Sittingbourne in Kent. Bowaters had decided to close the line in 1969, but were keen to see something of it preserved. Through the mediation of Captain Manisty, the company was introduced to Malcolm Burton, chairman of the LCGB, who jumped at the chance to operate the railway. The club was granted a lease at low rent for the line now christened the Sittingbourne & Kelmsley Light Railway. In its first summer of operation the railway carried more than 3,000 passengers. As the new line became established it was decided in 1976 to separate the railway company from the LCGB.[177] The Leighton Buzzard Light Railway was similarly a conversion to passenger use of an industrial line. The Iron Horse Preservation Society, formed in 1967, took out a lease of about two miles of the 2ft gauge railway that had linked the local sand and gravel quarry with the main railway. The society planned at first to create a railway on an American theme, but the members voted instead for a British industrial narrow-gauge atmosphere for their railway. They changed the society's name to the

In the early days on the Sittingbourne & Kemsley Light Railway most trains paused for a photo stop. Bagnall locomotive *Triumph* poses on 4 September 1971 in surroundings that belie the industrial origins of the railway.

(Gordon Brown)

Pixie, a Kerr Stuart 0-4-0 saddle tank, was one of the first locomotives to arrive on the Leighton Buzzard Railway. It makes its way across the road on 26 May 1975.

(Les Folkard/Online Transport Archive) (LF293-21)

Leighton Buzzard Narrow Gauge Railway Society, and operated at weekends from 3 March 1968. By 1973 the railway was established. The society had secured an extended lease, and it reconstituted itself again, this time as an industrial and provident society, as a means of limiting its members' liabilities.[178]

Among the newly built narrow-gauge railways was what might be regarded as the first heritage railway to be built from scratch. The Lincolnshire Coast Light Railway originated with a group of enthusiasts who in 1958 secured for preservation some of the locomotives and stock from the Nocton Estate railway, an extensive system built to serve a large potato-growing estate. A site was found at Humberston on the north-east coast of Lincolnshire where the collection could be kept. A length of line was laid on which trains were first run in 1960.[179] The railway has grown and moved a few times since then.

During the 1960s and 1970s, groups wanted to use former standard-gauge routes for new narrow-gauge railways in England. The Hampshire Narrow Gauge Railway Society, formed in 1959, planned in 1961 to convert the Meon Valley (Alton to Fareham) branch from standard gauge to 2ft. By 1964, they had switched attention to converting the branch from Botley to Bishops Waltham.

The Rushden Railway Society in Northamptonshire planned to build a metre-gauge railway on part of the Higham Ferrers branch. A narrow-gauge conversion was later proposed for the Lyme Regis branch from Axminster.[180]

Ironically, the South Tynedale Railway, a success story as a narrow-gauge railway, was not intended to take that form. The South Tynedale Railway Preservation Society was founded in April 1973 by John Parker with a view to preserving the branch from Haltwhistle to Alston in Northumberland when BR announced its closure in 1975. Parker argued that money spent on roads and replacement bus services would be wasted; only a railway would maintain links through the winter. The society planned to take over the standard-gauge branch line and develop it as a tourist attraction and local amenity, but they were unable to raise the £200,000 to complete the purchase before BR's deadline of 1 September 1976. With the track lifted, the society instead relaid the line to 2ft gauge.[181]

The Seaton Tramway in Devon was created by Modern Electric Tramways Ltd, a company owned by Claud Lane, which had a business building battery-powered vehicles. Lane operated a 2ft gauge tramway in Eastbourne on which scaled-down versions of standard 'Preston' design tramcars were run. The closed branch line from Seaton to Colyford and Colyton offered the opportunity to expand business with longer rides. The line was rebuilt to 2ft 9in gauge, the Eastbourne tramway closed and the new Seaton Tramway opened in 1970. For the first few years the trams ran under battery power, but overhead supply was completed in time for the 1974 season.[182]

The Launceston Steam Railway was built as a narrow-gauge railway on an old branch line in Cornwall.[183] It was promoted by Nigel Bowman, and opened in 1983. Two more new railways on old routes were the Wells & Walsingham Railway and Bure Valley Railway in Norfolk, both built to miniature gauges. The Wells and Walsingham Railway was built at 10¼in gauge along four miles of a former Great Eastern branch line, and opened in 1982. The Bure Valley Railway was opened in 1990, a 15in gauge line built on trackbed bought by the local authorities.

Proposals for a preserved railway in Northern Ireland were being developed in the mid-1970s. The North West of Ireland

Railway Society in 1974 proposed a line of 3ft gauge between Victoria Road and Craigavon Bridge, Londonderry, a distance of a mile. It was to be known as the Foyle Valley Railway. The railway project did not proceed, however, a museum being opened instead.[184]

The Isle of Man Railway had a complicated life through all of this period. The owning company ran into difficulties during the 1960s, and the railway was likely to close in 1966. The railway company said it would consider sympathetically any proposals from enthusiasts, and the Isle of Man Steam Railway Association was formed in April 1966 with a view to taking the line on. Another rescuer came along, the Marquess of Ailsa, who took a twenty-one-year lease on the line in 1967. With the backing of the Isle of Man Steam Railway Supporters Association, Lord Ailsa had charge of the railway for four years. He terminated the lease from 1 March 1972, at which point the Isle of Man Railway Company took the line back. However, the operation was severely reduced in scale. By 1975 it was running trains only on the section between Port Erin and Castletown, with no prospect of a return to Douglas, a state of

Most of the Seaton Tramway cars are of relatively new construction, built or adapted to the 2ft 9in gauge of the tramway. Car No.2 was built in 1964, based on the type A design of London Metropolitan Tramways. (Chris Marsh)

Sea Lion epitomises Victorian steam engineering on the Groudle Glen Railway, 16 September 2012.

affairs that continued for the next couple of years. By the end of 1976 the possibility of the government taking the line over was being discussed, although the Isle of Man Steam Railway Supporters Association formed a company as a potential alternative operator. In the interim, the island's government subsidised the railway for services on the line from Douglas to Port Erin in 1977. That year the railway became an election issue on the island. Following that, the island's government took over the steam railway from 1 January 1978 and merged it with the Manx Electric Railway, which had passed into government hands in 1957. The two together have since then been run as the island's tourist railways.[185] The small Groudle Glen Railway is a more conventional preserved railway. This 2ft gauge railway, which once ran to a zoo built by the coast, was restored by volunteers of the Isle of Man Steam Railway Supporters Association during the 1980s. The first trains ran on a short length of line in December 1983, and the bulk of the railway reopened in 1986.

Part Three

THE HERITAGE RAILWAY
1980-2000

Goathland

Chapter 8

FROM PRESERVED RAILWAYS TO HERITAGE RAILWAYS

At Alresford, Mid-Hants Railway, on 2 September 2003, BR standard 4-6-0 No.73096 awaits departure.

A new magazine, *Steam Railway*, was founded in 1979. The number of active railway preservation projects, either operational or in development, then stood at forty-eight. By the time the magazine celebrated its twenty-fifth anniversary in 2004, fifty-one more preservation projects had been established and were still active.[186] Table 3 shows a number of those that opened during the last two decades of the twentieth century, a time of rapid growth in railway preservation. Barely a month passed without a new scheme being launched or a new extension being put in hand. Ambitions grew as major projects were planned. Long dreamed of, the rebuilding of the Welsh Highland Railway became

a real prospect, and inspired many as construction proceeded.

Ambitious projects were not confined to building new railways and extending existing ones. Major new facilities such as workshops, stations and exhibition halls were built at many lines. These developments were part of the maturing of an industry: the initial pioneering phases on many railways were over and new projects were needed, for the benefit both of preserving the historic collections and of the passengers.

Ambitions were fuelled and encouraged, and their fulfilment made possible, by a huge increase in demand for the services offered by preserved railways. Throughout most of these years the economy was growing strongly, and this was reflected in the turnover and traffic on most preserved railways. After the difficulties of the 1970s, numbers of passengers grew, slowly at first – the early 1980s were not easy – but by the end of the century there was strong growth. The Mid-Hants Railway, to take one example, carried 52,000 passengers in 1977; in 2004 numbers were 130,000. The three-millionth passenger since the railway opened was carried in the summer of 2005.[187] The West Somerset was another railway that struggled through the early 1980s – on 'the verge of financial meltdown' according to one recent assessment.[188] Traffic grew in the first few years after opening, but dipped from 84,000 passengers in 1980 to as low as 51,000 in 1983. But gradual recovery began. In 1989 116,000 passengers were carried, with a steady rise to 154,000 in 2000.[189] By this time, the business footing of this and most other lines was sounder.

As they have grown, preserved railways have by and large succeeded in throwing off the perception of being grown men

TABLE 3	
Some preserved railways opened, 1980-2000	
Railway	**Opening, first section**
Brecon Mountain	1980
Welsh Highland Heritage	1980
Llangollen	1981
Gwili	1978
Bo'ness & Kinneil	1981
Midland Railway – Butterley	1981
Foxfield	1982
North Staffordshire	1982
Wells & Walsingham	1982
Groudle Glen	1983
Lavender Line, Isfield, Sussex	1983
Launceston	1983
Pontypool & Blaenavon	1983
Teifi Valley	1983
South Tynedale	1983
Gloucestershire/Warwickshire	1984
Telford	1984
Cholsey & Wallingford	1985
Downpatrick & County Down	1987
Leadhills & Wanlockhead	1988
Bodmin & Wenford	1989
Vale of Rheidol	sold by BR 1989
Bure Valley	1990
Amerton Railway	1992
Chinnor & Princes Risborough	1994
Kirklees	1991
Caledonian	1993
East Kent	1993
Elsecar	1994
Northampton & Lamport	1996
Churnet Valley	1996
Spa Valley	1996
Dartmoor	1997
Welsh Highland	1997
Vale of Glamorgan	1997
Lincolnshire Wolds	1998
Great Central (Nottingham)	1999
Keith & Dufftown	2000

Preserved railways have made sights common that were unheard of in the days of British Railways and beyond. The S15 class 4-6-0 was a southern type of locomotive. Some members of the class have seen service on the North Yorkshire Moors Railway, where their power has been valuable for tackling the steep gradients. One, No.825, arrives at Pickering in the pouring rain on 13 September 2010.

playing trains, to become accepted by public bodies as serious businesses having a part to play alongside the main railway network. Large figures bandied around for the railways' contribution to local economies (£18m at the North Yorkshire Moors Railway, for example) made authorities keener to encourage their growth.

So enthusiastic did some authorities become for their local heritage railway by the end of the century that they looked for expansion beyond what the railways were themselves considering. North Yorkshire County Council commissioned a feasibility study in 2000 into the southward expansion of the NYMR from Pickering to Malton. Its optimistic report encouraged local businesses to press for that development, although the extension is not, so far, high on the railway's list of projects. Local authorities encouraged the East Lancashire Railway to extend from Heywood to Castleton; the railway does see that as important for the growth of its business. More recently, the Embsay & Bolton Abbey Steam Railway has received local backing for feasibility studies into extending to

Skipton, and at the other end of its line local community supporters have been keen to extend the line to Addingham, in preference, it was said, to a cycle track.[190]

Another consequence of the greater acceptance from public bodies was that grant-aided funding became available in larger quantities, sums of millions of pounds being regularly discussed in ways that the early preservationists would not have imagined (and might well have treated with suspicion). Such generous funding allowed heritage railways to expedite projects by employing contractors where formerly they would have relied on volunteers. The ambitious rebuilding of the Welsh Highland Railway was almost entirely the work of contractors, but many smaller projects have also been carried out in this way. Contractors get the job done more quickly, but there are prices to pay.

The range and character of preserved railways grew with their numbers. Steam has remained the dominant motive power, undoubtedly a crowd-puller. But this period saw the rapid growth in the preservation of diesel and electric locomotives and multiple unit vehicles, and they became major features on many lines. The use of different types of motive power was one way by which railways sought to establish their niche in the market. The Great Central Railway's windcutter train was an example of the ways in which heritage railways kept up the momentum of preservation and museum projects. A train of 16 ton mineral wagons was assembled to give an insight into freight operations of the past.[191] Developments such as educational facilities and display galleries all added to the diversity. When another new magazine was launched in 1999 it set out, its strapline said, to cover 'the total preservation scene', not steam only. The name of this new magazine, *Heritage Railway*, recognised another change in the times, as what were once preserved railways began to be called heritage railways. Heritage and environment were major themes in the development of leisure activities – one could take degree courses in heritage management – and soon preserved railways were included in the nation's heritage, and, wisely, sought to benefit.

This new nomenclature had the added advantage of drawing into its embrace a much wider range of railways and businesses, many of which could not easily be described as preserved railways. These included some long-established railways, such as the Romney Hythe & Dymchurch, the Fairbourne and the Snowdon Mountain Railway, which were never preserved in the general understanding of the term but operated with original equipment. There were also the increasing number of railways built from scratch, sometimes on an old industrial or rail site, but whose main claim to heritage status was their use of steam locomotives. The Amerton Farm Railway was one example, which opened in 1992. The Apedale Valley Light Railway is a more recent example, a narrow-gauge line built by the Moseley Railway Trust at Apedale Heritage Centre, a mining and industrial centre in north Staffordshire; it opened in 2010. To the preservation purist these railways lack authenticity. As Denis Dunstone suggested, many of the new railways of the 1990s were more re-creation than preservation. The managers of most of those businesses would agree. Their aim was to tap the leisure market, using 'heritage' rather than preservation as the draw. A new generation of community railways, such as the Wensleydale Railway, would also fight shy of being classed as preserved lines, but were happier with the 'heritage' tag.[192]

Another significant step in this process was the merger in 1993 of the Association of Railway Preservation Societies with the Association of Independent Railways (AIR). The AIR was the older body, formed as the Association of Minor Railways to represent those railways not included in the grouping of 1923. By the 1970s only a few of those original members were left, such as the Derwent Valley Railway, but new members had joined, several of them also members of the ARPS. Amalgamating the two groups brought together the commercial sector as well as the more purely preservationist groups. The blurring of distinctions had been under way for some time, in, for example, the decision of the freight-only Derwent Valley to operate tourist excursions in 1976. They were short-lived, and withdrawn in 1979, but the trend of development was clear.[193] The ARPS recognised the changing order by renaming itself the Heritage Railway Association from 1 January 1997.

Alongside these developments came new approaches to the business of running the railways. One cause was the larger number of public bodies – planning authorities, development

agencies and the like – with which the railways had to deal, each demanding mission statements, business plans and statements of core objectives. A more commercial attitude to the operation and management of the railways was, however, but another step along the path trodden from the very first season of railway preservation back in the 1950s. As soon as traffic carried exceeded the volumes carried in pre-preservation days, the railways were faced with the need to manage the new markets, to bring the infrastructure up to the standards needed for large-scale tourist traffic and to provide attractive facilities such as catering. To justify such large expenditure, they had to attract yet more passengers and business to the railway. That in turn needed a more professional approach to management and marketing. The *Railway Magazine* commented: 'The problem for the successful preservation society is to reconcile the starry-eyed idealism of its founders and volunteers with the hard-headed business sense of the commercially minded officers and paid staff of its railway.' That was written in 1972 when the Dart

The Kirklees Light Railway is a line of 15-inch gauge built on a former standard-gauge route at Clayton West, near Huddersfield. It opened in 1991. *Hawk*, one of the six locomotives, was built in 1998. It is an 0-4-0+0-4-0 tank engine of a Kitson Meyer pattern. 7 March 2016.

(Gail Coster)

Valley Railway became a public company, but similar sentiments would be valid at any time since.[194]

Although there was a prevailing air of expansionism throughout the railway preservation/heritage movement, it has certainly not all been plain sailing. There were still many projects that failed to get off the ground: the Market Drayton and Audlem line was one.[195] Not all railways experienced doubling of their traffic. Some remained roughly constant, some even experienced falls in passenger numbers. On the Talyllyn, the peak year was 1973, long before heritage had been invented, when 185,574 passenger journeys were recorded. Figures remained in that region for a few more years, but entered a long-term downward trend by the early 1980s. By 2007 the figure had reached 94,473. After rapid growth in its first decade of operation, the Welshpool & Llanfair reached a peak in passenger numbers in 1975. Despite the extension to Welshpool, traffic declined during the 1980s, before climbing back in the 1990s, fluctuating at figures still below those of 1975. These two railways are in relatively remote parts of the country, and in areas not among the most fashionable for tourism, emphasising the importance of location in attracting custom.

This period saw some schemes that failed or were but a faint hope in the 1960s and 1970s brought back to life. The old ambitions of a mainline railway from Leicester to Nottingham were rekindled with the opening of a steam centre at Ruddington (see p. 149). When a group of enthusiasts formed the Lynton & Barnstaple Railway Society in 1962, they decided that 'in view of the expense involved and the dubious value of reopening, this was considered out of the question'. Instead, the society aimed to collect relics and engage in research. Things were changing at the end of the 1970s: a new group, the Lynton & Barnstaple Railway Association, formed in 1979, was reported to be buying land with a view to reopening the railway from Lynton to Blackmoor Gate. After many frustrations during the 1980s and early 1990s the association bought Woody Bay as the first concrete step towards rebuilding the whole route between Lynton and Barnstaple. The first stretch of line, 400 yards out of Woody Bay station, opened on 17 February 2004. Extension brought the line to a mile in length, which in three years carried 100,000 passengers. That gave the association a strong base from which to launch its plans in 2007 to rebuild nine miles of railway from Lynton to Blackmoor, with new stations, locomotives and coaches, a project costed at £29m.[196]

In 1970 the first suggestions that the Epping–Ongar line might be a good subject for a heritage scheme entered public discussion, and the Essex Railway Society was formed to pursue such aims. London Transport at that time was still operating the line, unwillingly, perhaps, and discussed with Essex County Council turning the line into a steam tourist railway. London Underground in the event kept the branch going until 1994; as soon as it closed preservation proposals were revived by the Ongar Railway Preservation Society.[197]

New lines

The number and range of the new heritage railways of the 1980s and 1990s were so great that it is hardly possible to point to a 'typical' project. There were projects in all parts of the country, some short, others long; some were standard gauge, some

Pannier tank No.L92 trundles through the Chiltern countryside with the 3.00 pm train from Chinnor. 13 March 2016.

narrow gauge, and the Downpatrick & County Down Railway was the first preserved railway of the Irish gauge of 5ft 3in.

Perhaps the Chinnor & Princes Risborough Railway would qualify as a typical small branch line. It is 3½ miles long, operating on a relatively small scale at weekends and bank holidays, attracting 20,000 or so visitors a year. The railway originated in 1989 after the closure of the line to Chinnor cement works, the last remaining section of the line that once went to the small town of Watlington. As so often happened, someone wrote an article, this time in the parish magazine, to suggest the railway should be saved. A preservation group was formed in the September of that year, which, with strong local support, raised the £125,000 asked by British Rail for the line. The local support has been the mainstay since then, giving the railway debt-free finances, and a society membership rising to 1,000 by 2005.

It took several years of painstaking work before the new railway was ready to run its first trains over a mile of track from Chinnor station on 20 August 1994. Extensions followed to reach Horsenden in 1995 and Thame Junction in 1996. That left the railway 850 yards short of Princes Risborough station, and, although good relations with Chiltern Railways and Network Rail have been established, and a temporary connection was made, the permanent link allowing through running has yet to be completed. At the other end of the line there are ambitions to extend to Aston Rowant, making the railway five miles long.[198]

The Swindon & Cricklade Railway was another born from a small local initiative. It came from an unlikely source, again a not unusual occurrence: Mrs Joan Gibbs wrote to her local newspaper, the Swindon *Evening Advertiser*, in 1978 to say that, in view of the town's considerable heritage as a railway centre, it was a 'disgrace' that there was no steam railway serving Swindon. She sparked a debate and a public meeting was called. Sixty people came, who resolved to form the Swindon & Cricklade Railway Society. They planned to open a steam heritage railway on the old Midland & South Western Junction route. Passenger trains had last run on this route in 1924, so the objective was not the reopening of a railway so much as the creation of a museum or heritage railway for the town. The local authority, then called Thamesdown Borough Council, but more recently becoming Swindon borough, owned much of the

trackbed. They proved willing to lease the stretch of line from Moredon, on the outskirts of Swindon, to Cricklade, a distance of 4½ miles. A base was established at Blunsdon, about halfway along the route. It was a derelict site, but by 1984 the society ran its first steam trains over 200 yards of track. Progress continued slowly. The next extension did not come until 1995, when half a mile northwards to Hayes Knoll was opened. New sheds and workshops were built here, completed in 1999. Meanwhile, there are plans to extend southwards towards Swindon. The railway has remained small-scale, operating only at weekends. The society is likewise small, with 600 members, mainly based locally. It has kept itself debt-free, and commitment from the membership is strong, with a high proportion, twenty per cent, actively engaged in the work of restoration.[199]

Plans to preserve the railway from Grimsby to Louth were launched as soon as the East Lincolnshire line closed in 1980. A society and company were formed, and within a few years a base was established at Ludborough station, agreement was reached to lease the line and an application for a Light Railway Order was submitted for the whole route.[200] The local authority

The Swindon & Cricklade Railway opened its extension to Taw Valley Halt, on the outskirts of Swindon, in 2014. Great Western 2-8-0 tank engine No.4247, visiting the line from the Bodmin & Wenford Railway, prepares to run round its train at Taw Valley on 2 May 2016.

secured the route at the Grimsby end for a new road, leaving what became the Lincolnshire Wolds Railway with powers to rebuild ten miles of line, the first section of which opened from Ludborough in 1998.

On a different scale, Gloucestershire Warwickshire Railway has grown into a major heritage railway. Its success has been due to a singularity of purpose and a carefully staged growth, laying the foundations by acquiring the freehold to the line before embarking on expansion.

The Gloucestershire Warwickshire Railway Society was founded in 1976 not with the intention of buying a railway, but to act as a pressure group to persuade British Rail to retain the line from Honeybourne to Cheltenham. In this it signally failed, and in 1977 the society was reconstituted as a charitable trust with the objective of reopening the railway. A lease on Toddington station yard was taken out in 1981. Foundations for the project were laid with the securing in 1983 of a Light Railway Order for the whole of the line of fifteen miles between Broadway and Cheltenham, followed by the purchase of the line in 1984. The first train service, started in April 1984, was a modest operation over just 700 yards of track at Toddington. From those beginnings the railway has grown through a series of incremental extensions, until, in 2003, Cheltenham Racecourse station was reached, officially inaugurated by the Princess Royal. In the same year the railway won the Heritage Railway of the Year award. This careful approach allowed the railway to avoid heavy borrowing. It did not seek major grant-aided finance, and, even with a line of ten miles, it has remained staffed by volunteers, although it does not operate every day even in midsummer.[201]

Other railways with a long 'pre-history' include the Churnet Valley Railway. The North Staffordshire Railway Society set up a working museum at Cheddleton station in 1974 to save it from demolition, the line having closed to passengers in 1965.[202] Sand trains continued to run along the line, part of the route from Macclesfield to Uttoxeter, until 1988. After the line closed in 1993, the society, through Churnet Valley Railway (1992) plc, acquired seven miles of railway in 1996 between Leekbrook Junction and Oakamoor. Trains ran two years later.[203] Rapid progress was made, with trains running to Consall from 1999,

and to Kingsley & Froghall from 2001. Ambitions to extend northwards to Leek, southwards to Alton (for the theme park at Alton Towers) and south-eastwards on to the Cauldon Low branch stalled because raising the finance was a slow process. Sewerage pipes beneath the trackbed between Oakamoor and Alton did not help.

The Bodmin & Wenford Railway is another project launched in this period that has become one of the leading heritage railways. It was started in 1984, operating its first trains in 1990. Extensions have created a line running from Bodmin General to Bodmin Parkway and Boscarne, with ambitions to reach Wadebridge. However, the railway was thwarted in its plans to reopen to Wenfordbridge in 1997 by a local campaign against the award of a Light Railway Order.[204] The Plym Valley Railway, also in the West Country, was launched in the early 1980s, with high hopes of building 'a major new heritage railway' extending from Marsh Mills near Plymouth to Yelverton. Lack of funds

Electro-diesel No.73129 shunting at Toddington, Gloucestershire Warwickshire Railway. 3 September 2005.

and other developments along the route meant that progress was very slow, and the project was considerably curtailed. It was not until 2001 that the first trains ran along 712 yards of track. Extensions in 2008 and 2012 took the railway to a length of 1½ miles from Marsh Mills to Plym Bridge Halt.[205]

The preserved railway movement grew in Ireland during this period, with half a dozen railway projects set up during the 1990s. The Alford Valley Railway had preceded them by a few years, opening in 1979. Not all survived: three miles of the Tralee & Dingle Railway opened in 1993, but ceased operating after 2000, and the Clonmacnoise & West Offaly Railway, a venture of the Irish Turf Board, closed in 2008. Others, however, have been establishing themselves. The Fintown Railway in County Donegal, opened in 1995, the West Clare in the mid-1990s, and the Waterford & Suir, at ten miles one of the longest projects in Ireland, was founded in 1997 and operated its first trains in 2002. At the other end of the scale, the Cavan & Leitrim revival is based on a museum opened in 1993, with half a mile of running line added two years later. Most of these lines are of the 2ft and 3ft gauges common in Ireland, but in 2003 a short section of the Listowel & Ballybunion Railway's Lartigue monorail was recreated.

Extensions

While new railways were being established and projects launched, established lines were extending their operations [Table 4]. Railways established in the 1960s and 1970s extended to reach their original objectives. The Welshpool & Llanfair reached Welshpool in 1981. The Severn Valley Railway got to Kidderminster in 1984, the Mid-Hants reached Alton in 1985 and the East Lancashire opened their extension from Bury to Ramsbottom in 1987. The Dean Forest Railway took longer to reach Parkend, one of the original objectives. This extension was opened in 2005, thirty-five years after the preservation society was founded. The Battlefield Railway is a smaller railway established in the 1970s with a running line from Shackerstone to Market Bosworth in Leicestershire, opened in 1973. It added an extension of 1½ miles in 1992 to reach Shenton, close to the site of the battle of Bosworth, from which the line took its name.[206] The Nene Valley Railway expanded beyond its original limits, adding a westward

TABLE 4
Extensions, 1979-1990

Railway	Extension	Opening
Welshpool & Llanfair	Welshpool	1981
Ffestiniog	Blaenau Ffestiniog	1982
Battlefield	Shenton	1982
Mid-Hants	Medstead	1982
Severn Valley	Kidderminster	1984
Mid-Hants	Alton	1985
Llangollen	Berwyn	1985
Nene Valley	Peterborough	1986
East Lancashire	Bury-Ramsbottom	1987
Avon Valley	Oldland Common	1988
Llangollen	Deeside	1990
Llangollen	Glyndyfrdwy	1993
Launceston	Newmills	1995
Llangollen	Carrog	1996
Peak Rail	Rowsley South	1997
Gloucestershire Warwickshire	Gotherington	1997

extension to Yarwell Junction. It achieved its ambition of running into Peterborough itself, finally acquiring the extra 1½ miles of route from the city's development corporation, allowing a new station to be opened in 1986 by HRH Prince Edward.[207]

The Earl arriving at Welshpool. The first coach is one of those acquired from the Zillertalbahn in Austria.

Projects evolve
The Embsay & Bolton Abbey Steam Railway now has a running line of five miles in the Yorkshire Dales between the two places in its title. When the preservation project was founded in 1969 by

Single-car railcar No.M55006 at Shackerstone, Battlefield Line, 4 September 2015.

Pannier tank No.1369 approaches Buckfastleigh, South Devon Railway with its train of mainly 1930s Great Western coaches. 9 April 2016.

the Embsay & Grassington Railway Preservation Society, the aim was ultimately to preserve the branch line to Grassington. First it set up a museum of local railway interest at Embsay station, to finance which it was proposing to issue £5 bonds in 1969. Meanwhile the Grassington branch gained a new lease of life as a freight branch serving stone quarries. The preservation group's focus changed instead to the closed line from Embsay to Ilkley, which it reopened in stages as far as Bolton Abbey, reached in 1997. In the process the society changed its name to the Yorkshire Dales Railway Society, later converted to a charitable trust. In the background, the trust continues to have ambitions for the Grassington branch should the stone traffic cease.[208]

The South Devon Railway was a new name for an established railway. By 1989 the Dart Valley Railway Company had had enough of losing money on the railway from Totnes to Buckfastleigh. It was too much for a commercial organisation to withstand, and the company withdrew in 1990, leaving the volunteers of the Dart Valley Railway Association to keep the line running. Closure of the line was averted by the volunteer groups pooling resources. Dumbleton Hall Locomotives Ltd, one of the locomotive owners on the line, had charitable status and articles of association that allowed it to operate a railway. It negotiated a lease of the line from 1 January 1991, and changed its name to the South Devon Railway Trust. From a neglected part of a larger organisation, the South Devon transformed the line into a Great Western-themed branch. Vigorous fundraising and a successful share issue secured a long-term lease, with the prospect of converting to freehold.[209]

Trials and tribulations

Railway preservation projects have rarely run smoothly: lest it should seem that railway preservation had entered a phase of ever greater achievement, there were still many setbacks, compromises and failures.

After getting established in 1973, the Chasewater Railway soon found itself eclipsed by the growth of the Severn Valley Railway, which, set in more attractive countryside and with a longer line, attracted passengers and volunteers more easily. The small group running the line was overwhelmed when the causeway that took the line across a canal reservoir suffered erosion so severe that in 1982 the line was forced to close. Members drifted away, leaving a rump determined to carry on. They fought back, forming a new Chasewater Light Railway and Museum Company, registered as a charity, to take over the assets of the previous company and preservation society in 1985. Work on rebuilding the causeway started in 1993, and took just over a year to complete one of the biggest of civil engineering works in railway preservation. In 1995 a new Norton lakeside station was opened. At the Brownhills end of the line, meanwhile, the new Birmingham relief motorway, now open as the M6 Toll, had taken the station site. However, this was turned to advantage as sums in compensation were successfully negotiated that in turn could be used as matching funding for a grant from the European Regional Development Fund. With nearly £2m available the railway overhauled its facilities, with a new Brownhills West station as a heritage centre in which all its rolling stock could be stored under cover. An eastern extension to Chasetown (Church Street) was also built, to bring the line up to two miles in length. Although another period of closure had to be endured while the new Brownhills station was built, the railway emerged, from being a poor relation in the preservation world, as now one of the better-appointed lines.[210]

A group formed to save the line from Barnstaple to Bideford after it closed in 1982 had their hopes dashed quickly by Devon County Council, which wanted to create the 'Tarka Trail' footpath and cycleway using the trackbed. The railway group turned instead to the Torrington to Bideford line, again without success. A third project emerged, the Bideford & Instow Railway, which has restored the signalbox at Instow, and a short stretch of track at Bideford station, on which rides were sometimes offered. Even this did not prove a secure base from which to grow. The Bideford site has been too restricted, and the local authority unwilling to allow expansion beyond the short running line of 220 yards. Indeed, it sold some of the land over which a railway might have been restored for housing. All hopes of restoring the line towards Barnstaple have had to be abandoned, although a centre has restarted at Bideford. Ambitions have since concentrated again on Torrington, where the station was already privately owned by one of the project's supporters and operated as a railway-themed restaurant. The Tarka Valley Railway Group, founded in 2008, hopes for a running line of about a mile from this base, and in 2013 gained planning permission for the first section alongside the path and cycleway.[211]

The efforts of the Southwold Railway Society, founded in 1994 to revive the narrow-gauge railway that ran to the town from Halesworth until it closed in 1931, have met with much opposition from local residents and councillors. A scheme put forward in 2003 met such opposition that it was withdrawn. Revised plans submitted in 2007 and again in 2012 fared no better.[212]

Shortly after the line from Frome to Radstock was closed in the early 1990s, the Somerset & Avon Railway Association proposed to reopen it. It seemed an ideal candidate for a heritage-cum-community operation, but progress was limited. The association was succeeded by the North Somerset Heritage Trust and the North Somerset Railway Company, which in 2010 persuaded the Department for Transport and Network Rail to accept the case for the line's reinstatement as part of the national network rather than a heritage railway. That still did not lead to anything, and in 2014 another new group, the Somer-Rail Trust, took over the campaign.[213]

Preservation of parts of the Cambrian Railway near Oswestry turned into a success story despite the fact that two groups were involved, which for a time were bitter rivals. The Cambrian Railways Society was founded in 1972 to study and preserve the heritage of the Cambrian Railway. It established a base in Oswestry, the old headquarters of the railway, where it built up a museum collection that gained registered status at the end of 2004. The society's ambitions turned to establishing an operating railway on the Nantmawr branch line. After nine years of negotiation the society succeeded in 2004 in buying the freehold of 1½ miles of the line from Network Rail.[214]

Some society members argued that the line from Gobowen to Oswestry, part of the Cambrian Railway's major routes, offered the better prospects. They established the Cambrian Railways Trust in 1997–98 with a base at Llynclis station, only about a mile from the Nantmawr branch, and secured the backing of Shropshire County Council, which agreed to buy the line between Gobowen and Blodwell from Network Rail. This was completed in 2008.[215] Meanwhile the two rival camps each claimed that theirs was the only viable project and that the other had no chance of success.

The standoff between the trust and the society ended in 2006, and the two agreed to co-operate. The trust started operations over the first mile of track between Llynclis and Pant, and the society continued with its plans for the line from Llynclis to Blodwell and the Nantmawr branch. Two years later progress was so encouraging that the trust, which always harboured ambitions of expanding well beyond Pant, was negotiating with the Welsh Assembly for the protection of the trackbed to Bullington Junction. The longer-term prospect was thus held out of developing a heritage railway as far as Welshpool.[216] The trust and society merged in November 2009 to form Cambrian Heritage Railways. The Nantmawr branch had become the responsibility of the Tanat Valley Light Railway Co, which progressed with restoration so that the first steam-hauled brake van rides could be operated on 7 November 2009.[217]

Chapter 9

EXPANDING HORIZONS

Welsh Highland Railway

Nothing exemplifies better the expanding horizons of the heritage railway movement than the rebuilding of the Welsh Highland Railway (WHR). One of the more spectacular and ambitious of railways in Wales was the route from Dinas to Porthmadog through Snowdonia involving a steep climb from Beddgelert and through the Aberglaslyn Pass. The first section to Rhyd-ddu was built in the 1870s as the North Wales Narrow Gauge Railway, the remainder completed by the Welsh Highland Railway in 1922. The railway's operating history, however, was less spectacular: its short career ended in 1936. The story of its revival is considerably longer and more complicated, involving bitter rivalry between opposing factions staking claims to ownership, the twists and turns in the policies of local authorities and central government, and the sheer doggedness of enthusiasts.[218]

The dream of reviving the railway was among the earlier projects of the preservation era, encouraged initially by the fact that the Welsh Highland Railway Company was never wound up. A breakaway group of Ffestiniog society members founded a Welsh Highland Railway Society in 1961. The new society put in planning applications for rebuilding parts of the railway. Merionethshire County Council consented to the plans for two miles from Ynys Fach to Pont Croesor, but Caernarvonshire turned down the application relating to the line in its county, from Nantmor to Beddgelert. The society also sought the support of the Wales Tourist Board, a move that was not welcomed by the Ffestiniog's management. Allan Garraway did not relish the prospect of competition on his doorstep, and there were suspicions later that the Ffestiniog's desire to buy the Welsh Highland trackbed was so as to keep it closed rather than rebuild it.[219] The immediate backing from the tourist board was not forthcoming, but the enthusiasts pressed on to incorporate their society as the Welsh Highland

Railway (1964) Ltd, a company limited by guarantee.[220] *Russell*, one of the locomotives from the old Welsh Highland, was secured, and some work started on the trackbed at Beddgelert. However, the continuing existence of the original company became a hindrance: the legal problems involved in winding up the business delayed progress, and deterred the raising of finance. Rival bidders for the trackbed appeared from time to time, and the negotiations with the local authorities, some of whom were also shareholders in the company, merely added complications. The WHR (1964) Ltd came within a hair's breadth of buying the old business from the liquidator; but he died and the liquidation process became the responsibility of the Official Receiver. That left the way open for objectors and rivals.

Through it all the group of preservationists never gave up hope, although they were never sure what to do for the best. In 1969–70 they made an offer to the Official Receiver to buy the line after another buyer had pulled out.[221] In the mid-1970s they moved their centre of activity to Portmadoc, where they acquired a short stretch of line from BR on which to lay track. Merioneth County Council discouraged their efforts, saying they would 'ruin the Festiniog', instead pushing the group to rebuild the northern end of the line. A reversal of county policy in 1978 brought them back to Porthmadog.[222] In a major step forward, in 1980 the group secured a Light Railway Order for the operation of trains over a line less than a mile from a station in north Porthmadog to a terminus at Gelert's Farm on land that had been bought in 1974. The aim was to extend to Pont Croesor, but the society still faced an uphill struggle.

A growing economy, encouraging hopes of a bigger tourist market based on heritage projects in the 1980s, formed the background for the final success in launching the WHR's revival. New financial and entrepreneurial muscle was also brought in with the participation of the Ffestiniog Railway: 'In the mid-1980s the neighbouring Ffestiniog Railway became involved,' comments Barrie Hughes, a bland statement papering over a long period of difficult relations that were at times fractious and bitter, as the original Welsh Highland preservationists found 'their' railway being taken over by the Ffestiniog going behind their back. The FR made a secret offer to the Official Receiver in 1987 that outbid the offer already

Beyer-Garrett locomotive No.138 hauls an engineering train on the Welsh Highland Railway at Rhyd Ddu on 13 September 2003.

(Les Folkard/Online Transport Archive) (LF966-5)

made and accepted from Gwynedd County Council, acting for the WHR (1964) company, to whom it would lease the route.[223] The Official Receiver felt obliged to accept the FR's bid, which allowed that company to secure the legal rights to the WHR trackbed. When the deal became public, the outcry led to its being referred to public enquiry, which found in favour of the WHR (1964) company. But the Secretary of State for Transport in 1994 overruled that decision, favouring the FR because he thought it had more professional muscle to complete such a major project.

Losing the battle for the trackbed nearly destroyed the WHR (1964) company. It faced heavy legal bills and a dispirited, declining membership. During the course of the negotiations with the Official Receiver, a group of WHR members had formed Trackbed Consolidation Ltd to buy shares in the original company, the better, they thought, to protect the preservationists' interests. Failing to get the support of the 1964 company, this group eventually threw in their lot with the Ffestiniog.

The greater outcome of the process initiated by the Official Receiver was that the legal complications relating to the original WHR company were now resolved. The Ffestiniog management had a solid reputation, vision, a sound business plan and the ability to secure widespread political support. Such a combination meant that what had seemed the wildest of dreams – the project to create a forty-mile route from Blaenau Ffestiniog to Caernarvon via Porthmadog – suddenly seemed possible. It remained an ambitious scheme, needing capital sums then unheard of in railway preservation: £20m was then the estimate for building the railway of twenty-five miles from Caernarvon to Porthmadog. Grant-aided funding from development agencies, tourist bodies and lottery funds was from the outset expected to provide the major part of the capital. A public appeal was also launched; by the autumn of 2005 this had raised £1m, reckoned to be the largest sum so far raised by appeal for a heritage railway project.[224]

The railway that the Ffestiniog management sought to build was a tourist railway pure and simple. There was much that the enthusiast could enjoy and support, from the Beyer-Garrett steam locomotives imported from South Africa and the new coaches built for the line to the challenge of rebuilding the railway through Snowdonia. But there was little attempt at authenticity. It was really a new railway built, more or less, on the course of the old. The railway has been marketed mainly on the ride behind steam through spectacular mountain scenery.

The first fruits of the new momentum came with the opening of the section of railway from Caernarvon to Dinas in October 1997. This, extending beyond the original terminus of the Welsh Highland, was built on the former standard-gauge LNWR branch line. Before rebuilding of the original line could begin, a public enquiry was held, with the National Trust and the Snowdonia National Park Authority expressing reservations. Objections were successfully accommodated, and building continued, with the line from Dinas to Waunfawr opened in August 2000, and the next extension to Rhydd Ddu in August 2003. The rebuilding of the remaining thirteen miles to Porthmadog was launched in 2004, with the announcement of a £10.75m financial structure, the object being to complete the line in 2009. Included in the project was a new cross-town link at Porthmadog to join the Welsh Highland and Ffestiniog. The tracks were laid through the streets of the town in April 2008. At the same time the first trains ran through the Aberglaslyn Pass. Beddgelert was reached in 2009, and the line was completed in 2010. The first special through train from Blaenau Ffestiniog to Caernarfon was run on 2 April 2011.[225]

The resilience of the original preservation group of the WHR (1964) company came to the fore yet again. The shock and disappointment at having 'their' railway snatched away, and the bitterness of the ensuing dispute with the Ffestiniog gravely weakened the society, which lost members during the 1990s. Since then they have revived. The fact that they had the operating railway to Gelert's Farm provided a foundation on which to build and a useful negotiating tool when it came to making peace with the Ffestiniog. It took time: some factions in the FR were difficult to win round. Agreement was reached in 1998, under which the original group, now known as the WHR (Porthmadog), would extend to a junction with the main route at Pont Croesor and would rebuild part of the southern end of the line. The WHR (P) would also have running powers on to the southern section of the main route, and would receive a proportion of the ticket revenue. Whereas the Ffestiniog was running a tourist railway to Caernarvon, the WHR (P) took on the character of a museum railway. Having *Russell*, the sole surviving locomotive of the original Welsh Highland, and four of the coaches, the railway's heritage became 'our unique selling-point', in the words of the company chairman, James Hewitt.[226]

Now renamed the Welsh Highland Heritage Railway, it has yet to run regularly to Croesor. So far, its trains run as far as Pen-y-Mount junction with the Welsh Highland main line.

Other big projects

The Great Central Railway achieved its ambition to rebuild a double-track main line in 2000. Further development included the Quorn and Woodhouse signalbox, opened in 2006, and the large signalbox at Swithland, commissioned in 2012. Swithland controls main and loop lines to give a short section with four tracks, and together the two signalboxes recreate a form of main-line signalling all but lost on the national network. Financially, however, these developments were draining. Much of the capital was put up by David Clarke, a local businessman and long-term supporter of the railway trust and director of the company, who was determined that the line should achieve double-track running. He had his own family charitable trust through which money was channelled to the railway. Clarke's death in 2002 left the railway having to pay off an overdraft, which he had personally guaranteed. Staff redundancies and reconstruction of finances stabilised matters over the next few years while a new relationship was established with the David Clarke Railway Trust, which continues to be a major financial supporter.[227]

Despite the problems, the railway's ambitions were undaunted, among them the desire to reach Nottingham. A first stage towards achieving that end took shape when a group of members from the Main Line Steam Trust formed the Great Central Railway Northern Development Association in 1989. They set up the Nottingham Transport Heritage Centre at Ruddington to the south of the city. This later became the Great Central Railway (Nottingham). Rides were offered on a short line out of the heritage centre to 50 Steps Bridge, and in 1999 these services were extended to the East Leake branch, then still operated by Railtrack as a goods line. In March 2001 the GCR (N) bought the branch, giving it a line of 5½ miles to Loughborough Junction, within sight of the main Great Central. Still keeping the two lines apart was a viaduct over the Midland main line, which had been demolished only in 1979 after standing neglected since the Great Central had closed. The cost would be formidable: feasibility studies put it at £3m in 1996. Undeterred, the two Great Central groups set up the Great Central Development Company and Great Central Railway (Link) Ltd to raise money and develop the designs for a bridge.[228]

That was not the only major project on the Great Central. Part of the Swithland branch was taken over by Railway Vehicle Preservations Ltd where facilities for storage and restoration of coaches would be built.[229]

Peak Rail's aim always was to reopen the railway from Matlock to Buxton. For a time in the late 1990s it seemed as if this project would be overtaken by greater schemes promoted by Railtrack. The demise of that company took with it most of its expansion programmes, leaving Peak Rail intent on pursuing its original objective alone, if possible, by extending beyond its present terminus at Rowsley. There was an immediate obstacle in the need to rebuild the demolished bridge over the A6 road at Rowsley. That would also entail rebuilding the approaches to the bridge to take account of the raising of the level of the road since the bridge went. Feasibility studies put the cost at £6m, another major obstacle for the railway company. Some 'political pressure' would be needed to smooth the path.[230]

Chapter 10

FINANCING GROWTH

James Freeman, a professional manager from the bus industry, was general manager of the Mid-Hants Railway for a couple of years. He described it as 'an irrational business'.[231] To many, the preserved and heritage railways have always seemed bizarre, for they do not conform to standard business formulae of accounting. For example, they usually have more rolling stock than is needed for the basic operation. Some of it is heritage stock kept for preservation and used in moderation, but even the day-to-day stock is old, so that reserves are needed to cover for maintenance. The track is maintained to a standard far higher than it was as a secondary line under British Railways. That allows heavier locomotives and trains to run on the line, but at a cost. The economics of heritage railway operation have needed different approaches from ordinary services. Finance has always been a delicate balance, from the smallest hand-to-mouth operation to the multimillion-pound businesses. Yet there always has been a rationale to the business organisation.

The Talyllyn Railway Preservation Society adopted a simple business model (not that they called it any such thing in 1951). The membership subscriptions and other funds raised by the society made up the shortfall in the operating deficit, and the input of volunteer labour helped reduce the deficit by minimising labour costs. John Tonkyn explained how this had worked out in an article for the *Railway Magazine* in 1962, in which he reviewed the experiences of the first decade of preservation.[232] The Talyllyn had made an operating loss throughout the period, amounting to £15,523, the gap between income and expenditure having been made up by subventions from the preservation society. Income had, however, increased as a percentage of expenditure, from thirty-eight per cent to seventy-five per cent, achieved by carrying more passengers and by increases in fares (the cost of a return journey the full length of the line had risen from 2s 6d to 4s over the ten years).

As well as underwriting the losses, the preservation society had provided almost all the funds needed for capital expenditure. This was partly out of subscriptions, but mainly through other fundraising: special appeals and sales. The society's efforts included raising £1,558 for a new boiler for the locomotive *Dolgoch*. Support from individuals and organisations who had provided many of the railway's needs, either free or at reduced cost, had kept the railway afloat. These had included the gift of locomotive No.6, repairs to locomotive No.4, rebuilding of No.1 and numerous gifts of tools and equipment. Although the railway had got beyond the hand-to-mouth existence of its first few years, Tonkyn acknowledged that things were not getting easier: success of the preserved enterprise brought increased costs, as more and heavier trains increased wear and tear. Some items that had been repaired in the first couple of years already had to be renewed, new coaches were needed, locomotives were in need of overhaul. Projects then outstanding would require an estimated 4,625 man hours of volunteer labour, he noted.

Most of the other early railway preservation schemes sought to emulate the TRPS. The TRPS was fortunate in that it had control over the direction of the railway company through a holding company to which all shares owned by the estate of Sir Henry Haydn Jones were transferred at minimal cost to the preservation society. The society's nominees were in the majority on the boards of both companies, giving strong democratic control. Preservation society and railway company were effectively the same. The Talyllyn Railway Company was an existing independent business, but most preservation projects had to form a new company to run the railway. The Bluebell, the Kent & East Sussex and the Keighley & Worth Valley were among preservation societies that followed the same path as the Talyllyn in retaining control of their railway-operating companies. The Keighley & Worth Valley has had a very open democratic structure along the lines of a co-operative.

Not all societies achieved the same degree of control. This was a matter observed by a writer in the *Railway Magazine* in 1971 who noted the need for preservation projects to have proper constitutions to avoid the preservation society becoming only a supporters club to the railway company.[233] It was not so much a constitutional matter, however, as one of finance, the large sums involved in capitalising a railway preservation operation, which were often beyond the societies. When the Swanage Railway Society embarked on its project it would have to raise estimated capital of £105,000 to buy the whole line from Swanage to Worgret Junction. At the time, in 1974, the society had £1,000 in hand, having already spent the other £3,000 it had raised. The society members were asked for more money, and there were hopes of raising funds by commercial sponsorship and bonds.[234]

The Swanage Railway Society retained control of the railway company, but for other societies the sums and the complexities of getting the project established were too great. A greater degree of separation between the preservation society and the railway company often resulted. Other people provided the capital for the railway operating company. Alan Pegler bought the shares of the Festiniog Railway Company. The West Somerset Railway Company was founded by a group led by Douglas Fear, who put in the sums needed for the initial share capital. The West Somerset Railway Association had no shares in the company, and operated alongside but independently of it. Shares in the Strathspey Railway Company were initially held by the founder–directors and leading supporters of the line, and there were many similar examples. Although enthusiasts frowned on the 'commercial' nature of the Dart Valley Railway run by businessmen, more preserved railways had a similar ownership structure than they liked to admit. The Colne Valley Railway was established and owned by Dick Hymas. When he wanted to retire in 2006 he sold the business over the heads of the volunteer societies involved in its operation. The new owner, Darren Young, a property developer, came to an agreement with the Colne Valley Railway Society, allowing it to be responsible for the line's operations. The insecurity of the arrangement became clear when Young applied for planning permission to build houses on the Castle Hedingham station site in 2015. He terminated the agreement and served the railway notice to quit at the end of the year. Subsequent negotiations gave the railway a reprieve: Young agreed to sell the freehold of part of the station and the running line to the railway society.[235]

As has been seen (see p. 93-8), lack of society control could cause tension, and financing expansion was one area for

Without the financial commitment of its founders the Strathspey Railway might not have got off the ground. One of the treasures of the line is Caledonian Railway locomotive No.828, built in 1899. It is seen on 24 June 1996 with a train near Boat of Garten.

(Les Folkard/Online Transport Archive) (LF699-20)

disagreement. The preservation societies raised their money through membership subscriptions, appeals, trade sales and other fundraising efforts. The directors of the railway operating companies had to raise large sums to get the business going and to finance expansion. They bought shares, they raised capital through bonds and loans, often commercial loans through banks. The North Yorkshire Moors Railway secured a loan from the Alliance & Leicester Commercial Bank in 2006 to finance the purchase of rolling stock, the repair of bridges and other works.[236] Several companies have needed bank overdrafts to keep them afloat through the running season. These are expensive sources of capital, however, and have caused a few railways to run into trouble. The Mid-Hants was a notable example, whose overdraft had grown to unmanageable proportions as interest rates rose in the late 1980s. By 1992 the railway was rendered insolvent by the cost of servicing its debts. A 'whip-round' among the preservation society's members staved off bankruptcy; this was when James Freeman was brought in as general manager on secondment from Badgerline Buses in 1992 to bring the finances under control. His replacement in 1994 was the first woman chief executive on a heritage railway, Margaret Parker.[237]

In the 1970s offering shares in the railway operating companies to the public became a popular means of raising large sums for capital projects, such as extending the line, building sheds and repairing viaducts. The North Norfolk Railway Company was the first to do this, issuing a prospectus in November 1969: £16,000 of shares were offered, with the aim of raising £11,700 of that by 31 December. Ambition was exceeded, with 14,000 shares sold by the end of the year. The Llanberis Lake Railway soon followed suit, with plans for a public offer of shares alongside the conventional public appeal for funds.[238] The modest ambitions of the North Norfolk were surpassed by subsequent public share offerings. The Severn Valley Railway offered 150,000 shares at £1 each, which raised £56,000 within a few weeks in 1972.[239] The Bala Lake Railway Company sold shares through the press in its locality.[240] A share issue was a major means of capitalising the Great Central Railway in its early years, £150,000 being raised from its initial issue. Early successes brought some railways back for more. The

North Norfolk Railway made another successful offer of shares in 1975, quickly raising £27,000 out of the total of £30,000 of shares. The Severn Valley made a rights issue in 1976 to raise an additional £110,000 to finance covered accommodation for rolling stock.[241]

In contrast, the Winchester & Alton Railway's share issue was an embarrassing failure. It was hugely ambitious, offering 999,993 shares of £1, and with a full-page advertisement in The *Daily Telegraph* to promote it. The failure to attract more than a tenth of that sum in the required time prompted the *Railway Magazine* to write that this sent 'a clear warning to all railway preservation enterprises … that the climate has changed completely since the boom days when share issues were heavily oversubscribed'.[242] It certainly did: public share offerings became much less popular, but did not disappear by any means. Peak Rail sold shares in 1988. The South Devon Railway made a successful issue of shares to raise the capital to buy the freehold of its line, and in 2008 the Bluebell Railway launched an offer of 1,800,000 shares at £1 to help finance the extension to East Grinstead. Despite the shortfalls from some share issues, this has successfully raised money for capital projects. An alternative to shares sometimes adopted was a public issue of bonds, such as the £175,000 of bearer bonds sold by the Kent & East Sussex Railway in 1987.[243]

Sales of shares have largely appealed to altruism: many shareholders effectively treated their purchase as a donation to the railway. There is a very limited market for the sale of heritage railway shares – and other types of social enterprise. None of the companies are publicly quoted, although a few brokers will arrange a market. Only the very few commercial enterprises among heritage railways offered any prospect of a dividend, and shares in those companies were rarely placed on public sale. For the rest, a share issue tapped into funds from those unwilling or unable to become members of the preservation society; several companies have constitutions that preclude the payment of dividends. Rarely has the preservation society been in a position to buy shares and gain control over the company. Although the buyers of the shares are content to play the role of sleeping partner, they value their stake in the company and would not want to see their investment diluted.

When the North Norfolk Railway in 2006 encouraged its shareholders to transfer their holdings to the preservation society, to gain fiscal benefits from its being a registered charity, the directors found most shareholders preferred to hang on to their shares.[244] But there remains the risk that the independent body of shareholders might have interests divergent from those of the voluntary societies. For these reasons, share issues have not become a predominant means of raising capital.

The lure of grants

Raising funds for large projects, such as the restoration of locomotives and carriages or building renovation and construction, was never easy. In the first two decades of railway preservation, appeals to society members and supporters was almost the only means available. This could be long and arduous, as individual donations of modest amounts were gathered in. An appeal launched by Peak Rail in 2002 for £100,000 for a new engine took two years to reach £40,000 – even so, an impressive achievement.[245] That, and many public appeals before and since, have raised enormous sums for railway preservation.

In the 1970s a new source of funding became available – grants, mainly from public bodies. Preserved railways turned increasingly to grant-aid as a means of financing major projects, as this seemed to offer large sums from one or two organisations rather than the thousands of small donations to an appeal. For many large projects grants became almost essential if the railway was to achieve its ambitions without being overburdened with debt or unable to proceed because fundraising was slow.

Grant-aided funding led most preserved railways to adopt charitable status for at least a constituent part of their organisation. The first was the Kent & East Sussex, which converted its preservation society into a charitable trust in 1971. The society for the North Yorkshire Moors Railway did the same in 1974, and many more have followed suit.[246] Financial benefit prompted most railway preservation groups to adopt a charitable structure. Some of the funds raised by the trust qualified for tax relief or gift aid, but grant-aided funding was usually the major factor. Many grant-awarding bodies would only deal with charities. This was true of the lottery funds, and the realisation that the lottery could be a major source of finance prompted more heritage railways to form a charitable trust from the mid-1990s onwards. The Talyllyn was one, having to reconstitute its holding company as a charity when it applied for lottery funding for the redevelopment of its Wharf station.

As early as 1968, Allan Garraway at the Ffestiniog Railway investigated obtaining development grants for building new coaches. However, it was not until the 1970s that grant-aided funding really became available to preserved railways.[247] Since then, tourist boards, job creation schemes, development agencies, the European Commission and its agencies, lottery funds and local authorities have all become sources of substantial sums towards restoration projects, extensions of lines, and development and improvement schemes.

Among the first of the new sources for grant-aided funding were the tourist boards. The Development of Tourism Act 1969 allowed them to make direct grants. The narrow-gauge railways of Wales were perhaps the main beneficiaries of this change, for the Wales Tourist Board, having been supportive of the preserved railways for some years, was willing to receive applications for grants for capital projects. The Ffestiniog was one of the first to gain a grant, £36,350 in 1973 in support of developments at Portmadoc station. Over the course of the next twenty years the Ffestiniog received more than £460,000 in grants from the Board. The Talyllyn was another early beneficiary when it received a grant towards the Nant Gwernol extension.[248] Tourist boards in England were not far behind Wales in making grants to preserved railways. One of the first grants made by the English Tourist Board was to the new North Yorkshire Moors Railway in 1973. The Board lent the railway £15,000 and made a grant of a further £15,000. This was conditional on the railway operating a steam service throughout the operating season.[249]

Local authorities made grants to preserved railways at about the same time. However, the extent and nature of local council support has varied enormously, from generosity to indifference and even hostility. Much has depended upon the political, financial and administrative priorities of the moment. Among those making financial contributions has been the North Riding County Council, a strong supporter of the nascent North Yorkshire Moors Railway. The council made a number of grants, as well as buying the freehold of the railway with a loan, which the company was to repay over a period of twenty-one years.[250] Welshpool Borough Council was a generous supporter when the Welshpool & Llanfair Railway launched its appeal to buy the freehold of the line in 1974.[251] More recently, in 2008, Torfaen County Borough Council made a large grant of £500,000 from the Heads of the Valleys Programme towards the cost of extending the Pontypool & Blaenavon Railway by 1¼ miles to Blaenavon High Level.[252]

The job-creation schemes introduced in 1975 to take people off the unemployment register gave several railways cheap, bulk labour. Administered through the Manpower Services Commission, grants allowed people to be employed for specific projects on short-term contracts, usually no more than twelve months. One of the early recipients was the West Somerset Railway, which had a grant of £50,000 to employ forty-five people for six months on preparing the line for its opening in March 1976. The Kent & East Sussex was another early beneficiary from the scheme, securing a grant that introduced the first employees to an otherwise voluntary railway. They took on twelve people to maintain the structure of the line in 1976. Another, bigger grant allowed the railway to employ forty people between November 1976 and September 1977 for track maintenance and bridge work in preparation for extension of the line. Several more grants to preserved railways followed; almost all operating lines and active restoration projects received something under the scheme. In the first nine months of the scheme, the total made available to railways came to £360,000. The Ffestiniog received £100,000 to support its deviation project, the North Norfolk gained support for extension work and the Colne Valley Railway won a grant of £33,000 to employ fifteen people to help build this new project. The Midland Railway Trust received £20,000 spent on laying track on their line at Hammersmith in Derbyshire. Although the labour thus acquired was on a short-term contract, it was no less welcome. The Manpower Services Commission projects on the Kent & East Sussex brought forward work on their next extension to Wittersham Road, including the rebuilding of Newmill Bridge at considerably lower cost than commercial contracts would have entailed. And as that extension opened, a further grant allowed a start to be made on the next stage towards Northiam.[253]

The Ffestiniog Railway was again a pioneer in being the first to get European funding, receiving a large contribution to the costs of the FR's final extension into Blaenau Ffestiniog, completed in 1982. Local authorities were involved and applied pressure to get a new joint BR/FR station at Blaenau.[254] Since then, grants from the European Union have been a feature of the funding for a number of railway projects, including the Weardale Railway, and the Embsay & Bolton Abbey, recipient of £70,000 in 2006.[255]

The 1980s introduced a new Derelict Land Grant, which was useful for some railways in their initial restoration stages. English Heritage was prepared to aid repair and restoration work on listed buildings. The Severn Valley Railway received £200,000 from them towards repairs to the Victoria Bridge at Arley in the early 1990s.[256]

During the 1990s, grant-aided funding grew sharply. The establishment of the National Lottery in 1994 introduced a major new source of funds. The Heritage Lottery Fund (HLF), one of the official 'good causes' dispensing the income from the lottery, included railway preservation within its remit. Grants from the HLF were available for projects that conserved collections of heritage material and improved access to them. Projects to rebuild or extend railways were not eligible. Even with that exclusion, many projects on the preserved railways fell within the remit. The restoration of locomotives, carriages and other objects of undoubted historical value, the conservation of old buildings and construction of new in which collections could be housed securely and with viewing facilities for the public, and education projects, could all gain HLF support. Some very large sums could be obtained, sometimes more than £1m. In total, the fund dispensed £40m for railway preservation projects in its first eight years.[257]

Lottery funding has allowed several restoration projects to proceed that might otherwise have been waiting years for finance. The range of possibilities is wide. Among the early recipients of a substantial grant was the Welshpool & Llanfair, with an award of £786,000 in 1997 for the overhaul of its two original locomotives, restoration of carriages and the building

A view from the footplate of Kent & East Sussex Railway *Terrier* No.32670.
(Roy Brigden)

of an engine shed. Restoration of the Gresley 'quad-art' set of coaches owned by the Midland & Great Northern Joint Railway Society and based on the North Norfolk Railway received £341,000 of lottery funding. In contrast to this wooden-bodied train, built before the Second World War, was the class 126 diesel multiple unit at the Bo'ness & Kinneil Railway, the restoration of which was also supported. Building construction and refurbishment projects have received lottery funding where educational value, or improved 'access' to historic collections, can be shown. Less frequent have been grants for railway extensions, but the Kent & East Sussex got money from the Millennium Fund for its extension to Bodiam in 2000.[258]

The completion of the Welsh Highland Railway was one of the biggest grant-aided projects in the heritage railway world. Indeed the foundation of the Ffestiniog Railway's business plan for the rebuilding was based on securing the bulk of the funding through various local, national and European agencies, and FR's likely ability to achieve that contributed to the politics of the decision in their favour. The Welsh Assembly, the European Fund for Regional Development and other public bodies together contributed about fifty per cent of the £30m total capital cost. The opening of the Weardale Railway in 2004 was made possible by grants of £3.5m from the One North East development agency, the Government Office for the North East, the European Union and the HLF.[259] After ten years of waiting, this railway was brought into operation in a few months. The Keith & Dufftown Railway, established in 2001, brought its eleven miles of railway rapidly to operable condition through grants from the European Regional Development Fund and from the local authorities, keen to encourage tourism.

Private trusts have also played a part. The trust founded by the late David Clarke, former president of the railway, has been a major benefactor of the Great Central Railway, without which several major developments would not have taken place.[260]

Grants are not without their problems, however; they can be a double-edged sword. Preparing applications can be arduous, as is the wait while they're processed, so that it might take almost as long from inception of the project to receipt of funds as a public appeal. Grants can offer a railway too much at once, inflating ambitions and costs beyond what perhaps should be reasonable. The *Railway Magazine* raised concerns early on, when grants under the job-creation scheme were being handed out: 'it is a far cry from the early days of railway preservation, when "self-help" and "do-it-yourself" was the order of the day.' The writer wondered whether some preservationists might think that railway preservation would 'cease to be a challenge if they allowed others to do all the work for them'.[261] He was not far off the mark, for there was disquiet among the 'Deviationists' on the Ffestiniog when grant-aided funding introduced more professional contractors to the work on the extension to Blaenau Ffestiniog. The contractors speeded up progress, of course, but at a price.[262] More recently, the recipient railway has been expected to dance to the tunes of the official funders, with their policies for regeneration and public access, demand for 'transparency' and performance indicators, not all of which sit comfortably with the railways' accountancy.

Although these grants might relieve the railways of some anxieties about their funding, they can introduce pressure. Usually there is a need for matching funds to be found, which means the railways have to divert funds into the grant-aided project. Grants are usually made for capital projects, and some funds might have to be moved from the railway's revenue accounts into capital accounts to meet the funder's conditions. That project might then go ahead more quickly, but others into which the railway's finance might have gone may be held back. Strict conditions about the timing of a project can be attached to a grant award, which puts pressure on the railway to find finance and labour, again often at the expense of other needs. This happened to the Talyllyn when the deadline of May 1976 set by the Wales Tourist Board for the completion of the Nant Gwernol extension approached.

While the managers of the railways were busy meeting the demands of the funding bodies, the bands of volunteers, from which most preserved railways grew, could feel alienated from 'their' railway. The new structure of management and charitable trusts, monitoring and compliance procedures brought on by grant funding have not always been welcoming to the members of the preservation societies. Despite all these concerns, grants are an established major source of finance, but they have not entirely supplanted appeals and other sources.

Running the railway

At the AGM of the West Somerset Railway in 1982 the chairman said the company was bankrupt by any conventional reckoning, but 'You are not dealing with a conventional situation and it would be wrong to judge by those standards.'[263] That statement encapsulated the problems with running heritage railways. They are not conventional businesses, and it is well-nigh impossible to turn a profit by normal standards of accounting. However, that has not absolved railway managers from attempting at least to cover basic operating costs, preferably to earn a small surplus. It is not possible to fly in the face of conventional accounting forever. Losses on the West Somerset had been mounting: a deficit of £46,071 in 1976 resulted in cuts to winter diesel railcar services, and two employees accepted voluntary redundancy. Accumulated losses forced the West

Somerset in the early 1980s to rethink the business plan once more. The shareholders were called on for more money, thoughts of running trains to Taunton were put on ice and services restructured until financial stability was achieved. In 1996, for example, there was a surplus of £6,750. On a turnover of £944,000 that was still far less than other businesses would expect.[264] Almost all heritage railways have been through similar processes. Marketing initiatives, ancillary businesses, subventions from preservation societies and the input of voluntary labour are all used to deal with the fact that it is difficult to make the business of running trains pay, especially when they use old technology that costs a lot to maintain.

The Talyllyn Railway continued to make a loss on the business of running trains beyond the years about which John Tonkyn wrote in the *Railway Magazine*. The preservation society was still making a subvention to balance the books, of more than £33,000 for 2006. Indeed, in the thirty years since 1980 a profit was made by the railway operating company on only five occasions: 1984, 1988, 1990, 1993 and 2009. However, taking the rate of inflation over intervening years into the reckoning, the society's financial contribution to balancing the revenue account had become a smaller proportion of the total. The difference is explained by the growth of traffic, higher fares and ancillary trade.[265]

In the first season of operation by the preservation society, 15,628 single passenger journeys on the Talyllyn Railway produced a gross income of £704 1s 4d. By 2007 turnover had reached £750,000 and the number of passengers 94,473 on a railway that had grown more slowly since 1980 than many, and was now dwarfed by the leaders of the heritage railway world.[266]

Whatever the scale of organisation, making a profit on the railway operations has been difficult. The Ffestiniog suffered large deficits in the late 1990s, before recovering to a surplus of £400,000 for 2003.[267] The Llangollen had a deficit to control in 2003. The early years were problems for many a preserved railway. The Severn Valley Railway had an accumulated deficit of £34,406 by the end of its 1975 accounting period. For that year the railway had an operating surplus of £1,663. That was largely accounted for by a film contract. Two years later the railway recorded a similar result, of operating surplus and loss on group accounts.[268] The North Yorkshire Moors Railway had only been operating a few years when the chairman's annual report in 1974 said that the extension of services to Pickering was threatened by the high costs of track repairs, at £21,000 against a budgeted £6,000. Two years later the national park authority bought the trackbed from the North Yorkshire Moors Historical Railway Trust, thus releasing capital to support the railway's operations.[269]

Often it is the extraordinary items that tip the balance. Large-scale maintenance, whether charged to revenue or capital account, can devour money. The Severn Valley Railway, which has several major engineering structures, has regularly faced this problem. In the very early days of the preserved railway's existence, expenditure on one of the bridges contributed to an operating loss of £24,000 for the year 1973. Between 1994 and 2004 the Severn Valley spent £1.8m on engineering and infrastructure projects alone. Repairs and maintenance to Victoria Bridge cost £200,000 in 1994, and a further £363,000 ten years later. Maintenance of Oldbury Viaduct costing £208,000, repairs to station roofs at £133,000 and £66,000 for stabilising the banks alongside the River Severn were other major items of expenditure. All of this was routine, budgeted expenditure, but the heavy storms of July 2007 were exceptional. The railway was overwhelmed by flood waters, resulting in damage that needed £3m to repair. Special appeals for funds were launched.[270]

Despite the difficulties, preserved railways have striven to at least break even. The secretary to the Festiniog Railway Company, Francis Wayne, noted in 1962: 'In railway accounting terms we have approximately broken even, but we know that our whole undertaking has been improved out of all recognition…. We must, however, recognise that we are discussing the resuscitation of commercial failures.' The gap between income and expenditure remained a problem, he acknowledged, and its elimination was essential to the 'future viability of the undertaking'.[271]

Railway managers and promoters have always taken a sunny view of prospects, especially when getting established. The Swanage Railway Society in the 1970s estimated that operating the branch line they had not yet acquired would bring in £86,000 a year, against which were to be set £79,000 of expenses.[272] A feasibility study into plans to revive the branch line from Alnmouth to Alnwick in Northumberland in 2007 took a similar approach: operating costs, it said, could be covered by 10,000 passengers a year.[273]

The fine balance of breaking even on the operating account, the need to meet extraordinary bills and financing capital requirements have led to periodic financial and managerial crises on heritage railways. Overwhelming debts, capital restructuring and boardroom problems have added dramas to heritage railway life. There was a funding crisis in the infancy of the Swanage Railway in 1974 when £50,000 was needed mainly to buy from British Railways the track that had not been lifted from the branch and other permanent way materials. Heritage railways have remained prone to such problems: as Bob Scarlett discovered in the early 1990s, cost control on most railways was lax to the point of non-existence. Departmental budgets were rarely set, and the volunteers who ran things got their own way.[274] Eventually the financial crises and near-bankruptcies tipped the balance, and proper accounting and reporting structures have been put in place for most railways to allow them to reach the beginning of the twenty-first century on a reasonably sound footing. Many recorded a group operating surplus, although rarely as large as the Dart Valley Railway plc, which reported £358,000 on the Paignton & Dartmouth Railway in 2005.[275] Talk of the North Yorkshire Moors Railway cutting back its operations had long gone; instead, another share issue was made to finance services to Whitby.[276]

Volunteers and professionals

One of the founding principles of railway preservation was voluntary labour; it was a key contribution to balancing the books. Without it, most railways would not have been preserved. For the volunteers put in the hours clearing the track, making stations usable, repairing and cleaning coaches, and raising money before a single train had run. Once the railway has been preserved, the volunteers have maintained and operated it. Running the railway has needed skill and discipline: preserved railways have kept the traditional structure and hierarchy of cleaner, fireman, passed fireman, driver and so on, not only because it is a part of the preservation ethos but also because it allows skills to be learned and the railway to be run safely. Railway preservation societies have generally attracted

Washing the carriages, Grosmont.

a high proportion of people with professional expertise, so the volunteers also provide legal, engineering, surveying, financial and a host of other services. The benefits are incalculable, although that has not stopped people quantifying them. In the early years of the Ffestiniog Railway's preservation, up to 1962, it was reckoned the society had contributed more than £10,000 and more than 200,000 hours of volunteer labour. As with all voluntary organisations, about one in ten of the membership counted as regular workers, but there was a larger body of occasional volunteers, and those who did odd jobs from home. Volunteers were the bedrock of the railway preservation movement, and by and large have remained so.

In the early days running a railway with volunteers was exciting, but one drawback was what more recent times have called an 'image problem'. It was very difficult to shake off a perception that the preservationists were nothing but a bunch of bumbling amateurs, steam romantics and dreamers. There was some truth in that, for in the early days the preservation societies were made up of predominantly young men with limited experience. They were members of the Ian Allan 'locospotters' generation who found in the preserved railway an outlet for youthful energy and self-expression. Listening to their reminiscences, you could be forgiven for thinking that work on the railways was one long scouts' camp full of japes. That impression did travel and influenced the attitude of officialdom in BR, local and central government to the detriment of some schemes: the Kent & East Sussex, for one, had to revamp its management with people of greater professional experience to get taken seriously. The impressions of amateurism influenced the railway enthusiast world for many years, affecting the arguments over proliferation of preservation schemes. The Bluebell should undertake a professional cost-benefit analysis of its proposed northern extension, it was said in the 1970s, as if the Board, by then of wide professional experience, had not thought of the implications.[277]

It was difficult to shake off the perception of lack of seriousness, but in reality the volunteers operating a public service on a railway

Coaling the locomotive, Wallingford.

quickly had to adopt a professional attitude. Safety, training, the company rule book and working one's way up the grades to achieve the responsibility of engine driver were all taken seriously. It worked eventually, and voluntary work on the railway came to be seen as valuable work experience, even by those with no interest in railways. The army came to do exercises, and young men from borstal and open prison were sent for a week's character-building and job preparation.

By the 1980s the young men had become mature and responsible, as befits the operators of a public service. They had been joined by many others of equal professionalism. Some were paid staff. As the preservation movement grew, so its use of employed labour increased. Some railways were run entirely by volunteers – and still are: for example, the Tanfield and the Swindon & Cricklade. Most employed at least a few key staff. The Talyllyn set the tone. The preservation society inherited a few employees, paid Tom Rolt to manage the line and took on one or two additional seasonal staff in the first years. The Bluebell started out with just a general manager and two employees, everything else being in the hands of volunteers. Often the staff were drawn from corps of volunteers and the preservation societies, which could ease tensions between staff and volunteers. But many managers were employed from outside the railway's supporting society, especially as numbers grew.

Numbers of paid staff grew as the traffic and business of the railways built up. It became common for the management and administration of railways to be in professional hands, but other operational functions also gained paid staff. The expansion of operating seasons often meant staff had to be taken on to cover for times when volunteers were not available.[278] The Talyllyn by 1967 had two paid managers, nine other staff and three seasonal employees. The rapid growth of the Ffestiniog into a business of substance meant that it took on larger numbers of employees. In 1977, when the company recognised trades unions, there were thirty-eight staff who joined the National Union of Railwaymen.[279] By 1992 there were seventy-two members of staff. Many of the new standard-gauge railways built up numbers of staff in the 1980s and 1990s. The North Yorkshire Moors Railway became the biggest employer among heritage

OPPOSITE:
Taking on water, Havenstreet, Isle of Wight.

railways with about a hundred staff at peak times. Employment on a preserved railway was not secure. There were many seasonal staff; many were on short-term contracts, often through grant-aided projects; they were vulnerable to redundancy whenever the railway had a bad season. Almost every railway with paid staff has been through financial upheavals resulting in staff redundancies. And the railways have not always been good at handling those difficulties.

'One of the many good things about the FR is its capacity to behave as a business concern and at the same time to let its members have a full share in its decisions,' wrote Gerry Fiennes in 1973. Maintaining the balance between commercial needs and the goodwill of the volunteers became important, and was not always as straightforward as Fiennes implied. There has often been tension between staff and volunteers. The preservation society and its volunteers might have saved their railway and their jobs, but some of the established employees on the Talyllyn still despised the volunteers who came to run the trains in the 1950s. They were not only bumptious, they were English. But it is between the volunteers who provide the labour and the professional managers that the greatest problems have arisen. The manager wanting to run everything smoothly has often seen the volunteers as little more than a nuisance, lacking discipline and as likely as not to break or lose the equipment. The volunteers become frustrated with management's perceived officiousness. Several railways have experienced these problems, one of them the Ffestiniog, in contrast to the happy optimism of Fiennes' remark. The core volunteers have from time to time felt alienated and taken for granted by the management of company and trust. Sometimes the frustrations burst into the society's journals. Paul Lewin, the general manager of the Ffestiniog Railway in the early 2000s, spoke of the volunteers putting their efforts into peripheral activities as a result of that feeling of separation, creating a 'doughnut' railway.[280] At the heart of the problem is the question of ownership and control. The voluntary societies that do not own their railways have limited say, and at times this has been a serious problem.

The management of the Lakeside & Haverthwaite over the years turned the line into a professional tourist operation,

The Dartmouth Steam Railway employs more staff than some preserved lines.

The afternoon sun reflects off the side of the train. Lakeside & Haverthwaite Railway, 8 September 2004.

directing its activities to run alongside the other attractions of Windermere, especially the lake steamers. At the end of 2008 the company made a break with the volunteer organisations that once were at the core of efforts to preserve the line, and gave the Lakeside Railway Association and the Furness Railway Trust notice to quit their base at Haverthwaite. Both groups were shareholders in the L&H company, but did not have the controlling interest to allow them to go against the management decision.[281]

Despite the professionalisation, the disagreements, the share issues, the covenant schemes and the grants, the volunteer has remained essential at most heritage railways. Volunteer labour for restoration work, for some aspects of operating, retail and catering has remained prominent. Most of the preserved railways have originated from a voluntary group, and at their heart there remains a voluntary society or charitable trust, whose members are engaged in fundraising, with all the established methods of sponsored walks, second-hand book sales and so on contributing their share.

Chapter 11

THE CHANGING MARKET

P reserved railways are almost exclusively passenger railways. Although many harbour ambitions to provide a transport service for their local communities (see Chapter 13), most of their income comes from leisure travellers – holiday-makers and day-trippers. As the railways have grown, many have become significant local businesses. By 1973, the Ffestiniog Railway was reckoned to be the fifth-largest tourist attraction in Wales, and the English Tourist Board in 1991 reckoned that steam railways accounted for three per cent of the market for all commercial leisure attractions.[282] The market has grown, but it has also changed: by the 1990s it was different in many respects from that in which the Talyllyn and Ffestiniog set out as preserved railways in the 1950s. It has become a very competitive sector, in which a wide range of more or less historical attractions offer their own 'heritage experience'. For the heritage railway, business was more than simply running trains: it was developing a range of money-making activities, especially those with 'value added', such as Santa trains at Christmas or driver experience days.

Leisure and tourism

For the preserved railway, tourism and leisure rule supreme. They provide the bread, butter and most of the jam of the railway's livelihood. This was always so. The Talyllyn Railway was already a line for the holiday-maker before the preservation society took it over. Preservationists recognised that they had to cater for this market, but some were more willing than others. Allan Garraway would annoy members of the Ffestiniog Railway Society by reminding them that he was not running a railway mainly for their benefit. The tension between preservation to museum standard, the enthusiasts and the tourist trade has been present throughout the history of preserved railways. Some railways, such as the Welsh Highland, are tourist railways almost exclusively. Others have retained their preserved railway

Always a favourite is *Bluebell*. Although that was never its name on the 'real' railway, it would be impossible for the Bluebell Railway to give it any other identity now. It is with South Eastern & Chatham Railway No.592 in more authentic livery at Sheffield Park, 2 September 2013.

character, with a less commercial service, and have paid a price in their bottom line. All, however, depend on the tourist and leisure market.

Marketing as a result is likewise directed mainly at the leisure market, and once again the tension between the authentic and the commercial has been prominent. Marketing of heritage railways has generally appealed to the nostalgic – recapturing a 'lost age'. It has stressed the romance of steam, the benign and friendly guards and porters found in *The Railway Children*. It has played upon the railway and its rural landscape – 'Escape to the Moors', reads the publicity for the North Yorkshire Moors Railway. Names and nicknames adopted by the railways – 'Bluebell', 'Poppy', 'Watercress' – evoke that idyllic rural image. Other aspects of the historical significance of a railway are ignored, as when the Kent & East Sussex Railway emphasises its closeness to Bodiam Castle and the 'unspoilt countryside' of the Weald. That's what the tourist

Creating a period atmosphere at the stations: Chinnor, Dunster. (Chris Marsh)

needs to know, rather than anything to do with Colonel Stephens, the past owner who gave the line its character.[283]

Marketing and publicity have had to become more attuned to the times. Posters and leaflets distributed by volunteers to hotels and guesthouses were once the mainstay. They remain useful, but have become modest in comparison to websites and social media. Websites continue the trend to cater more for the leisure traveller than the enthusiast or historian, as many give more information about the countryside and days out than the history of the line.

The leisure market has expanded, and it has changed character. The tourist season has lengthened, on the whole to the heritage railways' benefit. When the first railways were preserved, the five-day working week was far from universal and paid holidays for most were no more than two or three weeks. Traffic on the preserved railways had a marked peak of a few weeks, coinciding more or less with the school summer holidays in July and August, the time when most families had their holiday. The railways concentrated on this period, drawing in volunteers to run the daily trains. The operating season in those early years was restricted to May to September. It was not until its fourth year of operation that the Ffestiniog, for example, tried a few trains at Easter. By the 1960s there were already signs of change in the market. An early report prepared in 1963, on prospects for the rebuilding of the Tanybwlch to Blaenau Ffestiniog section, noted that efforts made by tourist authorities to extend the season were having an effect.[284] These were limited, however: more than half of the traffic on the Ffestiniog during the mid-1960s was still carried during the six weeks of high summer.[285]

The 1970s saw a much greater change, with the competition from overseas package holidays. Many places served by preserved railways, such as the coast of Wales, dropped in popularity as holiday destinations. The railways had to adjust their marketing strategies, but this took time. Gradually they redirected their marketing towards the growing trend of taking short breaks, and holidays that started and ended on days other than Saturday. This was a trend that accelerated with economic prosperity during the 1980s and 1990s: more people were taking a main holiday and going away at other times as well. With this development the tourist market significantly expanded beyond the traditional summer period. Families took half-term breaks as well, and those without families spread their holidays throughout the year, with self-catering becoming a bigger part of the market in many of the tourist areas served by heritage railways.

In the late 1970s, some preserved railways were running weekend services during winter months, among them the Severn Valley, the West Somerset and the Bluebell. As preserved railways became heritage railways during the 1980s and 1990s, the season for many became March to early November, plus Santa trains in December. Weekend-only operation expanded to daily as railways grew, and the weeks of daily working would in turn grow in number. Some of the bigger and busier lines are now effectively year-round operations, although none runs every day. The Ravenglass & Eskdale advertises 'steam trains in every month of the year'. The North Yorkshire Moors Railway is another that has something happening all year round. There are special weekends at all times of the year, and regular daily running from late March to the end of October. The Ffestiniog now has only a brief period in January–February when no scheduled trains run. Even then, some specials are operated.

The number of operating days on some of the busiest railways has reached more than 250, including the Santa services in December. These railways include the Ffestiniog and Bluebell, and other leading railways, such as the Swanage and South Devon, are not far behind. Most of the railways with the highest number of operating days are the long-established heritage lines. The years spent building up the market, a core of volunteers and staff, and a line and stock sufficient to withstand intensive operation, largely account for that. The newer and smaller lines tend to have fewer operating days.[286]

December has become one of the busiest months on most heritage railways, the result of the great popularity of Santa specials – family rides with Father Christmas handing out presents to the children. Almost every railway runs these trains on weekends from late November and through December, and a few run on additional days. The Santa special is a phenomenon that built up rapidly during the late 1990s. Its origins go back much further – to Santa riding in the brake van on the Bluebell Railway in 1962 and some special trains on the

Keighley & Worth Valley later in the 1960s. The Ffestiniog ran its first Santa trains in 1970, over just one weekend in December. By the mid-1990s they were becoming popular, but for most railways they provided no more than useful bonus earnings, and were run on perhaps two weekends in December. But on the Mid-Hants, Santa trains were already contributing nearly half the year's traffic income, and business on all railways soon took off. By the mid-2000s there were railways on which all Santa seats were fully booked by the end of the preceding January, turning these trains into major money-spinners. Booking tickets through the internet helped, and is now the means by which most sales are made. The traffic was considerable by the beginning of the new century: for Christmas 2005 the East Lancashire Railway was expecting to carry 25,000 passengers and the Severn Valley about 34,000. Railways were now looking for more spaces in their timetables: the Severn Valley Railway packed thirteen trains into 22 December 2014. Some railways even run Christmas Day lunch trains, and several have extended the operation to beyond Christmas with mince pie specials. The Weardale and Dartmoor railways introduced variations on the theme with their 'Polar Express' trains. In many ways the Santa phenomenon on heritage railways has run parallel with broader developments in the consumer economy: for much of the leisure and retail industries Christmas has become the most important season. Maybe, though, a ride behind a steam locomotive is one of the more wholesome Christmas activities, as the editor of *Heritage Railway* has suggested.[287]

Extending the operating season has been good for traffic and income most of the time, but it has put pressure on railways to maintain services. It can be difficult to recruit enough volunteers; paid staff have to cover, increasing costs. Engineering departments have also faced greater pressure, for what used to be closed seasons of five or six months for maintenance have been squeezed into a few weeks.

As well as extending the operating season, preserved railways have had to respond to the demands of modern consumer society. The market has become more competitive, with competition from other leisure activities and Sunday shopping, and customers have become more discriminating. In

Oiling the locomotive for the Santa special, Wallingford, 6 December 2014.

the early days of the Talyllyn, when a train broke down it was generally taken in good spirit by the passengers, many of whom would offer to help the train crew solve the problem. Sixty years on, heritage railways are viewed as professional operations, and problems result not so much in offers of help as in complaints that the family's day out has been ruined. Most passengers reach the railway in their comfortably upholstered cars, and expect similar standards of space and comfort in the railway carriages. For them, recreating a vintage atmosphere only goes so far.[288]

Christopher Awdry, president of the Talyllyn Railway Preservation Society, wrote in 2005, 'If the Talyllyn is to remain popular and successful we need to give our visitors the amenities they have come to expect.' He was voicing what had been recognised for many years. In 1975 J. Harrison wrote in the *Railway Magazine* that preserved railways must enhance people's visits – they could not simply carry them 'slowly to nowhere in particular'. If that meant that railways occasionally had the air 'more of the fairground than of the transport industry, no doubt this is inevitable'.[289] The purists, he thought, might not be happy, and they were not. But heritage railways

Heritage railways
need passengers in
good numbers
to keep the
trains going.

could not be the quiet country railways they had been when British Railways closed them. Large car parks, museums, shops, catering and other facilities had been provided. Track was relaid to handle larger and heavier locomotives and carriages and longer trains safely, and the demands of legislation on matters such as safety had to be accommodated.

And good car parks:
Chinnor station.

Ian Allan for some years ran a campaign for better facilities on preserved railways, especially toilets. He was the natural

Styles in tea rooms 1:
Chinnor, in an old Cambrian Railway
coach body.

Styles in tea rooms 2:
The Victorian tea room at Shackerstone station, Battlefield Line, has
period charm.

choice of dignitary for the formal opening
of the new toilets at Abergynolwyn on the
Talyllyn in 1991. The new terminus at
Raven Square built for the Welshpool &
Llanfair was designed to meet the demands
of modern tourist traffic. When the Talyllyn
redeveloped its terminus at Wharf station,
completed in 2005, a large new building

Welshpool's Raven Square station, with *The Earl* taking water. 24 May 2016.

was added to the site accommodating all the needs of the tourist, including improved shop, café, toilets and museum. It was a blow to the authenticist, for the original office building for the trans-shipment wharf from narrow gauge to mainline railway was dwarfed by the new construction. However, this development was typical of investments that all heritage railways were having to make from the 1990s onwards. In effect, many heritage railways built a new railway on the site of the old to cater for tourist demands.[290]

Special events

The special event has been a major part of the preserved railway's business almost from the beginning. The pioneering narrow-gauge lines were exceptions: the Talyllyn simply carried on running the established services, and the Ffestiniog similarly got on with running trains as soon as they could. But for almost every other preservation project the special event has been vital. First, events were a means of attracting the attention of the public, raising funds and keeping up morale among the society's members while they endured the frustrations of waiting for all the funding and formalities to be completed to allow trains to run. As soon as they were granted the use of a base on the line they planned to operate, most preservation groups set about organising special open days or weekends. After the railways were open, special events continued to be a feature of most railways' calendars, a means of pulling in the crowds and their money. 'Special events are definitely the key,' Dick Hyams, founder–owner of the Colne Valley Railway, was quoted as saying in 2004.[291]

The Bluebell Railway held a vintage transport weekend in October 1964. This was a community event in aid of a fund for swimming pools for handicapped children, of which the patron was the entertainer Richard Hearne (Mr Pastry).[292] The following year two 'Bluebell on parade' weekends in June and July were held, this time for the railway's own benefit. These events offered additional facilities for photographers, foreshadowing what was to become a popular theme on many

It's thirty-fifth anniversary gala day on the Swanage Railway, July 2014: steam engine No.34028 meets diesel No.D6515 at Corfe Castle.

preserved railways.[293] Special events grew in number and scale from the 1980s onwards, in common with many features of preserved railways, until by the turn of the century they had become a major part of the calendar.

For the Welshpool & Llanfair Railway special events became the means of counteracting relatively flat returns on ordinary traffic in the 1980s, and everywhere they could be a major contributor to a railway's income. Events accounted for eighty per cent of turnover on the Tanfield Railway by the end of the 1990s; this railway has a very limited number of operating days in the year, and runs special events on many of them. That might be an extreme example, but few railways would now wish to live without special events.[294]

Special events fell into two broad categories: those for the enthusiasts, and those aimed at the family market. For the enthusiasts, events featuring visiting locomotives, a special train service with unusual motive power, locomotives with different liveries and demonstration goods trains have been the standard. The Keighley & Worth Valley Railway lays claim to being the first to hold this type of event as opposed to a general open day. Their first enthusiasts' day was held on 19 March 1973, thereafter becoming an annual event, expanding into a weekend and later to two events a year.[295] Most railways have followed suit: in 2005 there were well over a hundred steam and diesel galas, enthusiasts' weekends and the like. Most railways held at least one, some two or three. The Severn Valley, for example, had two: a Branch Line Gala and an Autumn Steam Gala. Enthusiast events are based on such themes as steam or diesel power, branch lines or the trains of particular regions. To draw the crowds requires a concentration of attractions. Trains are run on an intensive timetable, with unusual pairs of double-headed locomotives. Numbers of locomotives to see are important. The Severn Valley's Autumn Steam Gala in 2004, bigger than most, featured thirteen steam locomotives in operation. Successful operation of these events usually requires more than twelve months of planning, to secure visiting locomotives, and, if possible, a railtour coming to the railway that weekend.[296] Many of these events have been very popular: the Severn Valley's steam gala in September 2002 attracted 7,000 visitors,

OPPOSITE:
The Mixed Traffic Steam Gala at the Nene Valley Railway on 13 September 2014. A draw for this occasion was a visit by *Tornado*, the recently built A1 class locomotive. One of the favourite pastimes at gala events is to pretend to be somewhere else. The much-loved, but closed, Somerset and Dorset Joint Railway is a favourite subject for re-enactments. Hence Wansford station bears a board for Midford, a station that used to be on that line.

on its own a significant contribution to the total traffic figures of more than 170,000 for that year. Set against that, however, the costs are great, especially when locomotives are brought in from outside. The financial returns have generally been acknowledged to be modest, the benefits coming from maintaining morale among the society members and publicity in the railway press. Even these have not always been enough to justify the activity. In recent years attendances have been variable; after declining numbers, a few railways dropped diesel galas in 2004–05.

More likely to yield financial returns are the events for the general public. Victorian days, wartime weekends, Easter egg hunts, murder mystery specials and, most especially, Thomas the Tank Engine events, have typified the family-oriented events. Wartime became a big theme during the 1990s, encouraged by the popular celebrations of the fiftieth and sixtieth anniversaries connected with the Second World War. Events drawing in other attractions, such as traction engines, vintage cars and the operation of vintage bus services, have grown, both for the enthusiast and general public events. The Tom Rolt Rally at Tywyn grew from small beginnings into one of the major events in the Talyllyn's calendar. The Keighley & Worth Valley has organised bus services in conjunction with the Keighley Bus Museum at its annual enthusiasts' weekends.[297] The more purist enthusiast has perhaps treated these with disdain, seeing them as dominated by stunts to pull in the crowds. For the most part, though, they have done just that, to the immense benefit of the railways' funds.

Thomas the Tank Engine, and all the other characters of the Reverend W. Awdry's books for children, became major money-spinners. Here, the Talyllyn took a leading part, having special links with Reverend Awdry and his son Christopher, who continued writing the books. Awdry's Skarloey Railway, featured in *Four Little Engines* and other books, had been based upon the Talyllyn, and during the early 1980s the railway dressed up some of its engines as Skarloey characters. Locomotive No.3 was the first, running as *Sir Handel* for the 1982 season. It ran in this guise for some years, to be succeeded by No.4 as *Peter Sam*, and more recently No.6 as *Duncan*. Whereas the Talyllyn claimed to have prior rights over the Skarloey characters, other railways had to buy licences from the copyright holders for engines to act as Thomas, James or any of the other characters from the books. Tiresome as that might be, it was usually worth it, for Thomas rarely failed to bring in the families, and has become a major contributor to the income on many a line. On the Kent & East Sussex, for example, twelve days of Thomas events accounted for twenty-two per cent of the railway's income for 2005. The growth of the internet is reflected in the large proportion of advance bookings made by online enquirers. Slight dips in attendance during 2003–04 caused some to fear the Thomas bubble had burst, but 2005 was showing a resumption of steady growth. There were 150 Thomas events at all preserved railways and steam centres that year. The bigger threat to these events has been the requirements laid down by the owners of the rights that could make it hardly worth running the event. Revised licensing conditions introduced in 2007 led several major lines, including the Bluebell, West Somerset and Bodmin & Wenford railways, to decide not to apply for licences in 2008.[298] *Ivor the Engine* has also made an appearance at some railways, a Peckett 0-4-0ST owned by Steve Atkins being decked out in this guise, and more recently Peppa Pig has been added to character-themed events, at the Great Central Railway among others.[299]

Special events contributed to the extension of the operating season on many railways, as winter galas were introduced into December, January and February. In the 2005–06 season, for example, the Mid-Hants Railway held an event at the end of December, the East Lancs and Great Central in January, and the Keighley & Worth Valley in mid-February.

Special train services

In 1974 the Kent & East Sussex was one of the first railways to run dining specials, trains that ran slowly along the line while serving the passengers a good-quality meal. The impecuniousness of this railway was forcing it to be innovative. It also had a couple of Pullman coaches. When they were bought in the early days of the preservation project they seemed a white elephant; now they came into their own. The premium fares that could be charged for 'wine and dine' special trains proved to be a useful source of income.[300] Many other lines have entered this market, and for some it has become a significant part of their total income. The Great Central in 2000 was operating dining specials with seven-course meals at a cost of £45 a head. Variations on the theme have included 'murder mystery' dining specials.[301]

Private charter trains run on most railways for tour companies, weddings and other occasions. One particular speciality has become the photographic charter when groups of photographers book the railway on which to set up shots that could not be achieved in a normal day's service. The participants on those occasions are almost all railway enthusiasts, many of whom like to recreate 'lost' scenes from

The dining special
being prepared at
Loughborough, ready
to leave on time.

past times on the railways. Locomotives are repainted and given the numbers of members of their class that were scrapped; stations and trains are set up in ways typical of decades ago.

The enthusiast market
'This isn't an enthusiasts' railway,' Dick Hymas, the owner of the Colne Valley Railway, declared in 2004.[302] Although most of those who run them are railway enthusiasts, heritage railways rely on the general public for their income. On most heritage railways railway enthusiasts account for no more than 5–10 per cent of fare revenue.[303] But they are the ones likely to become members of the preservation society, subscribe to share issues, support special appeals for funds and become volunteers. They therefore remain an important sector of most preserved railways' business, and activities catering for their interests are more or less essential, even if they do not yield the same returns as a family-oriented event. Some railways not in major tourist areas have to make the enthusiast market a greater focus of their business. The Great Central Railway is one of these. Leicestershire is not a major holiday destination, and a double-track railway is not in itself something that has great appeal to the general public. It has therefore been important for this railway to maintain its attraction for the enthusiast. Enthusiast galas and events for photographers have been among the mainstays of the railway's activities. The growth of the engine-driving experience courses in recent years has been a major benefit; by 2004, thirty per cent of the railway's income came from this source. Two years later the railway sold its 7,000th driving experience course.[304]

This might seem an easy market to tap: after all, the enthusiasts running the railway should understand what enthusiasts want. In fact, there are many pitfalls. Whereas the general family trade might be expecting good catering and station facilities, the railway enthusiast can be just as demanding in other ways. The world of railway enthusiasm is prone to fashions, just as any other, and spotting the trends can be difficult. The Kent & East Sussex Railway fell out of favour for some years, and was seen as a 'rather dull railway whose trains were mainly worked by industrial tank engines pulling Mk1 coaches'. It was not until the 1990s, when the introduction of a set of restored four- and six-wheeled carriages gave it a vintage Victorian atmosphere, that its popularity revived.[305]

What has attracted enthusiasts has been a sense of the authentic in the restoration of locomotives, rolling stock and the railway to create a period atmosphere. Enthusiasts also have a strong desire for something different that they have not seen before. To attract return visits, railway managements have been driven to ever-greater novelty, often at considerable expense. New and visiting locomotives, different liveries and photographic events creating opportunities for novel shots are among the attractions that have been developed. The desire for novelty has not always been compatible with the desire for authenticity, but there has always been a wide range of enthusiast opinion. Even the Talyllyn went in for novelty by painting locomotive No.4 in Great Western livery in 1985, a livery never previously carried by the engine.[306]

One of the problems faced by heritage railways has been catering for the modern traction enthusiast. The railways have large numbers of diesel and electric locomotives and multiple units. Although they feature on many occasions, their supporters

The driver gaining experience has successfully brought No.7802 *Bradley Manor* into Kidderminster station. 28 May 2016.

have often felt neglected, and that the emphasis is over-whelmingly on steam. The problem for the management of the railways, however, has been that diesel galas have not always proved successful, and for the general public the steam engine is undoubtedly the draw.

Film work

In 1961 the 'discovery' of the Bluebell Railway by film companies was reported. Several enquiries had come to the railway from producers of films and from advertisers.[307] Other preserved railways soon shared in this market. The Keighley & Worth Valley was used by a number of film-makers and advertisers, including, bizarrely, one that involved the covering of one of the locomotives with wallpaper. Early film contracts included *The Private Life of Sherlock Holmes* in 1969, but the choice of the railway as the location for filming *The Railway Children* had the most dramatic effect. In 1971 passenger numbers were 125,000 compared with 71,000 the year before, and traffic was boosted for some years as families flocked to see the Old Gentleman's

Popular with enthusiasts is ringing the changes by repainting locomotives in a different livery or giving them different names and numbers. Class B1 No.61264 spent its summer in 2014 on the North Yorkshire Moors Railway decked out as No.61034 *Chiru*.

carriage and the locomotive that pulled it. The continued popularity of that film has meant that the railway has never lost its association with it, with a beneficial effect on its traffic.

The expansion of the market for film location work prompted the Association of Railway Preservation Societies to draw up a national register of location facilities. Film location work has become a useful source of income for many preserved railways, mostly the standard-gauge railways. The Great Central is one of the popular lines for this, as it offers large stations and locomotives and stretches of double-track line, to create the illusion of a mainline railway of the type that most situations in films would need.[308]

Services to other railways

The privatisation of railways in the 1990s brought about new relationships between the heritage railways and companies working on the national network. The divisions between the sectors became blurred. Maintenance and servicing companies, for example, lent, or hired at low rates, equipment for use on the independent lines. Some found the heritage lines useful places to test new or overhauled machines before they entered mainline service. Some of those promoting railway preservation back in the 1960s had anticipated such developments. There were even one or two instances of preserved railways being used by other businesses for testing purposes. The Middleton in 1977 was the trial ground for a battery-electric 'Greenbat' locomotive built in Leeds for Hong Kong.[309] Such examples were few, and opportunities were not seriously opened up until the 1990s. Since then a number of preserved railways have seized the chance to develop new lines of business, and companies providing services to the mainline railway have found heritage railways useful bases for storage and testing of equipment, as Colas Rail have at the Nene Valley Railway.[310] The Great Central has secured a special licence for running at 60mph on its double-track sections to allow manufacturers to test locomotives and multiple units. The new Ecclesbourne Valley Railway has perhaps taken this business most seriously. The Wirksworth branch where it is based used to be used as a test track by Derby works, and the Ecclesbourne Valley built on this tradition. Testing work was made one of its target areas for business growth, and a subsidiary company, My Test Track.com, was set up in 2003 to handle this side of operations. Facilities offered to clients have included the installation of a stretch of flawed track so that machines to detect the faults can be tried out.[311]

Ancillary businesses

'Symbiotic' businesses to support and often cross-subsidise the railway have become increasingly important to heritage railways. All railways have catering operations, and many have become extremely good, with refreshment rooms offering high-quality food, specially made using local sources. A few railways have gone beyond the station refreshment room: one or two have bought a pub, and the North Yorkshire Moors Railway has taken over the café next to Pickering station.

Along with the preservation of the railways has been the need to maintain engineering skills and facilities. One of the results of the railway preservation movement has been in effect to preserve aspects of Britain's engineering industry. Those few railways, like the Ffestiniog or Talyllyn, which were complete entities before preservation, already had workshops. The rest have had to develop engineering capacity, at the very least sufficient for essential maintenance of locomotives, rolling stock and signalling. Many have gone much further and created well-equipped engineering workshops capable of undertaking full-scale overhauls, sometimes to the standard needed for operation on the main network. Growing alongside the railway preservation movement has been a small, specialist steam engineering industry, mainly servicing the railways and mainline operators. Some of these are independent businesses, such as the Old Flour Mill works in the Dean Forest. Others are based at some of the major steam centres outside of the operating railways, such as Didcot and the Tyseley Locomotive Works. On some preserved railways, meanwhile, the workshops had been undertaking work beyond the immediate needs of their railways. They might take in work for other railways, and often would do jobs for other local business and domestic customers, all of this earning useful additional income. In recent years a few of the heritage railways have taken this aspect more seriously and have built up their engineering workshops as fully fledged ancillary businesses. Cranmore on the East Somerset Railway is one of these. The Severn Valley Railway's Bridgnorth works has established a reputation for boiler work, and the Llangollen Railway has become the base for new locomotive projects. The Churnet Valley Railway decided in 2006 to set up a new engineering business. The South Devon Railway bought the long-established boiler-making business of Roger Pridham when he retired in 2010, moving it to Buckfastleigh, and the North Norfolk Railway bought Chatham Steam Ltd in 2013, transactions that gave those railways enhanced engineering operations. The main market for most of these engineering workshops is the heritage railway industry, but business does come from other sources from time to time.[312]

In 1997 the Mid-Hants Railway bought a set of coaches for operation on the main line. Its first railtour was run on 13 September that year from Alton to Bath via Guildford and Reading. The Mid-Hants became the first heritage line to run railtours on its own account using its own stock and, mainly, its own locomotives. This operation was very successful for a time, but in 2005 the 'Green Train' was sold to raise money for other restoration projects. The Scottish Railway Preservation Society ran special trains on the main line before they had their own railway and have kept some involvement with railtours since then.[313]

In October 1964 Minffordd British Railways station on the Cambrian Coast line became an unstaffed halt. British Railways appointed the Ffestiniog Railway as local agent to sell tickets for mainline trains from Minffordd, and later Portmadoc. Turnover by the end of the year had reached £148. German and Dutch visitors to the railway turned to the Ffestiniog's agency to book them through tickets including the ferry. In 1974 the Ffestiniog ran its first escorted tour to Switzerland, attracting seventy customers, and from there the ticket agency became a fully fledged international travel agency and holiday company. Ffestiniog Travel, a specialist in railway-related tours, is now one of the most highly regarded travel companies.[314]

Finding a niche

In a crowded leisure market, heritage railways sought new approaches to marketing, to create their 'unique selling points'. The railway that really wanted to make an impact and fill its trains had to be more active in engaging with the marketing

The North Yorkshire Moors Railway train snakes its way through Newtondale Gorge on the way to Whitby 7 September 2016.

Loughborough motive power depot.

methods of the late-twentieth century. Being a committed member of the tourist board and the chamber of commerce, holding press days and carrying out targeted marketing, such as promoting the railway to tour operators – all of these became important tools in the marketing armoury. Co-operative action between railways has been a useful means of promotion. The joint marketing panel in Wales has been most prominent , but it has been emulated elsewhere. A 'Steam Lines SE' group was formed in 1972 to promote the Kent & East Sussex, Romney Hythe & Dymchurch and the Sittingbourne & Kemsley railways. In the south west, a joint effort – 'Great Western Steam Railways' – was launched by the South Devon, West Somerset, Bodmin & Wadebridge and Dartmoor railways in 2007. Since the 1990s, the exploitation of the internet, both to advertise regular train services and special events, and to offer online booking, has been increasingly important.[315]

Projecting an image became important. The Dart Valley Railway Company used names as marketing tools for the line from Paignton to Kingswear. For many years it was the Torbay Steam Railway; later it became the Paignton & Dartmouth Railway and, from May 2010, the Dartmouth Steam Railway and Riverboat Company.[316]

Most railways have tried to market a particular character associated with their line. One of the most successful has been the West Somerset Railway, which adopted the image of a Great Western seaside railway of the 1930s–50s, transporting happy holiday-makers to the coast in uniform chocolate-and-cream carriages behind a steam locomotive. This needed investment in the infrastructure, locomotives and carriages, but the result was the transformation of a railway that was in severe financial difficulty in 1980 into a leading heritage railway by 2000. The Kent & East Sussex Railway sought to present itself as a country branch line with the character imparted by its one-time owner Colonel Stephens. The Isle of Wight Steam Railway made its collection of restored coaches a major feature, and the Great Central its mainline character.[317]

Part Four

The Modern Heritage Railway

On the footplate, Whitby.

Chapter 12

PRESERVED RAILWAYS IN THE TWENTY-FIRST CENTURY

As the twenty-first century began, the heritage railway movement seemed to be continuing its expansion at the rate it had during the last two decades of the twentieth century. Operating lines reported record-breaking traffic, new projects were being launched, developing projects reached the point of opening and established railways built extensions and other developments [Tables 5 and 6]. The post-privatisation railway network seemed to offer new opportunities for community services (Chapter 13). Local authorities became more supportive of railways that brought business to their local economies. They actively promoted some developments, such as getting the Cambrian Railway Society and Trust to settle their differences and supporting the Swanage Railway's park-and-ride. West Sussex Council sold the Imberhorne rubbish tip to the Bluebell Railway for £1 to help the extension to East Grinstead. Some have wanted to move more quickly than the railways themselves: councils, chambers of commerce and others have been actively pressing for the North Yorkshire Moors Railway to extend southwards from Pickering to Malton, something which has not been at the top of the railway's priorities.

There were, however, problems to be dealt with that could threaten the railways' stability: an economic downturn, increased regulation, shortages of volunteers and motive power.

Continuing expansion

There seems to have been no let-up in the number of new proposals and projects for heritage rail revival. The Bramley Line project for the railway from Wisbech to March began in 2004 and the Anglesey Central Railway in 2006, and the Amman Valley, Garw Valley and Yorkshire Wolds Railways are others in the process of development. The North Somerset Railway, a revival of a project to reopen the line from Frome to Radstock,

TABLE 5
Heritage railway projects and openings, 2001 onwards

Railway	Founded	Opening, first section
Keith & Dufftown		2001
Plym Valley	1982	2001
Garw Valley	1988	
Giants Causeway & Bushmills		2002
Wensleydale	1990	2003
Amman Valley	1992	
Eden Valley	1995	2004
Weardale	1993	2004
Wisbech-March (Bramley Line)	2004	
Lynton & Barnstaple	1979	2004
Ecclesbourne Valley	1992	2004
Epping Ongar	1994	2004
Gwendraeth Valley	2002	
Cambrian		2005
Somerset & Dorset, Midsomer Norton	1996	2005
Corris	1965	2005
Glyn Valley Tramway, Glyn Ceiriog	2005	
Don Valley	2003	
Ashover	2006 (1996)[1]	
Anglesey Central, Amlwch	2006	
Cleethorpes Coast		2006
Royal Deeside	2003	2006
Helston	1994	2011
Apedale		2010
Aln Valley	1997	2013
Mountsorrel branch (Great Central)	2005	2015
Penrhyn	2004	
Ribble Steam Railway	2001	2003 freight, 2005 passenger
Stratford & Broadway	2005	
Moorland & City	2009	
Yorkshire Wolds	2008	
Strathpeffer	2014	

[1] Ashover Light Railway Society formed as study group 1996; project to reopen line started 2006.

launched in 2005. The Vale of Berkeley Railway (Sharpness–Berkeley) was launched in 2011, and the Strathpeffer branch in Scotland is the most recent heritage railway project, announced in 2014.[318] Most of these projects followed a familiar pattern: years of patient accumulation of funds, negotiation with authorities and little apparently happening, interspersed with the occasional boost. After years of inactivity, the North Somerset project was given a fillip by a legacy in 2015. A few with stronger backing made more rapid progress. The Aln Valley Railway, boosted by support from the Northumberland estate and other bodies, in 2012 made rapid progress in its plans to revive the line from Alnwick to Alnmouth. There had been

TABLE 6
Extensions planned and completed since 2001

Railway	Extension	Opening
Avon Valley	Avon Riverside	2004
Bluebell	East Grinstead	2013
Bluebell	Ardingly branch	
Bodmin & Wenford	Boscarne Jct – Grogley	
Bodmin & Wenford	Wadebridge	
Bo'ness & Kinneil	Manuel	2010
Churnet Valley	Leek	
Dean Forest	Parkend	2005
Downpatrick & County Down	Ballydugan	
East Lancashire	Rochdale	
East Somerset	Shepton Mallet/Wells	
Embsay & Bolton Abbey	Addingham; Skipton	
Gloucestershire/Warwickshire	Broadway	
Gwili	Carmarthen North	
Kent & East Sussex/Rother Valley	Robertsbridge	
Launceston	Egloskerry	
Lincolnshire Wolds	North Thoresby	August 2009
Llangollen	Corwen	
Peak Rail	Matlock station	July 2011
Plym Valley	Lee Moor crossing	2008
Plym Valley	Plym Bridge	2012
Pontypool & Blaenavon	Blaenavon High Level	May 2010
Pontypool & Blaenavon	Big Pit	September 2011
South Tynedale	Lintley	April 2012
South Tynedale	Slaggyford	
Spa Valley	Eridge	2011
Strathspey	Grantown-on-Spey	
Swindon & Cricklade	Hayes Knoll-Meadow Lane	May 2008
Teifi Valley	Llandyfriog Riverside	April 2006
Telford Steam Railway	Ironbridge	

setbacks along the way since the project was started in 1995, but with funding and planning permissions coming together, the building of a new station for Alnwick got under way and there was limited operation in 2013. Further sponsorship brought the timetable for relaying track along the line forward to 2015.[319]

The Ecclesbourne Valley and Lynton & Barnstaple railways were two of the lines that opened, the first sections in 2004, with extensions in the following years. The Corris Railway ran its first trains in 2005, and the Eden Valley Railway at Warcop in 2006. The Moorlands and City Railway in Staffordshire, with strong financial backing, made more rapid progress, running some special trains not long after taking over the Cauldon Low branch in Staffordshire. Development since has been at a slower pace, as the MCR has joined with its neighbour and associate, the Churnet Valley Railway, in seeking planning approval to

At the Aln Valley Railway's new Alnwick Lionheart station on 6 September 2015, an Andrew Barclay diesel locomotive waits to give rides in a brake van along the short line then in operation. This locomotive was built in 1977 and supplied to Blyth colliery.

rebuild the railway to Leek. Proposed building development on some of the MCR's land held out the prospect of reopening to Leek by 2017.[320] The Epping–Ongar Railway, after years of frustrated ambitions and disputes, was purchased in 2008 by Roger Wright, an experienced operator of buses, and reopened on 25 May 2012.[321]

Existing railways pressed ahead with expansion projects [Table 6]. The Spa Valley Railway reached Birchden Junction in 2005 and followed that with an extension to Eridge in 2011, which broke new ground in that it involved running for a mile alongside the Network Rail line. The Lincolnshire Wolds Railway extended to North Thoresby in 2009; the Swindon & Cricklade Railway opened extensions at each end of its line in 2010; and the Pontypool & Blaenavon Railway opened its branch to the Big Pit mining museum on 16 September 2011. The South Tynedale Railway brought its extension to Lintley into use in April 2012, and, with a Heritage Lottery Fund grant awarded in 2014, planned for the next extension to Slaggyford, and even Haltwhistle, and the Llangollen Railway opened to Corwen on 22 October 2014. The Gloucestershire–Warwickshire

Future destination: the new station and signalbox at Broadway take shape in readiness for the Gloucestershire Warwickshire Railway's extension. February 2016.

Railway has been steadily advancing towards Broadway, and ultimately Honeybourne, despite the setbacks resulting from two serious landslips on its existing line. Trains are expected to be running to Broadway by 2018. The Gwili Railway has been progressing with its extension to Abergwili and Carmarthen North, and the Strathspey to Grantown on Spey.[322]

'Bridging the gap', rebuilding a bridge over the Midland main line at Loughborough to link the Great Central Railway with the GCR (Nottingham), was a long-held ambition (see p. 149). Estimated costs kept rising: £6–8m by 2006, £10–15m according to a later study. There seemed no hope, but suddenly, it seemed, things changed. With the impending electrification of the Midland main line, Network Rail proved willing to undertake the building of the bridge at a favourable rate, bringing completion of the project within reach. Two bridge spans rendered redundant by redevelopment at Reading were bought cheaply for the project. At first intended for the main bridge over the Midland, they have since been allocated to another bridge in the project. A public appeal raised £1m by the end of 2015, and grants from the David Clarke trust and other bodies gave encouragement to start the project. The 'pause' in the Midland electrification project, meanwhile, had necessitated a rethink of the timing, and the GCR decided to manage the project itself. The first sod was cut on 12 February 2016. A separate development saw the Mountsorrel branch, which had been bought by Railway Vehicle Preservations Ltd as a site for storage and restoration of carriages and wagons, developed into a fully fledged preservation scheme. There is strong community involvement in this project, which, as well as restoring a branch line to operation, includes local environmental and history education. Demonstration trains were run on part of the branch during galas in 2013; soon thoughts turned to running a limited number of passenger trains, for which a station was built at Mountsorrel and opened on 24 October 2015.[323]

One of the major projects of this period has been the Bluebell Railway extension from Kingscote to East Grinstead. Two objectives were achieved: the fulfilment of the society's original plan to reach East Grinstead and the restoration of a connection with the main line, which had been broken years earlier when the line to Horstead Keynes was closed. There were many obstacles: land had to be bought and planning permissions obtained. When the site of West Hoathly station came on to the market in 1975 a purchase fund was launched, Bluebell Extension Railway Ltd was set up and the long process of negotiating with local authorities and others began. A planning application submitted at the end of the 1970s was turned down on the grounds that a railway would not be in the interests of the farmers, foresters and horticulturalists who now occupied the trackbed.[324] The Bluebell persevered; a Light Railway Order covering the whole of the route to East Grinstead was obtained in 1985, and the first few miles beyond Horstead Keynes opened to West Hoathly in 1992 and Kingscote in 1994. The final link to East Grinstead, a distance of about two miles, was the most difficult and costly part, a major engineering and logistical project. Fierce opposition from two landowners delayed the completion of land purchase. Sainsbury's wanted the East Grinstead station site for a supermarket. Imberhorne (Hill Place) viaduct just outside East Grinstead needed extensive repair.

Most of the total bill of £4m, however, was the result of clearing Imberhorne cutting, which had been used as a rubbish tip. Thousands of tonnes of rubbish had to be dug out and sent to other sites. To achieve this the Bluebell had to rethink some of its policies; in particular, diesel locomotives were allowed on to this staunchly steam-only railway. The railway even bought one, a Rolls-Royce/Thomas Hill industrial locomotive. The diesels were there to haul spoil trains, but sometimes were pressed into passenger service. It was nearly twenty years before East Grinstead was reached, with the extension opening to the public on 23 March 2013. With that project completed, attention turned to the Ardingly branch.[325]

As well as extra mileage, expansion projects for new sheds, workshops, stations and museums have been completed or put in hand. Typical examples are the new station at Kidderminster and the exhibition hall on the Severn Valley Railway, and the turning triangle and new turntable installed on the West Somerset Railway. Engineering workshops with the capacity to handle major overhauls have been developed by the Mid-Hants Railway and the South Devon Railway among others. On the Great Central Railway new workshops, sheds and exhibition space have been planned for Leicester, based around the relocated shed brought from Workington. Projects to improve stations have gone ahead, such as rebuilding the overall roof at Pickering station.[326] Crowd-pulling special events have been mounted on a grander scale, such as the 'Steam, Steel and Stars' spectaculars at the Llangollen Railway held to raise money for building new locomotives – another of the features of the century.

More projects that seemed to have no hope in previous decades have been revived. A short length of track was laid at Whitrope on the Waverley route in 2005 and trains ran in 2012 – a far cry from the hopes of the 1960s (pp. 106-8), and the northern end of the line was rebuilt as part of the national network.[327] The Somerset & Dorset Railway Heritage Trust started developments at Midsomer Norton station, including a running line of about half a mile, with ambitions to rebuild south a further half mile towards Chilcompton.[328] The South Devon Railway and its supporters harboured ambitions to return to Ashburton. These seemed to be scuppered by Dartmoor National Park Authority's granting of planning permission for

The extensive concourse of the Severn Valley Railway's Kidderminster Town station was completed in 2006.

redevelopment of the station and its surrounding site, but there were sufficient dissenting voices for the railway's supporters to continue campaigning.[329] When the Penrhyn Railway was closed in 1963 some argued that it had a strong claim for preservation. That drew opposition from those anxious about the proliferation of preservation projects, including a strongly worded letter from Allan Garraway, general manager of the Ffestiniog Railway, who felt that the 'narrow margin of luck' that had blessed the successful operation of his railway, the Talyllyn and others, left little room for additional railways, including the Welsh Highland and Penrhyn. The proposals died amid these arguments, but in 2004 a new Penrhyn Railway Trust was set up to revive the line, starting from a base at Bethesda. In 1974 a group was formed hoping to restore part of the Glyn Valley Tramway. In 2005 the Glyn Valley Tramway Group bought a quarter mile of trackbed, following that with securing a lease on the old engine shed at Glyn Ceiriog in 2007 and formulating plans to run trains over three miles of line. By 2015 the group, now renamed the Glyn Valley Tramway and

Somerset & Dorset 2-8-0 No.53805 arrives at Pickering on 8 September 2009 before the overall roof was built.

After the roof was built: No.44871 simmers in Pickering with admiring crowds alongside. 5 April 2013.

Industrial Heritage Trust, had acquired more land and the first stretch of track was being laid.[330]

After the rejection of its original plans there seemed to be no prospect of the Kent & East Sussex Railway reaching Roberts-bridge. But a new Rother Valley Railway Company was formed in 1990 to revive the scheme of filling the link between the limit of the Kent & East Sussex operations at Bodiam and Robertsbridge. The first mile of track from the limit of the KESR at Bodiam was completed in 2010, and a limited number of trains ran in 2011. A start was made on rebuilding at the Robertsbridge end of the line, with a connection to the Network Rail lines installed in March 2015. The obstacle of the A21 road remained, but those behind the rebuilding were undeterred. Attitudes had been changing within planning authorities, with greater willingness to consider proposals for the railway; the promoters of the railway were even suggesting that a road crossing would be an effective traffic-calming measure. A planning application was submitted in late 2014.[331]

One of the aims of the Rother Valley's project is to reconnect the heritage railway with the main-line network. This has become an important consideration for heritage railways. A connection with the main network allows through trains to run on to the line and visits from special trains; it offers the prospect of timetabled connections with other train services, and makes the transfer of stock to and from the heritage line easier. With some owners of preserved locomotives unwilling to commit their valuable stock to road transport, heritage railways have become keener to gain access to the network. Establishing that link has been a major reason behind extension projects. It was the main reason for the Bluebell's pressing on to East Grinstead. The East Lancashire's decision to take on the branch to Heywood, which was reopened in 2003, also had the objective of connecting with the network.

Some extension projects have had the objective of completing the rebuilding of the route that the preservationists originally planned to restore. For others, the aim is simply to offer a better, longer, more attractive ride than the half mile or so with which the railway started out, or to stop the railway running from 'nowhere to nowhere', and to reach a destination that is more attractive and likely to yield greater numbers of passengers. The

Churnet Valley Railway hopes to get to Alton Towers. The Telford Steam Railway has extended 500 yards to Lawley, but has grander plans to take it from a minor line of half a mile to a major tourist railway, eventually reaching Ironbridge. The Avon Valley has plans for a four-mile extension to Newbridge, which will bring it closer to Bath. The East Somerset Railway has revived old plans to reach Shepton Mallet, but is casting eyes even further afield towards Wells.[332]

Downturn

Yet not everything in the railway preservation garden has been rosy: pressures and challenges to continued growth have been as great as at any time before. The general state of the economy worsened, posing new questions for railway management. The costs and pressures of maintaining heritage enterprises also grew. Among those affecting heritage railways have been the supply of motive power and the cost of fuel. The availability of volunteer labour became a cause of great concern, and the burden of regulation has grown. Obstacles in the way of new lines and extensions are perhaps greater, with footpaths, cycle tracks, housing and other developments often obstructing parts of railways long closed.

The economic downturn that began in 2007–08 seemed the most serious threat to the prosperity of heritage railways yet encountered. Traffic had been steadily increasing on most railways for about ten years. Now a tighter economy led to a decline. Most railways experienced a drop in traffic in 2008; for some the decline was more serious, especially those, such as the Welsh narrow gauge, which are relatively remote from centres of population. The Talyllyn, the pioneer, especially suffered, apparently left behind by the general growth of heritage railways.

High fuel prices reduced the number of journeys people were prepared to make, and the distances they were prepared to travel. They also contributed to the mounting operating costs: in many cases fuel costs in 2008 were twice what they had been the previous year. The high cost of diesel fuel prompted the Llangollen Diesel Group to offer its entire collection of locomotives for sale in June 2008. High costs and poorer traffic returns forced several railways to reduce the number of paid staff, in some cases enduring painful redundancies. The

Ffestiniog had to make nine staff redundant in 2008 following a fall in traffic of eight per cent. The Talyllyn had to cut the post of general manager in 2009, following an operating loss of £100,000 for 2008, and there were staff cuts at the North Yorkshire Moors and West Somerset railways among others. The Severn Valley was considering staff redundancies in 2010 after a difficult trading year, with traffic eighteen per cent lower than 2009, and total revenue down by four per cent.[333]

The recession was not a simple matter of decline in trade, however, and after some initial upset, the onward march of heritage railways carried on. A rise in the numbers of people staying in Britain instead of going abroad for holidays boosted traffic figures on many lines. For some, 2009 was a very good year: the Bodmin & Wenford Railway reported ticket sales up by forty-four per cent and revenue by thirty-two per cent. The years following brought good results, often setting new records,

Great Western Castle class No.5029 *Nunney Castle* on the West Somerset Railway in 2011.

(Matt Tapper)

on a number of railways. The South Devon Railway, from 100,000 passengers in 2007, was up to 107,000 in 2009 and nearly 112,000 in 2010. The North Norfolk Railway was breaking records in most years from 2010: 144,000 that year, and up to 157,000 by 2013. However, with the economy growing little, if at all, traffic figures and trading results varied widely. Whereas some railways, such as the Bodmin & Wenford, continued to break records, others, even among the 'first division', in some years carried fewer passengers. Business was showing greater fluctuation from year to year, although it was about a reasonably healthy mean.[334]

The only railway that had to cease trading because of business failure was the Weardale Railway. It crashed spectacularly – although it has been revived since. Interest in preserving this rural line in north-east England, which had been a freight-only branch since June 1953, had grown during the 1980s. The local council sponsored some summer Sunday passenger services to Stanhope between 1988 and 1992. When freight services to the cement works at Eastgate were withdrawn in 1993, the Wear Valley District Council immediately put its weight behind a campaign to revive the line. The Weardale Railway Society (later Trust) was founded to focus efforts, and to form the body through which the line might be acquired. Ambitious plans included daily passenger services for the local community, the provision of freight facilities, and the operation of steam trains for enthusiasts.[335]

The district council placed a revitalised railway at the head of its list of projects to bring new life and business into the valley following the closure of the cement works, announced in January 2002. The emphasis had shifted from community services to the railway's contribution to regional regeneration as a focus for tourism based on its proximity to the National Railway Museum's branch at Shildon, its historic associations with early railways in the north east and lead mining, and a number of other leisure attractions being developed along the route. Strong council support allowed the railway to put together substantial grant-aided funding from the agencies of local and national government, with which the trust could plan for a rapid reopening of the eighteen miles of railway from Bishop Auckland to Eastgate. The trust's deputy chairman,

Kevin Hillary, acknowledged: 'We are trying to achieve in less than five years what most lines of our size have had a thirty-year timeframe to develop.' Thoughts turned again to the possibility of commuter trains to Darlington. With the main emphasis now on the tourist market, the railway decided to use steam traction. Locomotives and rolling stock were hired from the North Yorkshire Moors Railway and other railways for the first operating season in 2004. The first stage of the line, 5½ miles from Stanhope to Wolsingham, opened on 17 July. All boded well. Crowds turned out in the rain for reopening day. Support for the trust grew, with membership rising from 500 to 1,000. In the few weeks of operation in the first season more than 14,000 passengers were carried.[336]

Then, just as rapidly, things went wrong. The main locomotive in use at the end of the summer season, a Peckett 0-6-0ST industrial engine, nicknamed 'The Mardy Monster', failed, with damage to its firebox, forcing the season's services to end prematurely. Ticket sales, including those for Santa specials in December, were lower than expected, and this, together with delays in the release of some of the grants, caused severe cash-flow problems for the railway. The operating company, Weardale Railways Ltd, was placed in administration on 5 January 2005. The administrators immediately laid off thirty out of the thirty-six employees of the company.[337]

It could be argued – and was – that the Weardale was overambitious. Instead of building things up gradually, as preserved railways tended to do, the largesse showered upon it from almost every agency in the north east allowed it to employ too many staff too early, and run costly services from the outset, while failing to secure suitable motive power. After the crash came the rescue: 'The goodwill remains for this railway to succeed,' a spokesman for One North East said, speaking for most of the public organisations supporting the Weardale Railway. Those groups engineered a new ownership and management structure. They decided the line could not be left to the small-scale preservation group, although the trust did retain an interest in the new company after Ealing Community Transport took a controlling interest in 2005.[338]

Ealing Community Transport sold their interests in the Weardale Railway to British American Railway Services (BARS) in 2009. Under their management, the whole line from Wolsingham to the junction with Network Rail at Bishop Auckland was upgraded preparatory to the introduction of new community services from Stanhope to Bishop Auckland in 2010, and steam-hauled heritage trains would run between Stanhope and Wolsingham. However, that did not guarantee security for the services: BARS suspended regular passenger services on the Weardale and Dartmoor railways in 2013 because they were losing too much money.[339]

The Weardale was not the only railway with financial problems. Managerial problems at the Teifi Valley Railway left the line with a 'road train' replacing the track at the end of 2014.[340] A greater threat to the survival of heritage railways, however, has been security of tenure. There have been a number of minor crises in the world of preservation when landowners have decided a heritage railway no longer fits their management. Although such problems were not new in that a number of preserved railways experienced difficult negotiations with the local authorities that owned the freehold in the 1970s and 1980s, there have been more since 2000. The small Swansea Vale Railway did close. After being unable to run any trains for about eighteen months, and with little prospect of securing a renewal of the lease on its property from the landlord, Swansea City & County Council, the Swansea Vale Railway Society decided at the end of 2007 to abandon its project. The line was lifted in 2009, and the society meanwhile transferred its assets to the Gwili Railway.[341]

Glamorgan Borough Council owned the Barry Island Railway, which it had set up with support from the Welsh Development Agency in 1994. The line was operated by the Glamorgan Railway Company from its opening in 1998. In 2008 the council withdrew its support for the company. An immediate effect was that the railway had to make Janet Small, its general manager, redundant. This upset for the railway ironically came at the same time as agreement was reached with Network Rail for bringing the mainline connection back into use, and the extension of the railway to a new terminus at Gladstone Bridge from 1 March that year. However, the council as landlord invited bids from other companies to operate the line under contract. Cambrian Transport Ltd (not connected with the society and trust at Oswestry) was the successful bidder, and the line reopened as Barry Rail Centre and Tourist Railway in September 2009. After failed attempts to reach an accommodation with the new operator, the Vale of Glamorgan Company moved its stock to the Garw Valley Railway.[342]

The Bowes Railway in north-east England has experienced very difficult times since 2008. Gateshead council withdrew its regular funding, leaving the railway dependent on Sunderland council's contribution, which did not cover all the bills. Vandalism, thefts and shortage of funds for wages and repair and maintenance to its structure and locomotives impaired the ability of the railway to operate, with the result that there have been periods when this historic site has suspended operations. In 2014 it seemed as though the railway might close completely, but gradually its fortunes revived during the following eighteen months.[343]

The difficulties experienced by the Sittingbourne & Kemsley Railway were prominent. M-Real, the successors to Bowaters, decided to close the paper mills and sell the site for redevelopment, and their plans did not include the Sittingbourne & Kemsley. The backing of the Heritage Railway Association succeeded in persuading Swale Borough Council to change its stance of indifference to offer public support for the railway, but this did not prevent the railway closing for some time; it was not until late 2010 that it ran some trains, with a more complete reopening a few months later. In the meantime, M-Real had sold the land to Essential Land LLP in 2010 before agreement had been reached for the railway to acquire the freehold of the land over which it ran and negotiate terms of access for the public.[344]

The Leighton Buzzard Railway faced threats from development proposals for their Pages Park station, which the railway does not own.[345] The Derwent Valley Light Railway Society was threatened with eviction in 2010 over disagreements about contractual payments and safety licences. The original railway had closed in 1981, but the Light Railway Order was transferred in 1987 to the Yorkshire Museum of Farming, which acquired the railway's land at Murton. A line of half a mile was reopened in 1993.[346] The North Norfolk Railway faced raising money quickly in 2000–01 to buy the freehold of its terminus at Sheringham when the landowner decided to sell and developers hovered, and the Colne Valley Railway has been served notice to quit by the owner of the freehold (see p. 152).

Volunteers and professionals

The voluntary core to the heritage railway movement has undoubtedly been a source of great strength. David Morgan has commented on the way that volunteers have maintained an independence of spirit within railway preservation that has kept it from becoming complacent.[347] A strong volunteer movement has had further benefits in adding political voice on occasion. When the proposals for costly changes to the inspection regime were put forward in 2006, the Heritage Railway Association was able to draw on support from large numbers of individual members of the railways in its lobbying of ministers and officials to get the proposals rescinded.[348]

The benefits and gains from volunteer involvement have not come easily. Building up membership of the preservation organisations from which volunteers are drawn has been a preoccupation from the earliest days of railway preservation. The Severn Valley Railway Association has had as many as 15,000 members, but most societies feel they are doing well with a quarter of that, and several have barely a thousand. Numbers fluctuate as casual members come and go, responding to changes in subscriptions. The Ravenglass & Eskdale Railway Preservation Society lost fifteen per cent of its members in 2004, down to 1,740, following an increase in subscription rates.

In common with almost all voluntary activity, the proportion of members of railway preservation societies actively engaged is small. The preservation movement was still young when concerns were raised about the supply of volunteers. The Bluebell Railway appeared to be struggling in the late 1960s, with a membership of 1,100, a quarter the size of the Ffestiniog's society. The North Yorkshire Moors Railway in 1975 reported that shortages of volunteers in that season had necessitated the employment of

Young and old working on the railway...

Painting the signalbox, East Cranmore.

Loughborough 'barrow boys'.

additional paid staff.[349] The ARPS should promote recruitment campaigns, it was argued in the 1970s. The end of steam on the mainline network was going to lead to serious problems, it was thought, for succeeding generations would know nothing of steam and would not be interested in preservation. That did not come to pass, and diesel and electric traction, and other aspects of railway operation, built up their own following.

Concerns about potential shortages in the supply of volunteers have resurfaced in recent years. Many of the founders of early preservation projects in the 1960s and 1970s were young – students and teenagers – and they attracted volunteers of similar age. By the 2000s that generation had aged with their railways, and it appeared that younger generations were not coming into railway preservation at the rate needed to replace their elders. Enginemen and signalmen in their seventies have become a not uncommon feature on preserved railways (75 is the limit allowed), and there are regular reports of shortages of volunteers at key times. Staff have had to cover for volunteer duties to maintain the service. Besides the ageing generation of volunteers, other reasons put forward have included the 'pensions crisis' and recession of the early twenty-first century,

Driver, Talyllyn.

Young firewoman,
Swindon & Cricklade.

which reduced the numbers of early retirers becoming available. When fuel prices are high, that is said to be a deterrent to volunteers who often travel considerable distances to their railways. Rarely mentioned is the effect of rising standards. Articles in preservation society journals sometimes reveal how railways short of volunteers in the early days of preservation would set barely trained youngsters to tasks that no one would dream of them doing in the twenty-first century. Proper training and supervision have raised standards immeasurably, but they have affected the availability of volunteer labour.

All of this has once again led to questions as to whether the heritage railway movement has passed its peak. 'Crisis' headlines have occasionally appeared about projects said to be in dire straits through lack of volunteers, which have not always advanced the cause, perhaps, for they have provoked vigorous defence from those involved. Retiring general manager of the Kent & East Sussex Railway, Graham Baldwin, added his concerns in 2014, noting the likely effect of higher retirement ages.[350] Several railways have taken vigorous steps to overcome the likely shortage of volunteers. Many have formed youth groups with some success, despite the bureaucratic hurdles erected by 'safeguarding' legislation. One particular concern has been the training of engineering skills needed for the maintenance and rebuilding of locomotives, carriages and other equipment. Several apprenticeship and training schemes have been set up by individual railways and independent groups. The Boiler and Engineering Skills Trust was set up in 2007. The Severn Valley Railway established a Heritage Skills Training Academy to train apprentices, the first being recruited in 2013, and the Mid-Hants Railway has an active apprenticeship scheme. Some consideration has been given to creating a national scheme to allow volunteers' skills learned on one railway to be made more readily available to any other railway, which could make it easier to keep volunteers in the preservation movement if they move to another part of the country, for example.[351]

Notwithstanding talk of shortages, many railways have remained entirely volunteer-run, and they tend to guard that status jealously. Among the largest is the Gloucestershire Warwickshire Railway. By 2005 the railway had an annual turnover of £750,000, was operating ten miles of railway and harboured ambitious plans for expansion. Apart from employing contractors sometimes for building and infrastructure work, the railway has adhered to a policy of control by volunteers, and has only recently appointed paid staff.[352] Smaller lines, such as the Swindon & Cricklade and the Tanfield railways, are often volunteer-only operations. For the lines that retained all-volunteer management and operation, among the benefits were greater commitment from their supporters and pride in what they did. The tension that can arise between staff and volunteers is absent, and there is often a feeling of greater control over finances. The financial turmoil that has sometimes beset lines with a large commitment to paid staff has generally passed them by. Their borrowings have been low, sometimes non-existent. Volunteer operation imposes limitations, however. Development is at a slow and steady rate, dependent upon the availability of volunteer labour, but, properly managed, that need not cause many difficulties. The extension of the Gloucestershire Warwickshire Railway has been about half a mile a year. This railway, in common with most all-volunteer lines, has remained mainly a weekend-only operation. Rarely do such lines have trains running daily, even at the height of the holiday season. They tend to retain the character of a preserved or museum railway, more than a heritage business. Not for them, either, the involvement in regular community transport services; or, at least, not yet. For there are possibilities for some of these lines, including the Gloucestershire Warwickshire when it reaches its junction with the national network at Honeybourne.

In that part of the heritage railway business that is run by purely commercial companies, shareholding can take on more the nature of a simple investment, and here the dangers of takeover by an unwelcome buyer are present. The directors of the Dart Valley Railway Company were involved in a long-running dispute with one of the shareholders over the direction of the company's affairs. David Barry, a businessman with no particular enthusiasm for railways or their preservation, had been buying shares in the DVR since 1996, as an investment, until by 2006 he had twenty-seven per cent and put himself up for election to the Board. His objective, he said, was to shake up the management and achieve greater returns to shareholders from the business, and this aroused fears that he would embark on asset-stripping, even closing the line to realise the property value. The Board staved off his election, but the underlying problem is unresolved, demonstrating the uncertainty to which the heritage railway business is exposed.[353]

Motive power

A recurring feature of heritage railway operation in the twenty-first century has been shortage of motive power, in particular of steam locomotives. The railway press regularly reports temporary problems of greater or lesser severity: the early summer of 2013 found the North Norfolk, Bluebell, Great Central and North Yorkshire Moors railways having a few weeks with fewer operational locomotives than they would have liked.[354] It has been the same almost every year, with few railways unaffected at one time or another. In 2004 the East Lancashire Railway was very short of steam locomotives, and lack of steam power contributed to the Weardale Railway's failure. In 2012, after hiring many of its home-based locomotives to other railways, the Llangollen Railway found itself briefly short of power for its own trains.[355] To overcome the shortages, and add variety to the operation, the railways hire locomotives from other lines and independent owners, which has created a minor branch of the heritage railway industry engaged in carting locomotives around the country.

Demand for motive power has increased. There are more heritage railways, running more trains over longer lines. They run longer and heavier trains. The major railways, such as the West Somerset and North Yorkshire Moors, run trains of six or seven coaches; even the smaller railways often run four-coach trains where once two coaches would have been enough. That has increased the demand for larger, more powerful locomotives compared to the smaller types. At the same time the supply of locomotives is inelastic.

To an extent this was not a new problem. Tom Rolt faced operating the Talyllyn Railway with one rather unhealthy locomotive, and one of the first actions of the preservation society was to seek additional power. The revival of the Ffestiniog a few years later was up against similar problems of motive power shortage throughout the first few years of operation. Another crisis in 1962 was resolved only by the hire of the former Penrhyn Railway locomotive *Linda*. This locomotive, together with her sister *Blanche*, was subsequently bought by the FR, bringing welcome relief to the locomotive department.[356]

However, matching demand and supply of motive power is a problem that is likely to recur. Preserved locomotives are all ageing, and need continual, expensive maintenance. Heritage railways have to tolerate rates of availability far worse than any mainline company, for at any one time most locomotives are likely to be out of service either for light maintenance or heavy overhaul. This applies to all types of motive power, but especially to steam. To cater for minor repairs, railways generally have more locomotives than might otherwise be needed. The Severn Valley Railway, for example, needs a minimum of seven steam locomotives available to operate its peak summer service. In practice, the aim is to have 10–12 locomotives available. The Swanage Railway requires three

Midland Railway class 4F No.3924 was the first locomotive to be bought for preservation from Woodham's scrapyard in Barry, South Wales. It arrived on the Keighley & Worth Valley Railway in 1970. It is seen in the yard at Haworth in 1974 alongside two former industrial locomotives of 'Austerity' type, with which many railway preservation projects began.

locomotives to operate the service; besides them there will be one in reserve, one receiving running repairs and one undergoing full overhaul. It only takes a few failures to tip the balance adversely: in 2000, the Severn Valley Railway had more locomotives out of action than expected because several suffered tube failures.[357]

Apart from the locomotives that the narrow-gauge railways already owned, the two main sources for motive power were British Railways and industry. In the 1960s and 1970s the supply of steam locomotives from both of these was abundant, and there was a prodigious effort at preservation. The buying and preservation of locomotives carried on in parallel to the preservation of the railways. Railway preservation groups concentrated on acquiring the line and bought a limited number of their own locomotives. Alongside, a multiplicity of organisations and individuals rescued locomotives, which were then placed on preserved railways under a variety of loan and hire agreements. Those acquiring the locomotives did not always place the operational needs of a railway high in their considerations. Availability, price and historic worth were of greater importance. Small tank engines were within the budget

Foremarke Hall, a locomotive rescued from Barry scrapyard, has been a locomotive based at the Gloucestershire Warwickshire Railway since 2004. It is at Toddington on 3 September 2005.

of individuals and small groups. As a result locomotives of limited practical value for operating trains arrived on preserved railways in some numbers. A letter to the Kent & East Sussex Railway Association's magazine in 1969 highlighted a concern that was typical for many railways. Its author questioned the wisdom of buying an ex-SE&CR class P locomotive because it was already 60 years old, and, therefore, going to be costly to maintain and likely to be of limited value for operational purposes. What was needed, he wrote, was powerful modern locomotives, such as the 'Austerity' 0-6-0 tank locomotives built in the 1940s and 1950s. British Railways had had a few, inherited from the LNER, and many more were used in industry. In the late 1960s they were becoming available for preservationists.[358] The Kent & East Sussex did buy two of these Austerity tank engines, as did many other preservation groups, and they justified that correspondent's faith, giving good service over

Another popular Great Western type of locomotive, the 'Manor' class was designed to handle the types of train railways such as the West Somerset now operate. No.7820 *Dinmore Manor* passes through Dunster in May 2000.

(Chris Marsh)

many years, although they were not especially popular with locomotive enthusiasts.

Useful, powerful locomotives were preserved in quantity as well, including some of the largest standard locomotives of the 1950s. The preservation effort was aided and prolonged by the fact that one of the scrap dealers to whom BR sold locomotives, Dai Woodham of Barry in South Wales, took his time in scrapping them. He was happy to sell them to preservation groups. There was criticism at the time that many of the purchases from Barry were of similar engines, but heritage railways have been profoundly grateful for the BR standard engines, the Great Western Halls, Manors and tank engines, and others that have been the mainstay of their operations.

The passing years have aged even the 'modern' Austerity and BR standard locomotives: by the turn of the new century the newest steam locomotives on heritage railways were 40 years old. With ageing locomotives the costs of maintenance and overhaul have risen steadily. The nature of preserved railway operation, with locomotives standing cold for several days between duties, especially on lines that run only at weekends, has not helped keep engines problem-free. The disappearance of steam from both the main railway network and industrial service meant that the engineering workshops went too. The heritage railway industry has had to recreate

In the queue for overhaul: 0-4-2 tank engine No.1420, sits in the yard at Buckfastleigh, April 2016.

Open-air restoration work on 34092 *City of Wells* at Haworth, 22 June 1974.

Most railways now have improved workshops, such as these at Sheffield Park, Bluebell Railway.

many of the skills of maintenance for steam locomotives. The Severn Valley and Mid-Hants are among the railways running engineering apprenticeship and training schemes. In 2014 a new apprenticeship programme for boilersmiths was launched with the support of the Heritage Lottery Fund.[359]

Most of the railways have their own workshops, some of them large, handling major overhauls and new manufacture. The Llangollen Railway's workshops are involved in new-build projects. The Severn Valley Railway can undertake boiler work. So can the South Devon Railway, after taking over the old-established boiler-making firm of R.K. Pridham, incorporating it into South Devon Railway Engineering Ltd. In addition there are independent specialist businesses, some old-established, such as Israel Newton & Sons, others new operations. All the workshops are small in scale compared with the old railway workshops, which adds to the cost of overhauls. More time is needed: what might have been six weeks at Swindon works is now several months, even years for an overhaul, as the time of volunteers and specialist workshops has to be found and finance raised. Add to these needs the impositions of new legislation, and it is easy to see how sums in six figures are common for major overhauls of large locomotives. One result is that locomotives are often out of action for years waiting their turn for overhaul. Some are placed in static displays. Most heritage railways have a museum building now, in which locomotives awaiting overhaul can spend time. Some go on loan to the National Railway Museum. However, pressure on motive power is often so great that railways fast-track some overhauls by contracting them out for professional restoration rather than rely on the pace of volunteer effort.

Meanwhile the supply of additional locomotives for heritage railways all but dried up. There are a few sources from which motive power might be found. One is the restoration of more locomotives to working order. Many have been bought for preservation, but have remained in disrepair ever since. About 200 steam locomotives were rescued from the scrapyard at Barry during the 1970s, but by the middle of 2006 only a little more than half of them had been restored to working order.[360] Of course, the reasons for the neglect of these locomotives were the same in 2006 as they had been for several years – shortage of money and manpower, and other projects had to take priority. Since then there has been a steady trickle of former Barry engines added to the restored and operational numbers. Great Western 2-8-0 No.3803 entered traffic in May 2006, twenty-three years after it was rescued from the scrapyard; restoration of BR Standard No.76084 was completed in 2013.[361] Even these newly restored locomotives add little, if anything, to the total motive power available to heritage railways. Locomotives fall due for overhaul every ten years or so, and some of the custodians have begun to wonder whether it is wise to continue operating their ageing engines. It is a question the East Anglian Railway Museum has asked of its Great Eastern N7 locomotive, for years a sturdy performer on preserved railways.[362] Some of the remaining scrapyard relics might never be fully restored. The interest of the pioneering spirits has moved on to new-build projects, for which some unrestored locomotives have become useful sources of major components.

To meet the operational needs of heritage railways, thoughts turned to using the bits of some of the derelict engines to

West Somerset

produce a useful locomotive. The ~~Severn Valley~~ Railway rebuilt a Great Western tank engine into a 2-6-0 tender engine of broadly standard Great Western pattern. It has been given the number 9351, a transposition of its former number, and the type of number that a Great Western 2-6-0 would carry. That was not enough to satisfy the more purist enthusiasts, who see this locomotive as a non-authentic intrusion. Less sentiment is attached to the standard industrial locomotives of the Austerity class. The conversion of one of these saddle tank engines built by Hunslet (number 2890 of 1943) into a tender engine caused less of a stir. This locomotive is based on the Mid-Hants Railway, where it goes in the guise of Douglas, one of the characters in Reverend Awdry's *Thomas the Tank Engine* books. This type of rebuilding is only a partial solution, however, for there can only be a small number of locomotives suitable for conversion, although the NBL Preservation Group has proposed creating 'new' locomotives out of scrap engines brought from South Africa.[363]

Another source of motive power is overseas. Preservationists have been importing locomotives and carriages for years, motivated both by the desire to rescue and preserve locomotives that might otherwise be lost and to acquire good working engines. The Welshpool & Llanfair was early in the field. Because its gauge of 2ft 6in is rare in Britain, it looked elsewhere for suitable motive power. It acquired a tank engine from Austria in 1969, and locomotives from Antigua and Sierra Leone in the 1970s, together with a number of carriages. Motive power for the revived Welsh Highland is mainly provided by locomotives imported from South Africa. Standard-gauge lines were acquiring overseas locomotives in some numbers during the 1970s. A Norwegian locomotive arrived on the Kent & East Sussex in 1973. Another of the early imports for the standard gauge was of an 'Austerity' 2-8-0 bought from Sweden for the Keighley & Worth Valley in 1972. Recently the railway has removed the alterations made to this locomotive while in service in the Netherlands and Sweden to restore it in its British form, returning it to service in 2007. The Nene Valley Railway, having a generous loading gauge, has made locomotives from overseas a special feature on the line. Other railways, including the Northampton & Lamport and the Churnet Valley, have

numbers of foreign locomotives. American locomotives of the S160 class, built for service in Europe during the Second World War, and several engines from Poland are among those to be found on these railways. Some British locomotives sold for preservation overseas have been brought back, including the standard-gauge Schools class *Stowe*, and a number of narrow-gauge 'Quarry Hunslets'. Overseas supplies are not inexhaustible, either, and there are limits to what can be accommodated in the British loading gauge.

The way out of the problems with motive power will ultimately be to build new locomotives. The narrow-gauge railways recognised this some time ago. In the 1960s the Talyllyn, experiencing difficulties finding second-hand locomotives that might be suitable for their unusual gauge, decided a new one might be the only answer. They sought tenders in 1966 from locomotive builders for what was expected to be the first narrow-gauge steam locomotive to be built in Britain since *Mannin*, built for the Isle of Man Railway in 1926.[364] In the event this order was not placed. Pressure on funds, a

One of the locomotives from overseas that has worked on the Nene Valley Railway. Swedish class B 4-6-0 No.101 awaits overhaul in Wansford yard.

A few of the S160 class locomotives brought over from America for service during the Second World War are now on heritage railways. No.6046 was visiting the Nene Valley Railway in September 2014.

slowing in traffic growth in the 1970s and the acquisition of a locomotive from Ireland that could be rebuilt deferred this decision. By the time this locomotive had been rebuilt as the railway's No.7 *Tom Rolt*, entering traffic in 1991, it was substantially a new construction.[365] The same thing happened with the rebuilding of Fairlie locomotive *Earl of Merioneth* on the Ffestiniog Railway in 1979; by the time it was finished the members of the preservation society decided it should be classed as a new locomotive. The Ffestiniog went on to build a completely new double Fairlie, *David Lloyd George*, in 1992, and a single Fairlie, *Taliesin*, in 1999.[366] In 2005 the revived Corris Railway built the new locomotive that the Talyllyn had not proceeded with all those years ago, to the same general design as their original No.4, which was now running on the Talyllyn. A 2-6-2 tank locomotive, *Lyd*, built to a design of the 1920s for the Lynton & Barnstaple, was completed in 2010.[367]

Railways on the miniature gauge did not have such a pool of old locomotives and had to build new. The lower costs of locomotives on this scale have helped. The Ravenglass & Eskdale built the first of the preservation era, the 2-8-2 locomotive *River Mite* of 1966. *Northern Rock* followed later, and a number of new diesel locomotives have also been built for the line. Locomotives for the Bure Valley Railway have also included many of new construction.

Apart from replicas of some of the pioneer railway locomotives for museum lines, it was not until the late 1990s that projects to build new steam locomotives for the standard gauge got under way. The first was the building of the new A1 class 4-6-2 *Tornado*. With the exception of a few rescued parts it was built from scratch. The success of this project seemed to open the floodgates, and before long a dozen or more new-build schemes were active. They included LNER Sandringham and P2, LMS Patriot, Great Western Saint and Grange and BR Clan and tank classes.

Common to all these projects, and a principal motivating force, is a desire to fill in gaps in the preservation record, for no examples of the Clan, A1 or Grange classes were preserved when BR withdrew them from service. The same is true of projects to build examples of diesel locomotives not otherwise preserved. The intention is not primarily to meet the motive-power needs of the heritage railways. Some, such as *Tornado*,

River Mite was the first of the new preservation-era locomotives on the Ravenglass & Eskdale Railway. Funded by the Ravenglass & Eskdale Railway Preservation Society, the locomotive was built in 1966.

Tornado, the new class A1 locomotive, completed in 2008, was built to run on the main line, but visits heritage railways in between railtours. It went to the Swanage Railway for its thirty-fifth anniversary gala in 2014, and is seen approaching Norden.

the Clan and others, are principally locomotives for the main line. Their enormous expense, and in consequence slowness of construction as finance is raised, makes these a luxury well beyond the average heritage line's budget.[368]

Other new-build projects are more rooted on the heritage railways. A project to build an Atlantic of LBSCR class H2 is based on the Bluebell Railway, and creation of a Grange 4-6-0, using a mixture of parts rescued from other standard Great Western engines and new construction, is based at the Llangollen Railway. There are some projects aimed specifically at the needs of heritage railways. The rebuilding of BR class 2MT 2-6-0 No.78059, which had lost its tender, into a similar class 2MT 2-6-2 tank locomotive is intended for work on the Bluebell Railway. The biggest exception among new-build projects has been the building of a BR Standard class 3 2-6-2 tank engine, described as 'the ideal locomotive to operate medium-sized branch lines'.[369] It was inspired by the recognition that heritage railways were going to need a fresh supply of reliable steam power as the original preserved locomotives grow older. The ambitions of the promoters of the project include building a batch of these engines. So far the work of raising the £1.5m needed to build one has been enough to occupy minds, but ultimately that need to find a source of additional power before the existing locomotives wear out might well turn thoughts back to such a project. Once the projects to recreate older classes have been completed, maybe one of the growing businesses of engineering firms serving the heritage railway industry will produce a new design of standard steam locomotive, incorporating advances in steam technology, which could be built in batches at lower cost per locomotive than the one-off projects. Such locomotives could be suitable for the day-to-day tourist operations of many heritage railways, allowing the older locomotives to be kept in reserve.

As well as the locomotives, maintaining supplies of coal is not as straightforward as it was in the early days of preservation, when orders could be placed with the pit for Welsh steam coal and Yorkshire coal to suit different boilers. Those pits have closed and most coal is imported; at the same time there are environmental campaigners who think all burning of coal should be stopped. Whereas the motive-power departments of heritage railways seem to be perennially short of steam locomotives, the supply of diesel locomotives and railcars has generally been in a better state. However, steam continues to be the mainstay and the draw for most heritage railways, which places the emphasis on maintaining availability of steam locomotives. A consequence is that, despite the strong following that modern traction can attract, enthusiasts for diesel and electric traction feel neglected. Electric locomotives and multiple units so far have no place to run on heritage railways, except behind steam or diesel power, although there have been plans to install a third rail on the East Kent Railway.[370]

There are similar pressures on other departments of the heritage railway operation. Most standard-gauge railways use former BR standard coaches for their regular trains, which were available in large numbers. These are now more than 50 years old and becoming more difficult to maintain, putting pressure on

The North Eastern Railway signalling and station furniture are an impressive sight complementing NER 0-8-0 No.63395 at Grosmont.

their availability for traffic. The railways will be looking for replacements soon. Narrow-gauge railways have also invested in completely new rolling stock. They had to: there simply was not enough coaching stock inherited to handle all the traffic, and no convenient source of second-hand coaches. A few coaches have been imported from overseas railways, such as the Austrian stock from the Zillertalbahn, brought to the Welshpool & Llanfair Railway in the 1960s, resulting from a growing friendship between the two railways. Most needs for extra stock on the narrow gauge have been met by new construction, a step taken also to satisfy demand for greater comfort and a smoother ride.

Besides the trains, other heritage equipment is becoming harder to obtain and maintain. Heritage railways keep to old standards of signalling, with semaphore signals controlled mechanically from old-style signalboxes. As the modernisation of signalling on the main network has gathered pace, so the supply of second-hand equipment has dried up. This is especially so for railways trying to maintain, for example, North Eastern Railway signals. The availability of such material more than 90 years old is very limited.

Chapter 13

COMMUNITY RAILWAYS

As was seen in the Introduction, there has always been a lively range of views about the objectives of railway preservation. One was that the railways should preserve the nation's public transport system, especially for rural areas. A leading exponent of this was O.H. Prosser, who had founded the Railway Development Association to campaign for improved community rail services. He believed that the transfer of branch lines unwanted by British Railways to new operators was vital for maintaining the provision of local transport, and for retaining feeder services into the mainline network.[371]

However, community services have proved to be a major problem for preserved railways, probably their single biggest area of failure. The history of railway preservation is littered with bold proposals to revive lines with the operation of passenger services for local commuters and shoppers, and goods services for local businesses. Sometimes whole projects have foundered on the rock of community services. More often a preservation group has been forced to cut its cloth to fit the tourist and enthusiast markets that are more likely to pay the bills for operating the line. Nevertheless, thoughts of running trains for local users have never gone away, and from the beginning of the new century have revived.

From the very beginning preserved railways had an element of local community involvement and service. Several drew a large proportion of their membership and support from their locality. For many it was a declared aim to provide transport services for local people. Some attempted to put this into practice. When the preservation society took over the Talyllyn there were still a few local people taking the train into Towyn on market days, and the town's tradesmen would send parcels back up the line for their farmer customers. Tom Rolt commented:

'Although from a revenue point of view this local traffic is negligible and it is upon the patronage of the holiday-maker that the railway has to depend for its bread and butter, we of the small permanent staff attached the greatest importance to it and did our utmost to ensure that, whatever else might happen, we should not let our regular passengers down.'[372]

This type of traffic continued, sufficient for the railway to run a once-a-week shoppers' service through the winters of 1951 and 1953. After a break of some years the service was reinstated in the winter of 1964 following requests from the residents of Rhydyronen. It was 'hardly a commercial proposition', but the service continued to run for a few years.[373]

In 1957 the Ffestiniog tried a winter service for local shoppers on Saturdays, but with traffic not forthcoming, this was quickly abandoned.[374] New railways could pick up some local traffic. Villagers from Llangower used the Bala Lake Railway to get into Bala in the 1970s because there was no local bus service. The Welshpool & Llanfair Railway's promoters hoped that they would be able to revive the coal traffic along the line, to give a year-round income.[375]

Several standard-gauge preservation schemes of the 1960s set out with the aim of running local community services. Some were plainly following the 'Prosser' line of thinking, attempting to provide a modern public service. The Vectrail Society, hoping to take over the lines from Cowes to Newport and Ryde on the Isle of Wight, proposed using new light rail vehicles powered by overhead electrification. This society set out to be railway revival rather than preservation as it was then practised. 'It must be emphasised that this is *not* a preservation society,' the group's chairman wrote. 'We believe that this line can be run in a modern fashion sufficiently cheaply and attractively to pay its way and prove that branch lines need not die out.'[376] Commuter services were part of the plans of a number of preservation proposals, among them the Westerham Valley, Hayling Island and Horsham & Guildford. These services would be operated using 'modern' diesel traction, and steam-hauled trains for enthusiasts and tourists would run at weekends between spring and autumn. Not openly stated, an element of cross-subsidy was implied in such proposals. These projects, however, all failed to get off the ground.

The Keighley & Worth Valley Railway Preservation Society aimed to provide a regular passenger service for the local people, who were strongly supporting the new organisation.

One of the railbuses used for the Keighley and Worth Valley Railway's community services. (Author's collection)

Tourist traffic was expected to provide only a small proportion of the revenue. By the time the railway opened six years later things had changed, and the railway was operating a more purely leisure service. The Kent & East Sussex had similar ambitions to run commuter trains, but had to abandon them and to concentrate on vintage and tourist trains to get over the administrative hurdles in the way of reopening the railway.[377]

Even more ambitious were schemes proposed when the Midland & Great Northern Railway was closed in 1958. Promoters aimed for a fully fledged public transport system over the whole of the M&GN system, or at least a substantial section of it, such as Yarmouth to North Walsham. But they had to settle for a short preserved railway, what became the North Norfolk Railway.[378]

The reasons for the failure of community-based projects at this time are not difficult to understand. The commitment needed to run commuter services all year round was a drain on a voluntary organisation that had struggled to get its first short section of line open for operation at weekends only. The rise and rise of road transport put paid to many dreams of running local rail services. People were buying cars, and roads were being built to accommodate them, some along the very branch lines the preservationists hoped to run. The owner of a mill at Ingrow asked at the public meeting that led to the formation of the Keighley & Worth Valley RPS how his men were to get to work without the local railway.[379] But most would have bought a car before the line reopened. The result of these changes was that, for many preservation projects, what had seemed a perfectly viable proposal to provide local public transport when formulated in the early 1960s had little prospect by 1970.

Public policy was not especially conducive to preserved railways' provision of community services. The length of time it took for a preservation project to get the authority to open meant that much of the impetus that might have produced a service for locals had dissipated by the time the railway actually opened. And when it did, the cash-strapped preservation society as likely as not had to settle at first for a short stretch of line, cut off from the main network and operated only at weekends. That hardly helped the shoppers and commuters. When the Keighley & Worth Valley project was being launched, the society's chairman, Bob Cryer, looked forward to a speedy resumption of services in 1965, expecting the railway to attract about fifty per cent of the 300,000 passengers British Railways claimed to have been carrying. This railway had a shorter wait than many, but transfer of operating powers still took much longer than expected.[380] Hopes of support from local authorities proved false dawns more often than not. The Clevedon & Yatton Railway Society, anticipating the possible running of the Clevedon branch, contacted the Minister of Transport in 1966 to seek clarification of the recent White Paper, *Transport Policy*, which stated that if local communities wished to retain transport services, they should expect to meet part of the cost.[381] Nothing came of that. Owen Prosser had high hopes that provisions under the Transport Act 1968, and again under powers announced in the early 1970s, would lead to local support for preserved railways. The Department of the Environment issued a circular to local authorities in 1973 that allowed them to make grants in aid of local railway services, which would be underwritten by the Exchequer. Prosser pointed out that the councils were not restricted to supporting only trains run by British Rail, and suggested a number of existing and potential preserved railways that might benefit from this regime.[382]

The application of these powers proved to be of little benefit to railway preservation. On the whole, local authorities were not willing to make annual grants in aid for socially desirable train services operated by bodies other than British Rail. It is understandable that they should be cautious about transferring their payments to an untried group supported by an amateur society. When the Stour Valley Railway Preservation Society suggested that they should take over the Sudbury branch and run the commuter services with the same local authority support given to BR, they found the councils unreceptive. However, the avowedly commercial Dart Valley Railway Company had the subsidy for the Kingswear branch cancelled by the Devon County and Torbay Borough councils in 1974. As a result, the winter service on the railway was suspended.[383] That is not to say that councils were never supportive of preservationists' efforts, but they tended to look to means other than the annual grant in aid. Somerset County Council offered to subsidise the West Somerset Railway with £10,000 a year, by reducing the annual rent for the line, provided the railway ran a year-round commuter service with a minimum of four trains each way between Taunton and Minehead. There was genuine willingness to proceed along these lines, despite objections of the Western National Bus Company that this would be an unfair subsidy. The West Somerset Railway, however, was unable to gain access to Taunton station.[384]

Therein lay the real problems for preserved railways in seeking to attract subsidy. They were rarely able to provide the service authorities were willing to support. It took too long to raise the finance, obtain the Light Railway Order or gain a connection with the national network. The exception was the contract that the Romney Hythe & Dymchurch Railway continued to receive to run school trains in the 1970s, as it had done twenty years before.[385] Preservation projects launched from the late 1970s to the early 1990s generally contained very little element of a community service in their proposals. They had to concentrate on their tourist and heritage potential.

Those railways that did operate local services in the 1960s and 1970s usually did so from their own resources. Inevitably, the community services they ran took second place to what was now the main business of running trains for tourists and enthusiasts. This meant that the local people were without a train service during the railway's off-season; even during the running season, ticket prices were too high for most local users, generally pitched for the tourist market and to meet the high costs of heritage steam trains. Services for shoppers and commuters, therefore, remained on the margins of the preserved railways' activities. Some ran a diesel-hauled market-day train. In its early years the Keighley & Worth Valley, to keep faith with its initial aims, ran most early-morning trains as a diesel railcar, and a service on winter Saturdays, again with railcar and aimed mainly at local travellers. More recently this railway has offered local residents' railcards, entitling them to a discount on the standard tourist fare. It also encouraged its visitors to come by public transport. Having an easy interchange with the national railway network at Keighley, on some days in the early 1980s half of the line's passengers arrived by train. The West Yorkshire Passenger Transport Executive at this time made a point of including the KWVR in the official public transport network of its region.[386]

A new era for community services?

Since the mid-1990s, following the privatisation of railway operations, interest in the operation of community services by heritage railways has revived. As passenger numbers on the railway network have risen, public authorities and train operators of all sorts have been looking at ways to meet demand. Freight operators have been pursuing similar aims. Preserved railways have been caught up in this with many an ambitious scheme. Commuter services, micro-franchising, partnerships with train operating companies, community rail partnerships and the creation of new local networks all entered the vocabulary of the heritage railway world. The support of local authorities, some of whom have initiated proposals for new community services, has been important.

In the early days of the project to preserve the Swanage Railway, one of the arguments put forward in its support was that the railway would ease traffic congestion. It was appropriate, perhaps, that one of the first signs of a new age for community rail projects was the successful establishment of the park and ride service on the Swanage Railway in 1995. Introduced initially by Purbeck District Council, trains ran from Norden into Swanage allowing motorists to avoid the section

of road through Corfe Castle and into the confined area of Swanage itself. As it built up, with the car park being expanded from 125 spaces to 500, the railway operated the complete service. Additional facilities were developed alongside the car park, including a children's play area and a museum of the local ball clay industry. In the first ten years of the park and ride service, 840,000 passengers were carried. In 2006 alone more than 40,000 passengers used these trains. Although this service was as much for the benefit of tourists coming into Swanage as the local shoppers, it marked a change of approach by both the railway and local authorities.[387]

The Swanage Railway has continued with its ambitions to extend operations to Wareham. These will be 'commuter' services of the type the local authorities always said they would support. Perseverance has paid off. After securing the permanent connection to the main line (p. 258-9), further grants have allowed the track on the branch to be upgraded and two diesel railcars prepared for the service, expected to begin in spring 2017.[388] Numerous other proposals for commuter

In anticipation of completion of the project to reach Wareham, on gala days the Swanage Railway ran demonstration trains up to the junction with Network Rail, such as this one on 12 July 2014.

services from heritage railways have been put forward. The East Lancashire Railway, it has been said, could provide a link to Manchester via Heywood and Castleton Junction, and local councillors have talked of running trains to Rochdale over the ELR.[389] Hopes of a local commuter service being revived along the Cholsey & Wallingford line have surfaced, as have proposals for similar services on the Severn Valley from Bewdley to Kidderminster, and from the West Somerset into Taunton. Partnerships with the franchised train-operating companies have also been mooted, most notably the idea floated by Chiltern Trains to run through services on to the Chinnor & Princes Risborough Railway. To do this the connection between the heritage railway and the main network would be restored. Various proposals to 'roll back the Beeching years' and revive former railways have included links with existing heritage railways. There was a proposal in 2010 by the CES Partnership to bring the line from Ripley in Derbyshire back into use, on which commuter trains would run to Derby, but with connections with the Midland Railway–Butterley included.[390]

New Generation lines

During the 1990s several new railway preservation projects began to be called 'New Generation' lines. What at first was a coinage of journalists soon became self-consciously adopted by the promoters of the railways themselves. When the Rhondda & Cynon Valleys Railway Society abandoned its plan to reopen the Treherbert to Blaencwm line after failing to gain the support of local authorities, it merged with the Bridgend Valleys Railway in preference to the Gwili Railway. 'As we are a New Generation group we wanted the money to go to a New Generation line,' explained the Rhondda society. The merged group, the Garw Valley Railway Co Ltd, was planning to reopen the branch line from Tondu to Pontycymmer.[391]

New Generation lines saw themselves not just as another group of preserved or heritage railways, but as offering something new. In particular they wanted to be more than railways for the tourist or even for the enthusiast, but to be more deeply rooted in their local communities. Provision of transport services for the community was, therefore, important; at the same time they hoped to boost the local tourist economy.

Support, and sometimes finance, from local authorities and regional development funds was important for several. Promoters of the lines were often from a younger generation that was less emotionally attached to steam, and they did not place such emphasis on steam traction. Some, such as the Keith & Dufftown Railway that opened in 2000, eschewed the use of steam traction until they held a steam gala in 2012. Others have succumbed to its attractions simply as a means of raising money. In reality many of the ambitions of the New Generation were not so far removed from those of the first generation of preserved railways, and they soon found it necessary to adopt some of their predecessors' methods, with special events for the enthusiast market, for example.[392]

A prime example of a New Generation line was the Ecclesbourne Valley Railway in Derbyshire. The company set up to run the railway, Wyvern Rail plc, described itself as a community-owned company, after making a public offer of shares directed especially at local people. The aim of the project was the reopening of the railway from Duffield to Wirksworth. This had closed to passengers as long ago as 1947, but the line had continued in use for many years for freight and as a test track for new and overhauled rolling stock from Derby works. From modest beginnings in the early 1990s, the Ecclesbourne Valley project grew rapidly in the following decade. After twelve years of negotiation a lease for the line was agreed with Network Rail in 2003, but, two years later, Wyvern Rail bought the line outright. Train services were reintroduced on a short stretch of line from Wirksworth to Gorsey Bank from 24 August 2004. Extensions, first to Ravenstor in 2005 and then to Idridgehay, opened in March 2008, were pushed ahead, assisted by grant aid from Derby and Derbyshire Enterprise, who contributed £95,000 towards these extensions. The railway's business has been planned with a mixture of community services, trains for the enthusiasts and commercial hire for test purposes. Wyvern Rail joined the Derwent Valley Community Rail Partnership. One of its contributions was to maintain Duffield station, where the railway joined Network Rail's Derwent valley route. Membership of the partnership allowed the railway to develop good relations with its neighbours, so that, when the remaining section of line to Duffield was

The Mid-Norfolk Railway Society kept a collection of stock at County School station in the 1990s, which was moved after trains started running at Dereham. The line of locomotives was there in July 1997.

reopened on 8 April 2011, the timetables on the Ecclesbourne and Derwent routes gave good connections.[393]

The Mid-Norfolk Railway, another of the New Generation lines, had a long gestation. Its origins lay in the establishment of the Fakenham & Dereham Railway Society in 1978 with the aim of taking over the freight-only line from Fakenham, building up the goods services and reintroducing passenger trains. It set up a base at County School in 1988, but, despite running several open days, did not make much progress. The Mid-Norfolk Railway Preservation Trust, formed in 1995, was the group that succeeded in buying part of the route, from Wymondham to Dereham, with the addition of the stretch to North Elmham purchased in 2001.[394] Trains started operating between Dereham and Yaxham in 1996, and through to Wymondham in 1999. The long-term aim remains to extend northwards from Dereham to reach Fakenham, to be achieved in stages: first to North Elmham, then County School. The railway has promoted a generally modern image, using diesel traction more than steam, partly a result of its establishment late in the day, when the availability of steam locomotives was more limited. It has attracted freight traffic, principally to the military depot at Dereham. It has also hosted works trains from Network

Rail and Direct Rail Services. In these ways, the Mid-Norfolk sees itself less as a conventional heritage railway, more a flexible provider of a variety of services.[395]

A new direction
The Wensleydale Railway started operations in July 2003. This was another that seemed to offer a new direction for community railways and for railway preservation. A local, community-based organisation was reintroducing passenger services to a line that was still part of the national network and was still open for goods traffic. The Wensleydale Railway Association, formed in 1990, had tried to buy the twenty-two-mile branch from Northallerton to Redmire when the end of limestone traffic threatened it with complete closure. The operation of occasional 'Dalesrail' trains under the auspices of Yorkshire Dales National Park, introduced in 1977, had encouraged hopes for the revival of the branch. The Wensleydale Railway Association, however, had difficulty raising funds, but after the Ministry of Defence used the line to transport equipment between Catterick Camp (near Redmire) and Salisbury, the association negotiated a lease of the line for ninety-nine years from Railtrack.[396]

The first services to be run by the new company were local commuter and shoppers' trains using old diesel railcars on the first twelve miles of the route, from Leeming Bar to Leyburn. An extension over the five miles to Bedale and Redmire was brought into operation from 1 August 2004. There was great public rejoicing at the inaugural services, but the harsher realities of operating community railways soon became apparent. In common with almost all lines seeking to regain a connection to the national network, achieving the objective of the junction at Northallerton has proved no easy task. Like preserved railways before it, the Wensleydale relied heavily on volunteer support to keep costs down and draw in local involvement. With its separated stretch of line it was not easy to cover costs, such that by the winter of 2005 it reduced services to weekends only and made ten out of seventeen staff redundant. At the same time an appeal went out to Wensleydale Railway Society members to help raise £100,000 to rebuild reserves. Part of the remedy lay in the introduction of steam power for some summer services, the hosting of special trains from the main line and holding special events for railway enthusiasts and families. In doing this, the railway aligned itself more with other heritage railways, and has been a success, pulling itself back from the brink, and allowing it to continue with its expansion plans. A new Northallerton West station was commissioned on 22 November 2014, which, although not next to the mainline station, marked a major step forward. In the longer term, there are ambitions to rebuild the line across the Pennines to Garsdale.[397]

The Dartmoor Railway, running over the fifteen miles from Coleford, the junction with the Exeter–Barnstaple line, to Meldon Quarry, was another that seemed to offer new hope for the development of community railways. The line, a freight branch serving the stone quarry, had been sold by British Rail to ECC Quarries in 1994. A few railtours were run on to the branch after it changed hands, which stimulated interest in a revival of passenger services. The breakthrough came when Devon County Council in 1997 sponsored trains on summer Sundays running along the branch and through to Exeter. The county council brought together other local authorities, ECC Quarries, and cycling and youth-hostelling groups and others to support the venture. The enterprise resulted in the restoration of Okehampton station, a model of conservation, and new stations were opened at Meldon Quarry and Sampford Courtenay in 2004. The railway was not a preserved or heritage line in the conventional sense. It operated under the Network Rail rule book, not a Light Railway Order, which among other things allowed it to run at higher speeds. However, it took on the characteristics of a heritage line with special events for enthusiasts and families and heritage trains run between Meldon and Okehampton or Sampford. ECC Quarries sold this nascent line in November 2004 to the ECT Group, a leading example of a new breed of social and community enterprise. ECT had been founded in 1979 as Ealing Community Transport, an industrial and provident society, operating three local buses, filling gaps left by larger operators. From those beginnings it grew into a business with a turnover of £22m and 650 buses, while remaining a not-for-profit company. The Dartmoor Railway under ECT's management continued to develop its community services in association with the county council and

First Great Western, and planned to operate regular through trains from Okehampton to Exeter.[398]

The Dartmoor was the ECT group's first venture into the railway business, but it became the foundation for expansion. RMS Locotec, a business formed in 1994 to hire and maintain locomotives and rolling stock, was bought, and in 2005 ECT took seventy-five per cent of the shares of the Weardale Railway Company, reconstituted after the failure of the initial preservation project. The Weardale reopened under the new management in August 2006. On these foundations ECT had ambitions to take on further community lines, until a change of heart at the end of 2007. The two lines were probably not yielding as much as ECT might have hoped. There were only 10,000 visitors to the Weardale during 2007, the company reported, compared with 35,000 needed to break even. ECT had also concluded that, whatever the rhetoric, the government was failing to support community railways. It therefore put all of its rail business up for sale. Although the Weardale Railway continued to operate, the Dartmoor Railway was closed, except for Sunday services from Exeter to Okehampton, which ran with support from Devon County Council. Fortunately for the two lines, a buyer was found reasonably quickly. On 4 September 2008 it was announced that British American Railway Services, a new subsidiary of Iowa Pacific of Chicago, was to take over ECT's holdings. Under the new management, the Dartmoor Railway was reopened on 10 April 2009 and expansion plans revived.[399]

The new owners had plans for the Weardale Railway that were just as ambitious. A new timetable of daily passenger services was introduced on 23 May 2010 from Stanhope to Bishop Auckland, where connections were offered to the mainline network. Steam-hauled heritage services were interspersed with this timetable – precisely the type of thing envisaged by many of the early generations of railway preservation when they hoped to run community services. As well as the passenger services, there were plans for freight traffic, which would underpin the finances of the line.[400] A daily schedule between Stanhope and Bishop Auckland was introduced in March 2010. However, traffic in volume failed to materialise, the regular commuter service was withdrawn from 31 December 2011 and the railway concentrated on heritage passenger trains.[401]

Traffic on the Weardale and Dartmoor railways continued to disappoint the owners, and all heritage and community services were abandoned on both in 2013. British & American Railway Services announced plans for luxury dining services instead. The Dartmoor Railway Supporters Association negotiated the running of a few charter trains on the Dartmoor Railway, and members of the Weardale Railway Trust started services on the northern line in June 2014. Services have continued in this modest fashion, with the Polar Express trains at Christmas time the biggest money-spinner. Meanwhile, the Dartmoor railway gets talked up as potentially part of a Dawlish coast diversionary route.[402]

Rail partnerships and micro-franchises

A few years after privatisation the idea of separating some local routes from the major train operating companies came to the fore – 'micro-franchising', it was called. The Strategic Rail Authority, a national co-ordinating body established in 2001, championed micro-franchising and held up the successful launch of the Wensleydale Railway as an example of what new businesses could do in running branch lines. In a consultation paper, *Community Rail Development*, published in February 2004, the SRA suggested that discrete local routes might be better off run by dedicated organisations rather than the larger train-operating companies.

Heritage railways were mentioned as potential operators of micro-franchised community railways, and their reaction was positive. The Esk Valley line to Whitby was among the candidates, and the NYMR promptly expressed interest in taking the line on. The Bodmin & Wenford Railway was interested in the Cornish branch lines to St Ives and Looe, and a group of Cornish enthusiasts formed Sterling Service Rail Link Ltd also with a view to partnership in the St Ives branch. Wyvern Rail, the operating company for the Ecclesbourne Valley Railway, and the Dartmoor Railway, were among others declaring an interest in the possibilities included in the discussion paper.[403]

The demise of the Strategic Rail Authority in December 2006 left this policy high and dry. The only thing to materialise has

been the agreement for the North Yorkshire Moors Railway to operate some through services from Pickering to Whitby. These have been tourist services, mainly steam-hauled, rather than community services. Trains from Whitby to Glaisdale, operated by the West Coast Railway Company on behalf of the NYMR, began running in 2005. From 2007 the NYMR was granted a safety case allowing it to run trains over Network Rail lines on its own account, and its first train, crewed by volunteers, ran on 3 April. The railway planned to run 100 trains through to Whitby during that year, with extra trains running along the line westwards to Battersby at weekends. These have been outstandingly successful. By 2013 more than half the NYMR's fare income came from the Whitby services, and the company invested in a platform and run-round loop at Whitby station to increase capacity; these were brought into use in August 2014.[404] The North Norfolk Railway plans to run similar services from its line to Cromer to begin in 2016.[405]

The ambitions of some of the heritage railways and community interests to revive local transport have not diminished, with many groups striving to follow in the footsteps of the Ecclesbourne

The new platform at Whitby built for the North Yorkshire Moors Railway comfortably able to accommodate the seven-coach trains used on the route.

The end of the line for the North Norfolk Railway at Holt, where No.65894 prepares to run round its train on 14 July 1997. Maybe this will become a stop on the Norfolk orbital railway.

Valley and Wensleydale railways. The Don Valley Railway is a community project founded in 2003 to run regular services from Stocksbridge and Deepcar to Sheffield city centre, using modern railcars, such as the Parry People Mover. It has the support of South Yorkshire Passenger Transport Executive and other authorities. Like some preservation schemes of the 1960s, there are thoughts of running heritage services at weekends.[406] Other projects include the Bramley Line Group, formed in 2003 to promote the rebuilding of the line from March to Wisbech, and CKP Railways, a company that wants to recreate the railway between Penrith and Keswick. The Berkeley Vale Railway has been promoted as a community project by the Stratford Broadway Railway Society, members of which were frustrated at the lack of progress towards Stratford, and sought a new interest. The group, renamed Sharpness & Berkeley Railway Ltd, plan to run tourist trains on the 4½ miles of railway from Berkeley Road junction to Sharpness, and to host freight traffic to the Berkeley and Oldbury power stations. They secured a lease from Network Rail from 4 March 2011.[407] In Norfolk an ambitious plan was launched in 2007 to create a Norfolk Orbital Railway. The Melton Constable Trust and the Holt, Melton Constable & Fakenham Railway Company aim to rebuild the railway between Holt and Fakenham to link the North Norfolk and Mid-Norfolk lines. In turn these would connect with Network Rail routes to Norwich and Sheringham to create the circle. In 2013 the first parcels of land were bought towards rebuilding the route from the North Norfolk Railway's Holt station towards Holt town.[408]

There is considerable goodwill in the twenty-first century towards heritage railways and their ambitions for community services. Talk of running trains from the West Somerset into Taunton, and the step-by-step moves towards running from the Swanage Railway to Wareham, keep hopes raised. The All Party Parliamentary Group on Heritage Rail suggested there was scope for greater support from local authorities towards the cost of providing community and 'public tourist transport' services. That there is more talk than action, however, is down to the fact that the problems for a heritage railway operating local community services are the same as they always have been. They are not cheap, even on a volunteer-run railway, they are not always compatible with a leisure and tourist-orientated operation, and, as the Weardale Railway has experienced, the traffic is not always there.

Freight services
Many of the preservation groups with ambitions for community services expected the carriage of freight to play a part. When the West Somerset was assessing the prospects in 1978 for running regular services to Taunton, one of the sources of trade it looked for was freight to Watchet. There were hopes of coal traffic on the Dean Forest Railway.[409]

The Middleton Railway was unique in carrying freight almost exclusively, linking the private sidings along its route with British Railways. Only when the businesses stopped using these links did the Middleton become a passenger-carrying railway.

Elsewhere, freight services have been an occasional activity, often a contract for a specific need. The Llanberis Lake Railway was used to carry materials for the laying of underground cables from the new Dinorwic hydroelectric power station. Trains were run during the close season for passenger services between 1975 and 1977.[410] Early in its history the Nene Valley ran trains for a boat builder carrying boats for a customer in France. It subsequently secured work from Cape Insulation Ltd: ten wagons a week carrying goods from Stirling to a warehouse at Wansford went via the NVR instead of transferring to road at Stamford. This deal was so encouraging that the railway produced a pamphlet to publicise its freight facilities to local businesses.[411] For some years Fitzgerald Lighting used the Bodmin & Wenford Railway to send wagons direct to the main network. So matters remained until in the aftermath of rail privatisation came the blurring of distinctions between heritage and main network railways, and a new interest in community railways.

The privatisation era has seen a readiness on the part of rail freight companies to take trains over heritage lines. English Welsh & Scottish Railway secured contracts to carry materials for sea defences at Minehead, which involved taking the trains along the West Somerset in the 1990s and again in 2010. Trains from Foster Yeoman's quarry likewise traversed the West Somerset carrying stone for road improvement works in 2004. GB Railfreight took trains of gypsum to East Leake via the Great Central (Nottingham). A demand for a large increase in insurance premiums, however, threatened those trains in 2003. Trains of military supplies have run to Dereham over the Mid-Norfolk Railway.[412]

The Ribble Steam Railway in 2004 became the first to operate a freight service for which it had tendered on its own account, as opposed to simply providing the rails over which one of the national freight operators ran trains. This railway is unusual in that it does not run through picturesque countryside but through 1½ miles at Preston docks. This was a new line, but at the same time a relaunching of an older project. The Steamport Museum had been based at Southport since 1973, but after twenty years the society running it was looking to expand. The impending closure of the Preston docks network in 1995 prompted the society to seek to relocate the Steamport collection with a view to running passenger trains. Sale of the land at Southport for development gave the society the cash to start work at Preston, with a new workshop built in 2001. While preparations were being made for the new Ribble Steam Railway to start operations, an approach was made to run trains of bitumen into the docks. This had been the traffic that had kept the branch open until 1995. Trials were made in 2003, which encouraged the railway, along with national freight operator English Welsh & Scottish Railway, to start regular services in 2004 running three times a week. A separate company, Ribble Rail, was set up to handle this traffic; the contract was renewed in 2014. Formal opening of passenger services on the steam railway came on 17 September 2005.[413]

A more open market for rail freight has encouraged the entrepreneurs behind new heritage lines to incorporate it into their plans. It is the primary aim behind the Moorland & City Railway in Staffordshire, founded by two of the Churnet Valley Railway's directors, Greg Wilson and David Kemp, in 2009. Their ambitious plans were to reopen the 22½ miles of railway line from Stoke-on-Trent to Cauldon Low. The railway does not describe itself as a heritage railway but wants to concentrate on freight services to quarries and cement works. At the same time it held out the prospect of heritage railway passenger services, in conjunction with the Churnet Valley, a promise underlined by the opening galas for the Cauldon Low line in November 2010. The close working relationship between the two organisations was further emphasised by backing from the MCR for planned extensions of the Churnet Valley to Leek and to Alton, and the CVR's raising funds to take a shareholding in its new neighbour company.[414]

The rebuilding of the Mountsorrel branch off the Great Central Railway has the carriage of stone from the neighbouring quarry as its intent. British American Rail Services, the buyers of the Dartmoor and the Weardale railways in 2009, have ambitious plans for the development of freight services on both lines. The carriage of coal from an open cast mine at Tow Law along the Weardale Railway began in 2011. An associated company, Devon & Cornwall Railways, received an open-access freight licence for the national network on 24 December 2010.[415]

Chapter 14

REGULATION AND RELATIONS WITH THE MAINLINE NETWORK

'The future of heritage railways is being threatened by new safety requirements, according to steam enthusiasts,' ran the opening to a report in the *Daily Telegraph* in February 2006 written by the paper's transport correspondent, David Millward.[416] The threat in question was a new regime of safety inspection introduced with the Railway and Other Guided Transport Systems Regulations 2006. These regulations, originating from the European Union, were likely to impose charges for inspecting work on the track that hitherto Her Majesty's Railway Inspectorate had done for nothing.[417]

This threat seems to have passed, but its moment of national prominence did highlight the heritage railway movement's growing concern that regulation could be adding a disproportionate burden. All the new rules of health and safety, disability and other aspects of modern life, especially those of European origin, seemed to be applied with little or no distinction between a small independent railway and an express main line. There were exemptions, but they were few. Preserved railways narrowly escaped being drawn into the franchising net when the legislation to privatise British Rail was before Parliament in the 1990s.[418]

Complaints about bureaucracy and regulation were made by witnesses before the All Party Parliamentary Committee on Heritage Rail. They had broad concerns about the growing burden of regulation and some of the restrictions imposed by Transport and Works Orders. The red tape involved in planning and other matters involving local councils had often been cited as frustrating enterprise. The parliamentary committee was given several examples of petty things, such as a need to provide an environmental impact assessment for digging a small trench, or the refusal of planning permission to remove some brambles to widen a gateway on the grounds that they were an 'ancient hedge'.[419] Despite the problems, some heritage railways have been creative and embraced the changes as opportunities. In particular they have had a good record in converting old carriages for disabled access.

Safety is a special concern. Heritage railways, in common with the main line, operate public services under statutory authority and are not exempt from safety regulations. Nor have the railways wished to be exempt. From the earliest days of preservation, the rule book, the traditional manual for safety, was adopted, along with the hierarchy of grades and training.

The administration of the statutory rules might seem to have become more complex, with departmental reorganisations in Whitehall. Her Majesty's Railway Inspectorate had been a branch of the Board of Trade, later the Ministry (Department) of Transport, staffed by retired officers of the Royal Engineers.[420] Establishing a relationship with the inspectors was important for all railway preservation projects, and for most the relationship was one of trust. The inspectors, as revealed in accounts from the early days of most preservation schemes, were always scrupulously fair; they were gently understanding of the ambitions of these amateur railwaymen, advising and encouraging them on how to proceed. But they would not let any compromise with safety pass.

In 1990 the inspectorate became a largely civilian body, part of the Health and Safety Executive. Out went the formality of 'Major', in came informal 'Mike' when dealing with inspectors. Alongside this came new regimes of detailed risk assessments and safety case compliance, with the need to show a 'paper trail', and the burdens of regulation grew. Even so, most heritage railways have continued good relations with HM Inspectors. The Railway Inspectorate was transferred to the Office of Rail Regulation (ORR) in 2004. As well as the inspectorate, the new Rail Accidents Investigation Branch of the Department for Transport began work in 2005, set up following some serious mainline accidents, and its remit included the heritage railways.[421]

The safety record of heritage railways has not been un-blemished. Concerns were raised in the 1990s. Major Poyntz of the Railway Inspectorate told the ARPS that, with twelve derailments on preserved lines in 1992 compared with eleven on the whole of BR, improvement was needed. Poor track maintenance seemed to be the main cause of derailments. 'Too many railways were investing in extensions, new buildings or garish locomotive paint schemes rather than in track maintenance,' Major Poyntz said. In the early twenty-first century the railways were again in danger of gaining a reputation for laxity, as there were several accidents involving passengers and volunteers. Volunteers were crushed in shunting accidents on the Gwili Railway in 2007 and North Yorkshire Moors Railway in 2012; there were accidents at level crossings on the Romney Hythe & Dymchurch and Wensleydale railways. The ORR prosecuted the Wensleydale and Telford Steam railways in 2012–13, and pressed heritage railways to improve their safety management.[422]

Statutory powers

A few of the oldest independent railways – the Talyllyn, the Ffestiniog and the Middleton – derive their authority from their original private Acts of Parliament, a fact of which they are proud. Most preserved railways are light railways under the terms of the Light Railways Act 1896. Light Railway Orders, statutory instruments issued by the Board of Trade and its successor departments, offered a cheaper and simpler process of authorisation than a private Act.

The preserved railways on the standard gauge all needed to get new orders converting what had been a railway built under a private Act of Parliament into a light railway. There was almost always a two-stage process to this. In the first, British Railways, as the incumbent operator of the line, had to apply for an order to create a new light railway. BR subsequently applied for an order transferring its powers to the new operating company. There have been a few exceptions. The Kent & East Sussex Railway had been built originally as a light railway. All that was needed in 1974, therefore, was a transfer order vesting the powers held by BR in the new Tenterden Railway Company. Heritage railways developed on former industrial sites applied for their own Light Railway Orders. The Mid-Hants Railway was another exception to the rule, in bypassing the British

Railways stage of the process and making a direct application for its Light Railway Order, granted in 1977.[423]

This process of transferring powers was longwinded and costly, and was one of the major reasons for delays in getting a new preservation scheme operational. Almost every group promoting a line has faced postponing hoped-for opening dates, in many cases several times, while they waited for the Light Railway Orders to be approved. At every stage in the process public notice had to be given. Objectors had to be allowed to make representations. There have often been some, and, although it has almost always been possible to reach agreement with the objectors, they have added to the frustrations and delay of getting the railway running.

The Transport & Works Act 1992 introduced a new system for the authorisation of new and altered railway works that was intended to be simpler. It was not introduced for the primary benefit of preserved railways but for much larger organisations. However, its provisions applied to all railways and tramways in England & Wales (Scotland retained the previous legislation). Light Railway Orders were now superseded by Transport & Works Orders. Although this might have been simpler for some works on the main line, it added bureaucracy for heritage railways, which now had to get Transport & Works approval and a licence to operate. The Chinnor & Princes Risborough was the first preserved railway to receive authorisation under this legislation. The last Light Railway Order was not issued until December 2012, when the Royal Deeside Railway received its order. The application process had been started under the Light Railway Act, and thus was completed.[424]

One of the main conditions imposed by Light Railway Orders was a speed limit of 25mph. For most railways this is no imposition: the costs of maintaining track for regular running at higher speeds are very high. The branch-line character of many lines makes a low speed natural. However, a few railways with track and signalling already at a much higher standard than a 'light' railway might like some relaxation of the rule. They are constrained in not being able to market anything other than a slow trundle. The only railway so far to have been granted permission to run at higher speed is the Great Central. Speeds up to 45mph are allowed on some occasions, and up to 60mph for testing purposes.

Dealing with big brother

One of the recurring themes in the railway preservation story has been difficulties in dealing with British Railways and its successors. For the early preservationists there was the problem of convincing the authorities that they were serious. With an established heritage railway industry emerging by the 1980s, that battle had by and large been won, although most new schemes still had to go through lengthy negotiations to secure their railway. Emphasis shifted now towards working with the network railway on such matters as marketing, through tickets and shared facilities, in particular a connection with the main line.

Attitudes had changed from distrust or hostility to being broadly sympathetic towards the operators of heritage railways. That did not mean that relationships became straightforward. There were the changes in ownership as the network passed from British Rail to Railtrack and then to Network Rail. Each change introduced new policy priorities, with different emphases from region to region. It still needed dogged determination, patience in negotiation and often a lot of money for heritage railways to secure their network connection, as the few examples in this and the following sections demonstrate.

Following privatisation in the mid-1990s, there was much talk of expansion and revival. Railtrack's Network Management Statement in the mid-1990s included proposals that would subsume some preservation projects in an expanding national network. The rebuilding to mainline standard of the Great Central Railway, the Gloucestershire Warwickshire Railway and the Matlock–Buxton line to create new through routes and diversionary lines were among these ideas.

The demise of Railtrack put these on hold, but Derbyshire County Council, owner of the land, pursued the Buxton project further by commissioning a feasibility study. The consultants, Scott Wilson Railways, concluded in 2004 that there was no realistic prospect of rebuilding this line to mainline standard. The costs, estimated at £100m, would be too great. Their report, however, left the door open for Peak Rail to revive their plans to rebuild towards Buxton, though the costs and other hurdles have prevented this so far. As it was, it proved a long and costly business to restore Peak Rail's link into Matlock station. The link was broken in 2007 when the building of a supermarket forced the heritage line to stop short at a new Matlock Riverside station. It was not until 2010 that an agreement was reached with Network Rail for a new line into the main station, which was opened on 1 July 2011.[425]

Maintaining a network connection

Preserved railways have wanted to maintain or restore connections for two main reasons. One is that the main line is a source of traffic, and for those wanting to run local amenity services, taking their passengers to a junction with the main line is a further consideration. Most passengers come to the heritage railway by car or coach party, and being without a connection with the main network is not necessarily a handicap. But the minority who arrive by rail are not to be sniffed at. The narrow-gauge Talyllyn Railway, whose station is a walk from the Cambrian Coast line station at Tywyn, received as much as twelve per cent of its traffic by rail at the end of British Rail operation, although the successor companies have not quite matched that. In 1970 the introduction of a Sunday service on the Cambrian Coast line had a marked impact on Talyllyn passenger numbers.[426] Closer connection, preferably cross-platform, clearly offers greater potential. The second reason for the standard-gauge lines to want a mainline connection is to allow movement of trains into and out of their railway. The ability to bring railtours on to the line and to move locomotives and coaches in and out by rail makes a big difference to revenue and costs for special events. The Bo'ness and Kinneil Railway is one that finds the connection invaluable for the transfer of the SRPS stock for mainline duty, although this railway, like several others, does not have a passenger interchange.

The operation of railtours to and from preserved railways developed during the late 1970s. The first train to work on to the Keighley & Worth Valley was on 8 October 1977. The Severn Valley, meanwhile, had sent its set of restored Great Western coaches out to the main line a few times that year. The Severn Valley Railway had been fortunate in reconnecting to the main

Type 3 diesel No.6700 returns home to the National Railway Museum using the connection from the North Yorkshire Moors railway to the main line at Grosmont.

line at Kidderminster with little difficulty, but some preserved railways have faced greater problems.[427]

Fluctuations in policy on the main line was one. Pressure on Network Rail to cut its costs in 2004 led to an announcement that it was to 'place on hold' all connections with independent railways. One of the casualties was the connection planned at Lydney Junction with the Dean Forest Railway. Protests from Gloucestershire County Council and Forest of Dean District Council forced Network Rail to reinstate that project.[428]

Network Rail did exempt the Swanage Railway, with which progress was already being made towards restoring the connection. This railway had faced major obstacles in restoring a connection to the main network. The original intention of the preservation society in the 1970s was to run regular community services to Wareham, and by and large the local authorities supported the idea. The slow pace at which preservation groups raised the finance meant that the railway had to settle for opening in stages from Swanage. The dream of running to Wareham never went away, but there remained the matter of restoring a link to the main line, and running powers for about three miles along the line to Wareham. Local authorities and the mainline operators remained supportive. A new Purbeck Rail Partnership (later Purbeck Community Rail Partnership) was formed in 1997, comprising all the local authorities, South West Trains, Network Rail and BP (later Perenco Oil UK), operator of Wych Farm oilfield. Before that, British Rail had donated track for extending the line, and held out the prospect of reconnecting the line at Worgret Junction. Development continued to be slow, and negotiations with BR and its successors had their ups and downs. Agreement was reached with Network Rail in August 2005, but it was not until 2008 that the link was put in place.[429]

This allowed a limited number of special trains to run on to the branch, the first of which ran from London in April 2009. A full connection for regular use still had to be established, and gaining access to Wareham was still far from settled. Indeed, the whole project was threatened when Network Rail in 2010 demanded £3m from the Swanage Railway as a contribution to major resignalling work at Worgret Junction. There was a limited time for this payment to be made, even though the work was not scheduled for 2012. The community rail partnership helped overcome this crisis for the railway: the local authorities agreed to back the scheme with financial guarantees. In the second half of 2012 the permanent connection to the branch was restored at Wareham, preparing the way for services to begin once the section of the branch between the junction and Motala had been upgraded.[430]

Network Rail's moratorium was gradually eased, so that, when the Bluebell Railway pressed forward with its extension, the national company offered free installation of a connection at East Grinstead. This did not include access to the station, however, and the Bluebell would have to build its own.[431]

The West Somerset Railway had its network connection upgraded when signalling was improved on the main line. The link, which had been limited to six trains a year, could now be used at any time. This revived talk of reintroducing a regular train service between Minehead and Taunton, which had been put on the back burner in the 1990s because of the high costs of building and maintaining a link.[432]

The Nene Valley Railway lost its connection at Peterborough East when resignalling was completed on the east coast main line. Fortunately it created a new route through the branch serving the British Sugar factory at Wansford that reached the main line at Fletton Junction, and in 2013 the railway completed the purchase of the freehold of this 1½-mile branch.[433]

One striking example of the difficulties of dealing with the operators of the modern rail network has been the link between the North Norfolk Railway and Network Rail at Sheringham. In common with most preserved railways, the North Norfolk had to run its station separately from the network line from Cromer, although the heritage line had the benefit of the original station, and Network Rail had an insubstantial bus shelter and platform. By the 1990s the revival of rail transport was encouraging thoughts of connecting the two lines. Everybody seemed to agree it was a good idea: the operators of the Cromer line, Network Rail, the Bittern Line Partnership and, of course, the North Norfolk, which wanted to see the development of joint running with trains from the heritage line running over the Network Rail line to Cromer. The two lines were separated by less than 100 yards, so the reinstatement of a few panels of track should, on the surface, have been simple. That was to reckon without the planning issues involved with reinstating a level crossing over Station Road, the railway taking land that had been developed as a public amenity, and Network Rail's safety regulations and engineering to connect this short stretch of railway to its signalling centre. In consequence, the costs threatened to price the project beyond reach, especially since the assumption was that the North Norfolk would bear all the financial burden. A report from the consulting engineers Ove Arup in 2004 quoted a sum of £4.8m; another from RMS Consultancy put the cost at a less pricey £1m.[434] Stalemate lasted for some years until Julian Birley, one of the North Norfolk Railway directors, broke it with the proposal that a tramway crossing could be put in. It would be for occasional use only, no more than twelve times a year, and it would cost only about £140,000.

This satisfied all parties, for the time being at least. The crossing was put in during autumn 2010 ready for a test run on 7 March

with a diesel locomotive, No.37194. The public inauguration was on 11 March, a gala occasion, when a special train hauled by 'Britannia' locomotive No.70013 *Oliver Cromwell* ran on to the North Norfolk from Network Rail's tracks.[435]

Chiltern Railways have shown interest in running trains on to the Chinnor & Princes Risborough Railway, but that backing has not been enough for a permanent connection with the network to be installed. Agreements were made about access to Princes Risborough station, but the annual maintenance charges to be levied by Network Rail were beyond the heritage railway's finances. A special connection was laid on to allow a special train to run on to the line on 3 July 2010, and then in September 2013 a permanent connection was put in, partly funded by local

The locomotive running round the train a few hundred yards from Princes Risborough station, the point at which the heritage railway has had to turn round.

businesses, allowing trains to run into a new platform 4 at Princes Risborough on 5 October. For the Embsay & Bolton Abbey Railway, the figure of £2.6m for installing twenty yards of track linking the Grassington branch with the line to Skipton has been a deterrent.[436]

Despite the problems, the number of heritage railways with connections to the network has increased as Network Rail and train operating companies have appreciated the benefits this can bring. In April 2011 the Ecclesbourne Valley Railway opened to Duffield to connect with the line from Derby to Matlock. The Spa Valley Railway in Kent brought its extension to Eridge into use in March 2011. This involved the Spa Valley line running for a mile alongside the Network Rail tracks to reach the station: an arrangement that no other heritage railway has so far achieved, although it took more than ten years of negotiations.[437]

Steaming On

Totnes

CONCLUSION

Heritage railways of the twenty-first century are a far cry from the beginnings of preservation on the Talyllyn when the small band of volunteers wondered if they were going to survive. Everything seems to be on a larger scale. When the fledgling Talyllyn preservation society, in desperate need of motive power, sought to buy the two Corris locomotives from British Railways, a sum of less than £50 was involved.[438] Now hundreds of thousands of pounds are regularly spent on the overhaul of large locomotives. In the first year of the North Norfolk Railway's operation, turnover was £113 and one train ran. By 2004 turnover was more than £1m. Even allowing for inflation, the change in scale is daunting.

Despite the large sums of money quoted for railway preservation projects, there is much about them that has not changed. Most projects start with a small group, who need patience to endure the years that it takes before their railway reaches the stage of running trains over its first half mile of track. There may be large grants available, but the small-scale fundraising – raffles, collecting bucket, sponsored walks and sales stands – remain at the heart of each preservation society's activities, large or small, old or recently established. The basic model of aiming at least to break even on day-to-day operation, with appeals and grants funding capital projects, remains now as it did fifty or sixty years ago. And volunteers are still the lifeblood of most heritage railways.

Expansion or overexpansion?

Throughout the history of railway preservation there have been those who have said that preservationists were overstretching themselves, that there was not enough room for another preserved railway and that the voluntary effort would be spread too thinly. Instead, the argument ran, projects should be consolidated. As soon as there was the prospect of more than one preserved railway these arguments were aired. As the Ffestiniog

Railway's supporters were negotiating agreement to take over this railway, some argued that the existence of the Talyllyn Railway a few miles away would very likely preclude success at Portmadoc. The official Railway Inspector expressed similar doubts.[439] When William Morris first sought support for the preservation of the Welshpool & Llanfair Railway he felt obliged to write, 'Although two other narrow-gauge railways have been taken over by enthusiasts, I feel there is still scope for a further undertaking of this nature.'[440]

Correspondence appeared in the railway press deploring the proliferation of preservation schemes. One of the earliest, from Mr H.G. Radcliffe in 1959, encapsulates many of the themes: 'One reads with amazement,' he wrote, 'almost every month, of the formation of yet another society to preserve yet another railway … one reaches the inescapable conclusion that the whole thing is in danger of being overdone.' Enthusiasts needed to be

Sixty years of change on the preserved railways demonstrated by the Talyllyn's Wharf station. The general layout is little changed, but the new building completed in 2005 dominates the scene. It is not to the taste of the purist, but the railway has gained excellent catering facilities and toilets, and a fine home for the Narrow Gauge Railway Museum – all things needed by the modern heritage railway. Would Tom Rolt have approved? The new locomotive named after him waits with a train.

'realistic of the situation' and recognise that branch lines that were never a paying proposition would be unlikely to succeed in volunteer hands. The next few years saw a steady flow of correspondence and articles expressing these worries about the overextension of the preservation movement.[441]

To counteract 'proliferation' the British Transport Commission should establish an official museum railway, it was argued. Co-ordination and co-operation to avoid overextension in the preservation movement was one of the main concerns of the ARPS in its early years. One of its officers wrote in 1969, 'Whilst not wishing to put a damper on the genuine enthusiasm of the new preservationists, I feel one must point out we are just about at saturation point. If more schemes are conceived, resources are going to be stretched to breaking point.'[442]

The heritage railway business expanded to the strain of continuing criticism. The launch of the Peak Railway project was 'sheer folly', wrote one in 1979. Those rebuilding the railway from Honeybourne to Cheltenham Racecourse were told in 1979 that this was 'pie in the sky'. Even some of the preservation movement's leaders suffered occasional bouts of anxiety. Michael Draper, general manager of the Severn Valley Railway, said in 1981 that the ever-growing steam movement was 'sowing the seeds of its own destruction'. David Madden, general secretary of the Association of Railway Preservation Societies, revived the argument that preserved railways were expanding too quickly for the market. Citing traffic peaks on such lines as the Talyllyn, he claimed that business was unlikely to grow to match the costs. The expansion of existing schemes was not exempt from this criticism. When the Bluebell talked seriously of extending northwards to regain a mainline connection in 1976, doubts were raised in public about whether the high cost could be justified.[443] The same arguments raged, if anything more furiously, over the preservation of locomotives. Individuals and groups were condemned for saving 'yet another rusting hulk'. There were some enthusiasts who clearly regretted that the scrap merchant, Dai Woodham at Barry Island, had not disposed of his store of locomotives quickly before preservationists rescued them. C. Tankard of the King Preservation Society defended the rescues in 1975 when they were in full flow, arguing that in years to come preserved railways would be glad of them. They were.[444]

In the twenty-first century, economic pressures, shortages of motive power and well-publicised difficulties at some railways have all helped keep the doubts alive. Robin Jones, editor of *Heritage Railway*, is of the view that 'by and large, no more major standard gauge heritage lines will emerge', and *Railways Illustrated* in May 2010 asked, 'Do we need more heritage railways?' Saturation point had been reached, the magazine argued, with pressure on storage for locomotives, insufficient cash and too few volunteers.[445]

The doubters have generally been ignored, as enthusiasts push on with each new scheme, for the railway preservation movement has always been an outpouring of free enterprise. Market forces have been the most effective determinants of what has been preserved because most of the money raised has come from private pockets. The projects that failed did so not because some central co-ordinator thought it was a preservation too far, but because the sponsoring group could not raise the money or get planning permission. Whatever the doubters might have said, any new preserved railway that reaches the stage of reopening has almost universally been welcomed into the fold, as the Helston Railway in Cornwall was, winner of a heritage award in 2011. For everyone wants to see a railway succeed and grow.

Changing the lamps.

The result of this riotously free-market approach has been an immense variety of activities, as railways have developed their individual characters free from corporate bulldozing. Appeals for co-operation and co-ordination of effort have often been ignored, for at every turn there have always been individuals whose enthusiasm and belief in a project have overridden any concerns for moderation and consolidation. This has resulted in a certain amount of fluidity, some might say fickleness, in the volunteer side of railway preservation. Many a new project has been started by a breakaway group from an existing line, those tired of the humdrum of keeping a railway operating and looking for the next big challenge. Some left the Talyllyn to get the Ffestiniog started. A group from the Dart Valley at Buckfastleigh set off in the early 1980s to found the Plym Valley Railway, which was planned to reopen the line from Marsh Mills, Plymouth, to Yelverton. When the high hopes of creating a major line had to be scaled back to a more affordable but very short line, a lot of the initial supporters left for the next project, taking their big engines. And so it has continued, as the pioneering spirits look for the next project.[446]

The heritage railway movement is populated by a mass of different businesses, preservation societies, charities, individual owners of locomotives and equipment, and organisations providing restoration and engineering services. They do not always get along. There have been some big egos among those who plough large sums into locomotive and railway preservation, and sometimes they clash. There have been many disputes between, for example, a hosting railway and a locomotive owner, causing the owner to go off in a huff, and perhaps the locomotive, after Henry the Green Engine, to sulk in the back of the shed. Another of the natural features of this free market is that not all will succeed. One project raises millions of pounds while another languishes or collapses altogether. Mostly, the successful project has been more focused in its objectives, determined in developing its business plan and effective in its methods of marketing and fundraising.[447] But, through it all, this mass of activity has been essentially dynamic in its effects.

Describing the heritage railway movement as a bastion of free enterprise would have pleased Tom Rolt. One of the attractions for him in the preservation of the Talyllyn Railway was that here was an expression of freedom from the heavy hand of the state at work in the newly nationalised British Railways. Nationalisation, he wrote, 'is administering the coup de grace to a conception of loyalty and service, to a sense of vocation …'. The 'planned state' had left few opportunities for individual enterprise, he thought.[448] Some of his associates, Pat Whitehouse among them, had similar views about the nationalised railway. Not that everybody involved was a market capitalist by inclination. Far from it. Most preservationists probably did not

approach the matter with much of a philosophy of economics or politics. Of those who did, there were as many of a more Fabian socialist mind who saw themselves as upholding some sort of worker control in the spirit of the co-operative movement, or who were maintaining local tradition and involvement against monolithic national bodies. The formation and management of companies were side issues.[449] This was the motivation that brought people such as Bob Cryer, a Labour politician, into railway preservation.

There are some who would like the state to play a greater role in the development of heritage railways. The All Party Parliamentary Committee on Heritage Rail thought the industry's contribution to the economy justified such action,

2-6-0 No.42968, a stalwart of Severn Valley Railway operations, runs round its train at Bridgnorth. 14 August 2009.

whereas others argue that state involvement to push ahead with developments such as extending the North Yorkshire Moors Railway to Malton would be in the national interest.[450] However, the state is unlikely to take more than a nominal interest in heritage railways for the foreseeable future.

Steaming into the future?

Looking back, Tom Rolt wrote of the Talyllyn Railway he encountered in the 1940s: 'Seen in its setting of mountains, this lost railway had a certain magical quality about it, which makes me wonder sometimes whether we did right to disturb it.' James Boyd had similar qualms.[451] The tension between preservation and development, to which reference has been made at times in this book, remains in the twenty-first century just as much as it was when Rolt and his colleagues took possession of their railway. The ramshackle quaintness could not survive. Despite all the attempts to create a 'branch line atmosphere', no heritage railway carrying thousands of tourists could operate in aspic.

Heritage railways have been transformed out of all recognition from their beginnings by the need for development. Paradoxically, their dynamism has resulted from a combination of looking forward to preserve the past. As the heritage railway movement evolves into a mature industry, it continues to fascinate and intrigue with questions about the direction of its future. Can the heritage railway movement continue to expand? There are barriers to this, one being physical. Railway lines closed by British Railways in the 1960s or 1970s have not been left, *Sleeping Beauty*-like, waiting for the preservationist to wake them. Land has been sold, and houses, factories, roads and cycle tracks have appeared on various parts of it, each use with vested interests ready to protect its current status. They view a railway scheme to be as much of a threat as any other development. The experience of those wanting to revive the Southwold Railway has shown how strong many of these interests are. The prospect of the Llangollen Railway's expanding eastwards towards Ruabon is limited by development on the course of the old railway, and a road blocks the North Norfolk's way from its present terminus at Holt to the town and beyond. The cycling charity Sustrans has become a serious competitor for disused railway lines, and has not always been well-disposed to railway revival schemes.

Nothing deters the committed. They dig out the rubbish tip for the Bluebell's extension. They work out ways of crossing the road towards Holt, with the local authority in 2012 declaring its preparedness to sell land to help that, a step towards the creation of the Norfolk Orbital Railway. Despite the obstacles, ambitions within the heritage railway movement seem to be boundless, with prospects apparently good for larger railways offering longer journeys. If projects such as the Don Valley get going, heritage railways might be running into city centres. The railways do not conform to the simple business pattern: they are part business, part consumption. As an industry, heritage railways remain small, their few hundred miles a tiny proportion of the national railway mileage. Yet they have made an impact and achieved recognition beyond their scale, encouraging prospects for further development. As long as there are individual enthusiasts wanting to spend their money on restoring a railway or a locomotive, this free spirit is likely to remain. For there are still dynamic individuals spotting the opportunities, seeking the railways waiting to be revived and persevering against the obstacles. For all of them, the example of the pioneers, without whose determination there would be far fewer locomotives, far fewer carriages and far fewer railways to run them on, remains an inspiration.

NOTES

[1] Figures from the Heritage Railway Association website, www.heritagerailways.com/visits_about.php.

[2] All Party Parliamentary Group on Heritage Rail, *Report on the Value of Heritage Railways* (July 2013) pp. 15-17.

[3] Tom Rolt, *Railway Adventure* (1971 edition) p. 43. *Talyllyn News*, No.206, June 2005, p. 40, letter from Mr O. Phillips.

[4] *Railway Magazine*, May 1972, pp. 266-7.

[5] Peter Johnson, *Immortal Rails vol. 1: the story of the closure and revival of the Ffestiniog Railway 1939-1983* (2004) p. 141.

[6] *Steam Railway*, No.299, July-August 2004, p. 40.

[7] O.H. Prosser, 'A New Deal for the Independent Railways', *Trains Annual 1967* (1966) pp. 89-96.

[8] *Railway Magazine*, December 1972, p. 653.

[9] *Heritage Railway*, No.63, July 2004, p. 6.

[10] See, for example, Dennis Dunstone, *For the Love of Trains* (2007) pp. 157-8.

[11] For Rolt's experiences in these activities see the first two volumes of his autobiography, *Landscape with Machines* (1971) and *Landscape with Canals* (1977).

[12] *Heritage Railway*, No.135 (March-April 2010) pp. 76, 77.

[13] Tom Rolt, *Landscape with Figures* (1992) pp. 7, 11.

[14] Alan Holmes, *Talyllyn Revived: the story of the world's first railway preservation society* (2009) pp. 16-19.

[15] A brass plaque was put up inside the hotel in 1985 and is now in the collections of the Narrow Gauge Railway Museum.

[16] *Talyllyn News*, No.205 (March 2005) p. 40.

[17] Tom Rolt, *Railway Adventure* (1971 edition) pp. 41ff, 100. *Talyllyn News*, No.241, March 2014, pp. 41-2.

[18] Tom Rolt, *Landscape with Figures* (1992) pp. 8-10.

[19] Tom Rolt, *Railway Adventure* (1971 edition), pp. 47-54, 59-60, 122-5. Alan Holmes, *Talyllyn Revived: the story of the world's first railway preservation society* (2009) p. 11.

[20] *Ibid*. pp. 61, 93, 120, 144-8.

[21] *Ibid*. pp. 118, 148.

[22] John L.H. Bate, *The Chronicles of Pendre Siding* (2001) chapters 1-2; military exercises, pp. 36ff.

23 Bate, *Chronicles*, pp. 9, 27. Michael Whitehouse, ed., *Preservation Pioneers* (2014) pp. 30-5. Michael Whitehouse, *Talyllyn Pioneers* (2016) pp. 49-50, 107.

24 John L.H. Bate, *The Chronicles of Pendre Siding* (2001) pp. 38-9, and chapter 2 passim. Alan Holmes, *Talyllyn Revived: the story of the world's first railway preservation society* (2009) pp. 46-51, 247.

25 *Railway Magazine*, December 1957, pp. 885-6.

26 Although it went to Blaenau Ffestiniog, the railway was incorporated as the Festiniog Railway Company, and that remains the legal form of the business. It was generally known as the Festiniog when the railway was preserved. References to this early period have retained the spelling of the time. Since then Ffestiniog has become the usual form for marketing the railway.

27 Allan Garraway, *Garraway Father and Son* (1985) pp. 110-11.

28 John L.H. Bate, *The Chronicles of Pendre Siding* (2001) pp. 8, 51.

29 R.C. Riley, 'Private Railway Preservation in Britain', *Trains 'Sixty-nine* (1968) p. 14

30 Peter Johnson, *Immortal Rails vol. 1* (2004) pp. 23, 25, 31, 33, 39-40.

31 Peter Johnson, *Immortal Rails vol. 1* (2004) pp. 41-62, 70, 76. Ian Carter, *British Railway Enthusiasm* (2008) pp. 151-2.

32 Peter Johnson, *Immortal Rails vol. 1* (2004) pp. 61, 63-77, 112. *Daily Telegraph*, 17 January 2015.

33 *Railway Magazine*, November 1956, p. 784, December 1957, p. 886.

34 Peter Johnson, *Immortal Rails vol. 1* (2004) pp. 79-82, 94, 107, 176, 214-16.

35 Ralph Cartwright, *The Welshpool and Llanfair* (2002) pp. 62, 65.

36 *Railway Magazine*, May 1956, p. 280, September 1956, p. 633, December 1956, pp. 796, 862, August 1959, p. 579, January 1961, p. 60, April 1973, pp. 168-70.

37 www.bluebell-railway.co.uk. *Railway Magazine*, April 1962, p. 226. *Steam Railway*, 305, December 2004 – January 2005, p. 45. Charles Loft, *Last Trains* (2014) pp. 99, 106-7, 115, 119-20.

38 *Railway Magazine*, March 1959, p. 212, August 1959, p. 578.

39 R.C. Riley, 'The Bluebell Line' *Railway Magazine*, April 1962, pp. 226-9. *Railway Magazine*, August 2010, pp. 19-21.

40 *Railway Magazine*, August 1959, p. 578. www.bluebell-railway.co.uk. Michael Whitehouse, ed., *Preservation Pioneers* (2014) p. 42.

41 R.C. Riley, 'Private Railway Preservation in Britain', *Trains 'Sixty-nine* (1968) pp. 19-21. *Railway Magazine*, January 1961, p. 66, April 1962, p. 229, December 1968, p. 735.

42 *Railway Magazine*, February 1962, p. 139, October 1963, p. 738, February 1966, p. 116.

43 Susan M. Youell, 'Third Century at Middleton', *Railway Magazine*, April 1961, pp. 223-9, 281. *Railway Magazine*, May 1962, p. 360, February 1964, p. 261,

August 1969, p. 489. R.C. Riley, 'Private Railway Preservation in Britain', *Trains 'Sixty-nine* (1968) p. 17.

[44] *Railway Magazine*, March 1967, pp. 170-1, July 2010, p. 21.

[45] *Railway Magazine*, April 1974, p. 167.

[46] *Railway Magazine*, May 1975, p. 249, comment by David Morgan.

[47] *Railway Magazine*, March 1962, p. 211, December 1962, p. 874, March 1963, p. 213.

[48] *Railway Magazine*, December 1965, p. 730, February 1966, pp. 115-16, March 1967, p. 169. Alan Bell, *Branch Line to Hayling* (1984) illus. 119.

[49] *Railway Magazine*, June 1968, pp. 325-7, January 1970, p. 44, February 1970, p. 107, June 1970, p. 301, July 1970, p. 401, September 1970, p. 526, November 1970, p. 637, January 1971, p. 46, May 1971, p. 278, August 1971, p. 450.

[50] *Railway Magazine*, November 1965, pp. 667-8.

[51] *Railway Magazine*, November 1965, p. 668, April 1966, p. 235, October 1966, p. 600. *Heritage Railway*, No.136, April-May 2010, pp. 64-5.

[52] Michael Harris, *Keighley & Worth Valley Railway* (1998) p. 28.

[53] *Railway Magazine*, January 1973, p. 47.

[54] Charles Lofts, *Last Trains* (2013) p. 168.

[55] *Railway Magazine*, April 1959, p. 281, June 1959, p. 431. *Heritage Railway*, No.90 (October 2006) pp. 80-85.

[56] O.H. Prosser, 'A New Deal for the Independent Railways', *Trains Annual 1967* (1966) pp. 93-4. The Chasewater branch was later successfully revived.

[57] *Railway Magazine*, November 1965, p. 663. Charles Lofts, *Last Trains* (2013) pp. 171-2.

[58] Lord Lindgren, *Hansard*, House of Lords, 18 March 1965, O.H. Prosser, 'A New Deal for the Independent Railways', *Trains Annual 1967* (1966) p. 95.

[59] *Railway Magazine*, January 1969, p. 3.

[60] Tom Rolt, *Landscape with Figures* (1992) p. 43.

[61] *Railway Magazine*, July 1971, p. 394, October 1972, p. 547, November 1972, p. 601, December 1972, pp. 659-60, June 1974, p. 307, November 1974, p. 567, July 2010, pp. 20-1.

[62] *Railway Magazine*, August 1968, p. 497, November 1969, pp. 652-3.

[63] *Railway Magazine*, November 1970, p. 593.

[64] *Railway Magazine*, May 1970, p. 282, June 1970, p. 349, December 1970, p. 693, March 1971, p. 168.

[65] W.J.K. Davies, *Ravenglass & Eskdale Railway* (2000 edition) pp. 112, 130. John L.H. Bate, *The Chronicles of Pendre Siding* (2001) pp. 149, 152. Peter Johnson, *Immortal Rails: the story of the closure and revival of the Ffestiniog Railway 1939-1983 vol. 2, 1964-1983* (2005) pp. 59-60. *Railway Magazine*, August 1977, p. 406.

[66] *Railway Magazine*, June 1973, p. 267.

[67] John L.H. Bate, *The Chronicles of Pendre Siding* (2001) pp. 176-86, 199. Peter Johnson, *Immortal Rails: the story of the closure and revival of the Ffestiniog Railway 1939-1983 vol. 2, 1964-1983* (2005) pp. 61-2. *Railway Magazine*, June 1976, p. 287. *Heritage Railway*, No.59, March 2004, p. 69. John Parsons, *Saving the West Somerset Railway: the branch line that refused to die* (2011) pp. 52ff.

[68] Peter Johnson, *Immortal Rails: the story of the closure and revival of the Ffestiniog Railway 1939-1983 vol. 2, 1964-1983* (2005) pp. 70, 91, 98.

[69] Peter Johnson, *Immortal Rails: the story of the closure and revival of the Ffestiniog Railway 1939-1983 vol. 2, 1964-1983* (2005) pp. 87, 90, 98.

[70] *Railway Magazine*, May 1972, p. 272, September 1977, pp. 420-3.

[71] *Heritage Railway*, No.98 (June 2007) pp. 86-91, *Railway Magazine*, July 2007, pp. 22-3.

[72] *Railway Magazine*, December 1972, p. 660, January 1974, pp. 43-4, October 1974, p 485, June 1975, p. 271, May 1976, pp. 265-6, August 1977, p.407, July 1979, p. 356.

[73] N. Pallant, *Holding the Line: preserving the Kent & East Sussex Railway* (1993) pp. 47, 91.

[74] *Railway Magazine*, August 1972, p. 439.

[75] *Railway Magazine*, February 1967, p. 111, April 1974, p. 164, November 1976, p. 594.

[76] N. Pallant, *Holding the Line* (1993) pp. 2-3.

[77] *Railway Magazine*, April 1961, p. 286, August 1961, pp. 582-3, September 1961, p. 661. N. Pallant, *Holding the Line* (1993) pp. 4-5, 7.

[78] *Railway Magazine*, February 1966, pp. 116-17. N. Pallant, *Holding the Line* (1993) pp. 72-4, 82.

[79] *Railway Magazine*, November 1964, p. 857, December 1964, p. 917, April 1966, pp. 233-4. N. Pallant, *Holding the Line* (1993) pp. 36-44, 72, 80.

[80] *Railway Magazine*, October 1963, p. 739.

[81] *Railway Magazine*, September 1961, p. 661, January 1968, pp. 50-1. N. Pallant, *Holding the Line* (1993) p.113.

[82] *Railway Magazine*, April 1968, p. 241.

[83] *Railway Magazine*, July 1968, pp. 431-2.

[84] *Railway Magazine*, June 1974, pp. 306-7, June 1975, p. 285.

[85] *Railway Magazine*, January 1976, pp. 10-12, April 1977, p. 178. *Heritage Railway*, No.63, July 2004, pp. 82-7.

[86] *Railway Magazine*, February 1959, p. 140, July 1959, p. 505, August 1961, p.583.

[87] *Railway Magazine*, September 1962, p. 588.

[88] *Railway Magazine*, March 1971, p. 161.

[89] *Railway Magazine*, April 1965, p.232. Dennis Dunstone, *For the Love of Trains* (2007) p. 95.

[90] Bob Gwynne, *Railway Preservation in Britain* (2011)*Railway Magazine*, March 1971, p. 161.

[91] *Railway Magazine*, February 1967, pp. 104-5. *Heritage Railway*, No.109, p. 41.

[92] *Railway Magazine*, July 1969, pp. 406-7.

[93] *Railway Magazine*, February 1971, pp. 61, 63, June 1979, p. 301.

[94] H.I. Quayle and S.C. Jenkins, *Lakeside and Haverthwaite Railway* (1977) pp. 29-42. *Railway Magazine*, November 1967, p. 664, April 1968, p. 241, July 1968, pp. 424-5, October 1968, pp. 622-3, May 1970, p. 287, November 1970, p. 637.

[95] Michael Harris, *Keighley & Worth Valley Railway* (1998) pp. 25-34. *Railway Magazine*, June 1962, p. 434, November 1964, p. 859.

[96] *Railway Magazine*, November 1969, p. 646. Michael Whitehouse, ed., *Preservation Pioneers* (2014) p. 41.

[97] N. Pallant, *Holding the Line: preserving the Kent & East Sussex Railway* (1993) pp. 60, 90.

[98] *Railway Magazine*, February 1973, pp. 99-100, May 1973, p. 253, August 1973, p. 381, July 1974, p. 365, December 1977, p. 613. *Heritage Railway*, No.97, May 2007, pp. 40-5.

[99] *Railway Magazine*, June 1966, p. 361, November 1967, p. 665, January 1968, p. 52, January 1969, pp. 48-9, August 1969, p. 475, January 1970, p. 52, May 1971, p. 276, May 1973, p. 215, March 1976, p. 158. Robin Jones, *Beating Beeching: Britain's railways fight back from the axe* (2013) p. 67.

[100] *Railway Magazine*, January 1974, pp. 12-13, February 1974, p. 99, March 1974, p. 149, June 1974, p. 271-3, June 1976, pp. 286-7, October 1976, p. 541, November 1976, p. 595, December 1976, p. 607, January 1977, p. 40, January 1978, p. 309, November 1978, p. 563, September 1979, p. 457.

[101] *Railway Magazine*, March 1966, p. 176, November 1966, p. 664, March 1969, p. 228, December 1970, pp. 657-9, July 1971, p. 394, September 2005, p. 16. Dennis Dunstone, *For the Love of Trains* (2007) pp. 90-1.

[102] *Railway Magazine*, June 1969, p. 344.

[103] *Railway Magazine*, August 1972, p. 440, May 1973, p. 253, March 1974, pp. 132-3, June 1977, p. 269.

[104] *Railway Magazine*, October 1977, pp. 509-10. *Heritage Railway*, No.65, September 2004, pp. 78-9, No.100, July 2007, pp. 34-9.

[105] *Railway Magazine*, October 1976, p. 500. Dennis Dunstone, *For the Love of Trains* (2007) pp. 38-40.

[106] *Railway Magazine*, December 1970, p. 693, July 1972, pp. 384-5, April 1974, p. 162, August 1977, p. 405, December 1977, p. 614. *Heritage Railway*, No.98, June 2007, pp. 86-91.

[107] *Railway Magazine*, January 1974, p. 43, May 1975, p. 213.

[108] *Railway Magazine*, June 1976, p. 317.

[109] R.C. Riley, 'Private Railway Preservation in Britain', *Trains 'Sixty-nine* (1968) pp. 21-2. *Railway Magazine*, December 1959, p. 880, November 1960, p. 816. Dennis Dunstone, *For the Love of Trains* (2007) pp. 78-9.

110 *Railway Magazine*, October 1969, p. 590, May 1973, p. 217.

111 *Railway Magazine*, August 1967, p. 475.

112 *Railway Magazine*, June 1968, pp. 370-1, August 1970, p. 467, July 1971, p. 394, July 1972, p. 384. *Heritage Railway*, No.100, June 2007, pp. 66-71.

113 *Railway Magazine*, December 1968, p. 737, September 1970, p. 524. Dennis Dunstone, *For the Love of Trains* (2007) p. 107.

114 *Railway Magazine*, March 1976, pp. 128-32, July 1977, p. 356, September 1988, p. 559. www.llangollen-railway.org.uk.

115 *Railway Magazine*, November 1969, p. 651, May 1970, p. 288, December 1972, pp. 660-1.

116 *Railway Magazine*, August 1978, pp. 410-11.

117 *Railway Magazine*, April 1975, p. 200, July 1976, p. 375, October 1977, p. 508.

118 *Railway Magazine*, October 1968, p. 623, December 1968, p. 735, April 1969, pp. 228-9, July 1970, pp. 410-11, March 1974, p. 150.

119 *Railway Magazine*, December 1975, pp. 620-1, July 1976, pp. 374-5, March 1978, pp. 126-9. Dennis Dunstone, *For the Love of Trains* (2007) pp. 104-5.

120 *Railway Magazine*, May 1972, p. 271, November 1972, p. 601. www.avonvalleyrailway.org.

121 *Railway Magazine*, July 1970, p. 411.

122 *Railway Magazine*, February 1974, pp. 99-100, August 1977, p. 407.

123 *Railway Magazine*, September 1971, p. 509, January 1975, pp. 41-2.

124 *Railway Magazine*, January 1974, pp. 42-3.

125 *Railway Magazine*, May 1979, p. 251.

126 *Railway Magazine*, October 1976, p. 539, June 1978, p. 311.

127 *Railway Magazine*, May 1976, p. 247.

128 *Talyllyn News*, No.205 (March 2005) p. 41. Robin Jones, *Beating Beeching: Britain's railways fight back from the axe* (2013) pp. 29-30.

129 *Railway Magazine*, March 1968, p. 181, June 1968, pp. 369-70, July 1969, pp. 363, 372-4, July 1979, pp. 320-2, March 2005, pp. 45-6. Michael Whitehouse, ed., *Preservation Pioneers* (2014) p. 48.

130 *Railway Magazine*, May 1972, p. 271, November 1972, p. 561, December 1972, pp. 620-4, March 2005, p. 46. *Heritage Railway*, No.142, September-October 2010, p. 72.

131 *Railway Magazine*, March 1969, p. 123.

132 *Railway Magazine*, April 1975, p. 159.

133 *Railway Magazine*, March 1969, p. 123.

134 *Railway Magazine*, November 1972, p. 575.

135 *Railway Magazine*, August 1969, p. 427, December 1970, p. 692, October 1971, pp. 562-3, May 1972, p. 229, June 1972, pp. 300-4, September 1978, p. 459, May 1979, pp. 226-9.

136 *Railway Magazine*, May 1974, p. 252, July 1974, pp. 365-6. *Steam Railway*, No.305, pp. 30-4.

137 *Railway Magazine*, February 1967, pp. 74-5.

138 *Railway Magazine*, October 1971, pp. 563-4, November 1971, pp. 619-20, April 1972, p. 215, April 1973, pp. 177-9, June 1974, pp. 274-5, June 1979, pp. 262-5.

139 *Railway Magazine*, January 2013, p. 10, September 2013, p. 63. *Heritage Railway*, No.179, August 2013, p. 53. John Parsons, *Saving the West Somerset Railway* (2011) pp. 32-3, 47-8.

140 *Railway Magazine*, January 1977, p.92, February 1993, p. 21, July 2011, pp. 32-3.

141 Michael P. Jacobs, 'The Isle of Wight's Fight for its Railways', *Trains Annual 1966* (1965) pp. 62-7.

142 *Railway Magazine*, April 1966, p. 234, May 1966, p. 290.

143 *Railway Magazine*, May 1966, p. 290, November 1966, p. 662, June 1967, p. 352, February 1968, p. 118, December 1969, p. 709. Michael P. Jacobs, 'The Isle of Wight's Fight for its Railways', *Trains Annual 1966* (1965) p. 67.

144 *Railway Magazine*, July 1966, p. 414.

145 *Railway Magazine*, October 1966, p. 596.

146 *Railway Magazine*, March 1967, p. 171.

147 *Railway Magazine*, May 1970, pp. 288-9, November 1970, p. 638.

148 *Railway Magazine*, February 1971, p. 110, August 1972, p. 438, November 1972, pp. 602-3, January 1976, p. 46.

149 *Railway Magazine*, April 1975, pp. 174-5, July 1976, p. 371.

150 *Railway Magazine*, March 1979, pp. 120-3, January 2016, p. 42.

151 *Railway Magazine*, August 1968, p. 498, September 1993, pp. 63-7. Foxfield Railway website, www.foxfieldrailway.co.uk.

152 See, for example, correspondence on the subject in *Railway Magazine*, April 1967, p. 224, May 1967, p. 287.

153 *Railway Magazine*, October 1974, pp. 518-19. *Heritage Railway*, No.138, June 2010, p. 45.

154 For example, *Railway Magazine*, August 1969, p. 468.

155 *Railway Magazine*, June 1968, p. 361, April 1971, p. 222.

156 R.A. Symes-Schutzmann, 'The Waverley Line – a new approach', *Railway Magazine*, May 1969, p. 262. *Railway Magazine*, May 1969, p. 241, August 1969, pp. 427, 468, October 1969, pp. 547, 593, November 1969, p. 646, December 1969, p. 702, April 1970, pp. 229-30, June 1970, p. 349, January 1971, p. 45, January 1972, p. 42.

157 *Railway Magazine*, May 2005, p. 12. *Heritage Railway*, 77, September 2005, p. 18.

158 *Railway Magazine*, December 1968, p. 736, June 1969, pp. 340-1.

159 For example, *Railway Magazine*, July 1966, p.413, August 1966, pp. 474-5, October 1966, p. 596.

160 *Railway Magazine*, February 1971, p. 112.

161 *Railway Magazine*, May 1970, p. 288, February 1972, p. 105, November 1973, September 1974, p. 433, December 1975, p. 609, September 1976, p. 483, May 1977, pp. 249-50, April 2005, pp. 15-16.

162 *Railway Magazine*, December 1957, pp. 885-6, December 1970, p. 693. John L.H. Bate, *The Chronicles of Pendre Siding* (2001) pp. 157-8, 177-85.

163 Peter Johnson, *Immortal Rails: the story of the closure and revival of the Ffestiniog Railway 1939-1983 vol. 2, 1964-1983* (2005) pp. 15-27.

164 *Railway Magazine*, June 1968, pp. 328-30, October 1969, p. 564, September 1978, pp. 423-4.

165 Peter Johnson, *Immortal Rails: the story of the closure and revival of the Ffestiniog Railway 1939-1983, volume 2* (2005) pp. 103-50. *Railway Magazine*, April 1955, p. 288.

166 *Railway Magazine*, September 1977, p. 457, January 1978, pp. 45-6. *Heritage Railway*, No.59, March 2004, pp. 66-9.

167 *Railway Magazine*, November 1961, pp. 797-8, November 1962, p.800, June 1963, pp. 385-9, July 1972, p. 347, November 1973, p. 543, July 1977, pp. 355-6. R.C. Riley, 'Private Railway Preservation in Britain', *Trains 'Sixty-nine* (1968) pp. 22-23.

168 Peter Johnson, *Immortal Rails: the story of the closure and revival of the Ffestiniog Railway 1939-1983, vol. 1* (2004) pp. 169-70.

169 *Railway Magazine*, April 1970, pp. 227-8.

170 *Railway Magazine*, May 1964, pp. 449-51.

171 *Railway Magazine*, February 1970, p. 65, May 1971, p. 277, July 1971, pp. 362-6, 393, September 1971, p. 508, May 1977, p. 214. www.lake-railway.co.uk.

172 *Railway Magazine*, November 1970, p. 593.

173 *Railway Magazine*, March 1974, p. 152, January 1975, p. 44, February 1975, p. 97.

174 *Railway Magazine*, February 1973, p. 99, December 1973, p. 638.

175 *Railway Magazine*, March 1967, p. 166, June 1967, p. 353, August 1967, p. 469, March 1970, p. 170, December 1971, p. 675, July 1973, pp. 368-9.

176 W.J.K. Davies, *Ravenglass & Eskdale Railway* (2000 edition) pp. 77-85. *Railway Magazine*, July 1953, pp. 481-6, September 1960, p. 589, October 1960, p. 738, December 1960, pp. 889-90.

177 *Railway Magazine*, October 1969, pp. 550-3, May 1970, p. 243, September 1970, pp. 525-6, January 1977, p. 40.

178 *Railway Magazine*, May 1968, p. 306, July 1970, pp. 368-70, October 1973, pp. 531-2.

179 *Heritage Railway*, No.124 (June 2009) p. 10.

180 *Railway Magazine*, June 1961, p. 435, June 1964, p. 529, March 1969, p. 125, November 1972, p. 605, October 1977, p. 480, June 1978, pp. 311-12.

181 *Railway Magazine*, July 1973, pp. 368-9, May 1974, p. 257, December 1974, pp. 688-91, February 1975, pp. 57-8, October 1976, p. 540.

182 *Railway Magazine*, March 1969, p. 125, April 1970, p. 229, February 1974, p. 99. Dennis Dunstone, *For the Love of Trains* (2007) p. 116.

183 *Heritage Railway*, No.140, August 2010, pp. 72-3.

184 *Railway Magazine*, December 1974, p. 615, February 1977, p. 93.

185 *Railway Magazine*, July 1966, p. 411, December 1966, p. 721, December 1975, pp. 599-600; November 1976, p. 593, December 1976, pp. 644-5. Dennis Dunstone, *For the Love of Trains* (2007) p. 75.

186 *Steam Railway*, No.300, August 2004, pp. 34-5.

187 *Railway Magazine*, September 2005, p. 54.

188 *Heritage Railway*, No.109, p. 35.

189 John Parsons, *Saving the West Somerset Railway: the branch line that refused to die* (2011) p. 154.

190 *Railway Magazine*, July 2005, p. 68, November 2006, p. 53, September 2009, p. 59. *Heritage Railway*, No.73, May 2005, p. 14.

191 *Railway Magazine*, April 2007, pp. 30-4.

192 Dennis Dunstone, *For the Love of Trains* (2007) p. 151.

193 *Railway Magazine*, October 1979, p. 507.

194 *Railway Magazine*, December 1972, p. 617.

195 *Railway Magazine*, April 1994, p. 22.

196 *Railway Magazine*, November 1961, pp. 811-12, August 1962, p. 574, November 1979, p. 559. *Heritage Railway*, No.65, September 2004, pp. 22-3, No.104, November 2007, pp. 10-11. www.lynton-rail.co.uk.

197 *Railway Magazine*, December 1970, p. 688. *Heritage Railway*, No.63, July 2004, p. 5. *Steam Railway*, No.300, August-September 2004, p. 32.

198 *Railway Magazine*, December 2005, pp. 40-4. www.chinnorrailway.co.uk.

199 *Heritage Railway*, No.70, February 2005, pp. 66-70. *Railway Magazine*, October 2006, pp. 20-21.

200 *Railway Magazine*, September 1988, p. 559.

201 *Railway Magazine*, February 2008, pp. 16-21.

202 *Railway Magazine*, November 1974, p. 568.

203 *Railway Magazine*, February 1994, p. 70, December 1994, p. 51.

204 *Heritage Railway*, No.143, October-November 2010, p. 78.

205 *Heritage Railway*, No.90, October 2006, p. 34. *Steam Railway*, No.411, February 2013, pp. 94-7.

206 *Steam Railway*, No.32, July 2006, p. 26. *Railway Magazine*, May 2008, p. 63, July 2008, p. 66. *Heritage Railway*, No.81, December 2006, p. 16, No.142, October 2010, p71.

207 *Heritage Railway*, No.98, June 2007, p. 90.

208 *Railway Magazine*, December 1968, p. 737, April 1969, p. 228, June 1969, p. 352. www.embsayboltonabbeyrailway.org.uk.

209 *Railway Magazine*, March 2005, pp. 46-7.

210 *Heritage Railway*, No.63, July 2004, pp. 40-44.

211 *Heritage Railway*, No.90, October 2006, p. 37, No.104, November 2007, p. 30,

No.140, August 2010, p. 27. *Railway Magazine*, May 2008, p. 66, September 2014, p. 68.

[212] *Heritage Railway*, No.98, June 2007, p. 21.

[213] *Railway Magazine*, September 2010, p. 61. *Heritage Railway*, No.191, July 2014, p. 21.

[214] *Heritage Railway*, No.65, September 2004, pp. 28-9. *Railway Magazine*, October 1972, pp. 548-9, January 2005, p.74.

[215] *Heritage Railway*, No.65, September 2004, pp. 28-9, No.77, September 2005, p. 22. *Railway Magazine*, September 2005, p.11.

[216] *Heritage Railway*, No.88, August 2006, p. 15, *Railway Magazine*, April 2008, p. 62.

[217] *Railway Magazine*, January 2010, p. 60, February 2010, p. 46. http://tvlr.co.uk

[218] Ian Carter, *British Railway Enthusiasm* (2008) chapter 6 gives a detailed account of the bitter dispute between the Welsh Highland Railway (1964) Ltd and the Festiniog Railway Company.

[219] *Railway Magazine*, May 1961, p. 359, October 1961, p. 738, April 1962, p. 287. Peter Johnson, *Immortal Rails vol. 1: the story of the closure and revival of the Ffestiniog Railway 1939-1983* (2004) pp. 169, 177.

[220] *Railway Magazine*, April 1964, p. 393.

[221] *Railway Magazine*, May 1969, p. 289, June 1970, p. 335.

[222] *Railway Magazine*, June 1975, pp. 312-13, June 1976, p. 319, June 1979, pp. 276-7.

[223] *Railway Magazine*, May 2005, p. 36. Ian Carter, *British Railway Enthusiasm* (2008) pp. 155-6.

[224] *Railway Magazine*, October 2005, p. 7.

[225] *Railway Magazine*, November 2004, p. 4, May 2005, pp. 37-41, June 2008, p. 9, May 2009, pp. 7, 69, June 2009, pp. 7, 64, April 2011, p. 88.

[226] *Heritage Railway*, No.70, February 2005, pp. 74-7, No.77, September 2005, p. 24.

[227] *Railway Magazine*, April 2005, pp. 16-17, October 2006, p. 58, March 2014, pp. 23-6.

[228] *Heritage Railway*, No.94, February 2007, pp. 36-7. *Railway Magazine*, July 1993, p. 42, April 2005, pp. 18-19, April 2011, p. 10.

[229] *Railway Magazine*, October 2005, p. 55.

[230] *Heritage Railway*, No.94, February 2007, p. 36.

[231] Personal communication.

[232] *Railway Magazine*, September 1962, pp. 615-17.

[233] *Railway Magazine*, April 1971, p. 179.

[234] *Railway Magazine*, March 1974, pp. 132-3.

[235] *Heritage Railway*, No.85, May 2006, p. 6. *Railway Magazine*, May 2015, p. 68.

[236] *Railway Magazine*, July 2006, p.54. *Steam Railway*, No.444, August-September 2015, p. 16.

[237] *Railway Magazine*, November 1994, p. 41.

[238] *Railway Magazine*, October 1969, p. 590, January 1970, p. 50, March 1970, p. 171, September 1970, pp. 524-5.

[239] *Railway Magazine*, April 1972, p. 214, June 1972, p. 333, July 1972, p. 385.

[240] *Railway Magazine*, June 1972, p. 332.

[241] *Railway Magazine*, August 1975, p. 415, November 1976, pp. 593-4, December 1976, p. 645.

[242] *Railway Magazine*, July 1975, p. 365, August 1975, p. 375.

[243] *Railway Magazine*, January 1988, p. 16, March 1988, p.150.

[244] *Heritage Railway*, No.90, October 2006, p. 59.

[245] *Steam Railway*, No.299, July-August 2004, p. 14.

[246] *Railway Magazine*, April 1974, p. 164.

[247] Peter Johnson, *Immortal Rails: the story of the closure and revival of the Ffestiniog Railway 1939-1983 vol. 2, 1964-1983* (2005) p. 39.

[248] John L.H. Bate, *The Chronicles of Pendre Siding* (2001) p. 174. Peter Johnson, *Immortal Rails: the story of the closure and revival of the Ffestiniog Railway 1939-1983 vol. 2, 1964-1983* (2005) p. 208.

[249] *Railway Magazine*, April 1974, p. 164.

[250] *Railway Magazine*, April 1974, p. 164.

[251] Ralph Cartwright, *The Welshpool and Llanfair* (2002) p. 90.

[252] *Railway Magazine*, March 2008, p. 9.

[253] *Railway Magazine*, June 1976, pp. 286, 319, November 1976, p. 595, December 1976, p. 607, March 1977, p. 144, April 1977, pp. 178-9, December 1977, pp. 614-15.

[254] *Steam Railway*, 299, July-August 2004, p. 74.

[255] *Railway Magazine*, November 2006, p. 75.

[256] Bob Scarlett, 'Management and Finance of Railway Preservation', *Management Accounting*, v. 72, No.4 (1994) p. 51.

[257] Dennis Dunstone, *For the Love of Trains* (2007) p. 144.

[258] Ralph Cartwright, *The Welshpool and Llanfair* (2002) p. 114. *Heritage Railway*, No.63, July 2004, p. 87.

[259] *Heritage Railway*, No.63, July 2004, p. 37.

[260] *Railway Magazine*, April 2005, p. 15.

[261] *Railway Magazine*, December 1976, p. 605.

[262] *Railway Magazine*, September 1978, pp. 424-5.

[263] John Parsons, *Saving the West Somerset Railway: the branch line that refused to die* (2011) pp. 93-4.

[264] *Railway Magazine*, November 1976, p. 595, December 1976, p. 607, March 1977, p. 150. *Railway World*, August 1997, p.10.

[265] *Talyllyn News*, No.215, September 2007, pp. AR12-13, No.227, September 2010, p. 10.

[266] John L.H. Bate, *The Chronicles of Pendre Siding* (2001) p. 19. *Heritage Railway*, No.110, April 2007, p. 47.

[267] *Heritage Railway*, No.59, March 2004, p. 70. *Railway Magazine*, December 2004, p. 78.

[268] *Railway Magazine*, August 1976, p. 431, July 1977, p. 356.

269 *Railway Magazine*, December 1974, pp. 614-15, May 1976, p. 264.
270 Cliff Thomas, 'The SVR – what does the future hold?' *Railway Magazine*, September 2005, pp. 14-20. *Railway Magazine*, May 1974, p. 251.
271 *Railway Magazine*, November 1962, pp. 793-4.
272 *Railway Magazine*, March 1974, p.133.
273 *Heritage Railway*, No.98, June 2007, p. 28.
274 Bob Scarlett, 'Management and Finance of Railway Preservation', *Management Accounting*, v. 72, No.4 (1994) p. 51.
275 *Heritage Railway*, No.100, July 2007, p. 18.
276 *Railway Magazine*, January 2006, p. 66.
277 *Railway Magazine*, March 1976, p. 151.
278 *Railway Magazine*, May 1973, p. 221.
279 *Railway Magazine*, April 1967, pp. 220-3, February 1978, p. 100.
280 *Heritage Railway*, No.59, March 2004, p. 69. *Railway Magazine*, August 2006, p. 56. Ian Carter, *British Railway Enthusiasm* (2008) pp. 130-6.
281 *Steam Railway*, No.357, December 2008, pp. 8-9.
282 *Railway Magazine*, May 1973, p. 218. Richard Sykes, Alastair Austin, Mark Fuller, Taki Kinoshita and Andrew Shrimpton, 'Steam Attraction: railways in Britain's national heritage', *Journal of Transport History*, v. 18 (1997) p. 157.
283 Richard Sykes, Alastair Austin, Mark Fuller, Taki Kinoshita and Andrew Shrimpton, 'Steam Attraction: railways in Britain's national heritage', *Journal of Transport History*, v. 18 (1997) p. 157-8. www.kesr.org.uk (accessed 13 March 2015).
284 Peter Johnson, *Immortal Rails vol. 1*: the story of the closure and revival of the Ffestiniog Railway 1939-1983 (2004) pp. 94, 211.
285 Peter Johnson, *Immortal Rails: the story of the closure and revival of the Ffestiniog Railway, vol. 2* (2005) p. 23.
285 *Heritage Railway*, No.127, August-September 2009, pp. 44-7.
287 Peter Johnson, *Immortal Rails: the story of the closure and revival of the Ffestiniog Railway 1939-1983 vol. 2, 1964-1983* (2005) p. 58. *Heritage Railway*, No.81, January 2006, p. 4. *Steam Railway*, No.318, January 2006, p. 18. *Railway Magazine*, Christmas 2013, pp. 62-7.
288 *Heritage Railway*, No.59, March 2004, p. 69.
289 *Talyllyn News*, No.206, June 2005, p. WRS2. J. Harrison, 'Thoughts on Preservation', *Railway Magazine*, February 1975, pp. 62-4.
290 John L.H. Bate, *The Chronicles of Pendre Siding* (2001) pp. 232-3.
291 *Railway Magazine*, August 2004, p. 77.
292 *Railway Magazine*, October 1964, p. 801.
293 *Railway Magazine*, April 1965, p. 238.
294 Ralph Cartwright, *The Welshpool and Llanfair* (2002) pp. 99, 102-5.
295 Michael Harris, *Keighley & Worth Valley Railway* (1998) p. 82.

[296] *Steam Railway*, No.305, December 2004, pp. 62-5.

[297] Michael Harris, *Keighley & Worth Valley Railway* (1998) pp. 53, 86.

[298] *Railway Magazine*, March 2008, p.63.

[299] *Railway Magazine*, July 2005, p. 61. *Heritage Railway*, No.86, June 2006, p. 30. *Railway Magazine*, November 2007, p. 79.

[300] *Heritage Railway*, No.63, July 2004, p.87. *Railway Magazine*, July 1975, p. 366.

[301] *Railway Magazine*, April 2000, p. 18.

[302] *Steam Railway*, No.305, January 2005, p. 30.

[303] *Heritage Railway*, No.97, May 2007, p.73.

[304] *Railway Magazine*, April 2005, pp. 17-18, *Heritage Railway*, No.85, May 2006, p. 27.

[305] *Heritage Railway*, No.63, July 2004, p. 87.

[306] John L.H. Bate, *The Chronicles of Pendre Siding* (2001) p. 214.

[307] *Railway Magazine*, April 1962, p. 229.

[308] *Railway Magazine*, August 1969, p. 478, September 1970, p. 525, April 2000, p. 18. Michael Harris, *Keighley & Worth Valley Railway* (1998) pp. 36-7, 41.

[309] *Railway Magazine*, October 1977, p. 510.

[310] *Railway Magazine*, April 2013, p. 11.

[311] *Railway Magazine*, April 2000, p. 18, March 2006, p. 67. *Heritage Railway*, No.77, September 2005, pp. 80-82, No.116, October 2008, p. 7.

[312] *Railway Magazine*, March 2006, p. 67, October 2010, p. 56, December 2013, p. 64.

[313] *Heritage Railway*, No.97, May 2007, pp. 44-5.

[314] Peter Johnson, *Immortal Rails: the story of the closure and revival of the Ffestiniog Railway 1939-1983 vol. 2, 1964-1983* (2005) p. 18. *Daily Telegraph* Travel, 5 April 2014, p. T12.

[315] *Railway Magazine*, November 1972, p. 604, November 2007, p. 74. *Heritage Railway*, No.97, May 2007, pp. 70-3.

[316] *Railway Magazine*, May 2010, p. 71. *Heritage Railway*, No.135, March-April 2010, p. 12.

[317] *Heritage Railway*, No.77, September 2005, pp.44-8, No.104, November 2007, p. 38.

[318] *Heritage Railway*, No.191, July 2014, p. 40. *Steam Railway*, January-February 2015, p. 32.

[319] *Railway Magazine*, April 2013, pp. 22-6. *Heritage Railway*, No.179, August 2013, pp. 82-7, December 2015, p. 75.

[320] *Railway Magazine*, March 2015, p. 73. *Steam Railway*, January-February 2015, p. 10.

[321] *Steam Railway*, No.444, August-September 2015, pp. 44-6.

[322] *Railway Magazine*, May 2008, p. 63, July 2008, p. 66, August 2010, pp. 54-5. November 2011, p. 92, May 2013, pp. 32-6, November 2014, p.11, March 2015, pp. 14-18, October 2015, pp. 22-6. *Heritage Railway*, No.81, December 2006, p. 16, No.142, October 2010, p. 71, No.159, January-February 2012, p. 35, April 2012, pp. 51-4. *Steam Railway*, No.32, July 2006, p. 26.

323 *Railway Magazine*, July 2013, pp. 7, 65, August 2014, p. 62, January 2015, pp.68, 70, August 2015, p. 6, November 2015, p. 11 January 2016, p. 74.

324 *Railway Magazine*, September 1975, pp. 464-5, February 1976, pp. 60-3, May 1976, p. 260, November 1979, p. 559.

325 *Railway Magazine*, August 2010, pp. 21-2, March 2013, pp. 28-32, May 2013, p. 6, November 2015, p. 77. Colin Tyson, ed, *Battle for Bluebell* (2013).

326 *Railway Magazine*, March 2008, p. 57, March 2011, pp. 28-31.

327 *Heritage Railway*, No.179, August 2013, pp. 92-3. *Railway Magazine*, January 2014, pp. 14-19.

328 *Railway Magazine*, January 2014, p. 59, March 2016, pp. 52-8.

329 *Railway Magazine*, December 2014, p. 66, February 2015, p. 64, July 2015, p. 80, August 2015, p. 72. *Steam Railway*, No.444, August-September 2015, p. 15

330 *Railway Magazine*, January 1964, p. 192, March 1964, pp. 319-20, May 1964, p. 457, June 1964, pp. 523-4, August 2005, p. 71, February 2015, p. 94. *Heritage Railway*, No.77, September 2005, pp. 66-9, No.104, November 2007, p. 15.

331 *Railway Magazine*, September 2010, p. 61, January 2013, pp. 28-32, February 2015, p. 65, May 2015, p. 62. *Heritage Railway*, No.140, August 2010, p. 12, No.179, August 2013, p. 38.

332 *Railway Magazine*, July 2005, p. 65, August 2005, p. 68, May 2007, p. 64, May 2008, p. 62, August 2008, p. 50, February 2015, pp. 33-7, December 2015, p. 77. *Heritage Railway*, No.81, June 2006, p. 34.

333 *Heritage Railway*, No.113, July 2008, p. 10, No.116, October 2008, p. 7. *Railway Magazine*, January 2009, p. 62, February 2009, p. 48, September 2009, p. 71.

334 *Railway Magazine*, December 2009, p. 66, September 2010, p. 54, April 2011, p. 68, January 2012, p. 70, March 2012, pp. 66-7, May 2012, pp. 8, 71, December 2012, pp. 36-40. *Heritage Railway*, No.159, January-February 2012, pp. 42-7.

335 *Railway Magazine*, August 1993, pp. 33-5.

336 *Heritage Railway*, No.63, July 2004, pp. 34-39, No.65, September 2004, pp. 14-15, *Steam Railway*, No.299, July-August 2004, p. 24. *Railway Magazine*, February 2005, pp. 10-14.

337 *Heritage Railway*, No.70, February 2005, pp. 6-7.

338 *Heritage Railway*, No.70 (February 2005), p. 7, No.73 (May 2005) p. 12. *Railway Magazine*, June 2005, p. 70, August 2005, p. 62, September 2006, p.58.

339 *Heritage Railway*, No.135 (March-April 2010) p. 16. *Railway Magazine*, May 2013, p. 10.

340 *Railway Magazine*, January 2014, p. 96.

341 *Heritage Railway*, No.104, November 2007, p. 31. *Railway Magazine*, December 2007, p. 63, December 2008, p. 55, November 2009, p. 96.

342 *Railway Magazine*, May 2008, p. 61, March 2009, p. 61. April 2009, p. 61, December 2009, p. 86.

[343] *Railway Magazine*, August 2008, p. 48. July 2013, p. 70, November 2015, p. 75.

[344] *Railway Magazine*, August 2008, p. 64, August 2010, p. 70, December 2010, p. 9, May 2011, p. 90. *Heritage Railway*, No.116, October 2008, pp. 6, 42-6.

[345] See *Heritage Railway*, No.85, May 2006, p. 6.

[346] *Railway Magazine*, September 2010, p. 60. www.lner/info/co/NER/derwent. www.legislation.gov.uk/uksi/1987/75/contents/made.

[347] *Railway Magazine*, November 2006, p. 79.

[348] *Railway Magazine*, June 2006, p. 68.

[349] *Steam Railway*, No.299, July-August 2004, p. 23. *Railway Magazine*, March 1976, p. 158. R.C. Riley, 'Private Railway Preservation in Britain', *Trains 'sixty nine* (1968) p. 21.

[350] For example, 'Windcutters in crisis', *Railway Magazine*, April 2007, pp. 30-4, and the reply *Railway Magazine*, May 2007, p. 36. *Heritage Railway*, No.191, July 2014, p. 16.

[351] *Railway Magazine*, May 1975, p. 248, June 2007, p. 24, November 2014, pp. 14-16. Phil Marsh, 'A Volunteers' 'Passport'?', *Railway Magazine*, September 2006, pp. 35-8. David Morgan. 'Passing on Knowledge to Apprentices is Crucial to Survival of Heritage Lines', *Railway Magazine*, March 2015, p. 77.

[352] *Heritage Railway*, No.85, May 2006, pp. 37-8.

[353] *Railway Magazine*, March 2007, pp. 3, 14-18.

[354] *Railway Magazine*, August 2013, pp. 66, 69, 71.

[355] *Railway Magazine*, December 2004, p. 72, August 2012, p. 69.

[356] *Railway Magazine*, December 2004, p. 72, August 2012, p. 69.

[357] *Railway Magazine*, September 2005, pp. 18-19.

[358] N. Pallant, *Holding the Line: preserving the Kent & East Sussex Railway* (1993) pp. 165-6.

[359] *Railway Magazine*, May 2014, p. 8.

[360] *Steam Railway*, October 2006.

[361] *Railway Magazine*, August 2006, p. 59, August 2013, p. 66.

[362] *Railway Magazine*, July 2015, p.82.

[363] *Heritage Railway*, No.77, September 2005, p. 70. *Railway Magazine*, May 2006, p. 65.

[364] *Railway Magazine*, December 1966, p. 726.

[365] John L.H. Bate, *The Chronicles of Pendre Siding* (2001) p. 232.

[366] Peter Johnson, *Immortal Rails: the story of the closure and revival of the Ffestiniog Railway 1939-1983 vol. 2, 1964-1983* (2005) pp. 151, 190.

[367] *Heritage Railway*, No.142, September-October 2010, pp. 22-3.

[368] *Railway Magazine*, January 2007, pp. 20-3.

[369] *Heritage Railway*, 98, May 2007, p. 32, No.137, May 2010, pp. 41-2. *Railway Magazine*, July 2007, pp. 50-1.

[370] Dennis Dunstone, *For the Love of Trains* (2007) p. 146.

[371] O.H. Prosser, 'A New Deal for the Independent Railways', *Trains Annual 1967* (1966) pp. 89-96.

[372] *Ibid*. pp. 84-5.

[373] *Railway Magazine*, February 1953, p. 134. John L.H. Bate, *The Chronicles of Pendre Siding* (2001) p. 111. Tom Rolt, *Landscape with Figures* (1992) p. 242.

[374] Peter Johnson, *Immortal Rails vol. 1: the story of the closure and revival of the Ffestiniog Railway 1939-1983* (2004) p. 102.

[375] *Railway Magazine*, June 1963, p. 386, April 1979, p. 176.

[376] *Railway Magazine*, May 1966, p. 290.

[377] *Heritage Railway*, No.63, July 2004, pp. 82-7.

[378] *Heritage Railway*, No.120, January-February 2009, pp. 35-6.

[379] Michael Harris, *Keighley & Worth Valley Railway* (1998) pp. 25-27.

[380] *Railway Magazine*, November 1964, p. 859.

[381] *Railway Magazine*, October 1966, p. 600.

[382] 'Railway Restoration with State Aid', by O.H. Prosser, *Railway Magazine*, April 1974, pp. 168-70.

[383] *Railway Magazine*, March 1974, pp. 150, 151.

[384] *Railway Magazine*, April 1974, pp. 175-6.

[385] *Railway Magazine*, April 1974, pp. 175-6.

[386] Michael Harris, *Keighley & Worth Valley Railway* (1998) pp. 50-3. *Railway Magazine*, October 1970, p. 580.

[387] *Heritage Railway*, No.77, September 2005, p. 5, No.94, February 2007, p. 6.

[388] *Railway Magazine*, May 2013, p. 64, July 2015, pp. 43-6. *Heritage Railway*, No.191, 2014, p. 48.

[389] *Railway Magazine*, July 2003. *Heritage Railway*, No.65, September 2004, p. 7, No.109, March 2008, p. 17.

[390] *Steam Railway*, No.299, July-August 2004, p. 28, *Railway Magazine*, February 2009, p. 47. *Heritage Railway*, No.146, January-February 2011, p.146.

[391] *Heritage Railway*, No.77, September 2005, p. 22.

[392] *Heritage Railway*, No.144, November-December 2010, p. 69. *Railway Magazine*, July 2013, pp. 26-30.

[393] *Railway Magazine*, October 2004, p. 9, July 2005, p. 61, May 2011, pp. 16-19. *Heritage Railway*, No.110, April 2008, pp. 20-21.

[394] *Railway Magazine*, April 1978, p. 459, June 1988, p. 356, July 2011, pp. 14-15.

[395] *Railway Magazine*, March 2009, p. 11, July 2011, pp. 14-18, July 2013, p. 64. www.mnr.org.uk.

[396] *Railway Magazine*, November 1978, pp. 527-29, March 1993, p. 33.

[397] *Railway Magazine*, August 2003, August 2005, p. 62, February 2006, p. 53, February 2012, pp. 21-5, January 2015, p. 90. *Daily Telegraph*, 30 June 2003. *Heritage Railway*, No.65, September 2004, p. 29.

[398] *Railway Magazine*, March 2005, p. 11, February 2007, 26-9. *Heritage Railway*, No.60, April 2004, p. 63.

[399] *Heritage Railway*, No.109, March 2008, p. 6, No.110, April 2008, p. 25, No.116, October 2008, p. 18. *Railway Magazine*, July 2009, p. 91.

[400] *Heritage Railway*, No.137, May 2010, pp. 50-3.

[401] *Railway Magazine*, March 2012, p. 64, *Heritage Railway*, No.159, January-February 2012, p. 18.

[402] *Railway Magazine*, May 2013, pp. 10, 67. *Okehampton Times* (www.okehampton-today.co.uk) 27 March 2013. Dartmoor Railway Supporters Association, www.dartmoor-railway-sa-org/news, 12 August 2013. *Heritage Railway*, No.191, July 2014, p. 23.

[403] Strategic Rail Authority, *Community Rail Development: a consultation paper on a strategy for community railways* (February 2004). *Heritage Railway*, No.60, April 2004, pp. 62-4.

[404] *Railway Magazine*, May 2005, p. 60, June 2005, p. 67, November 2005, p. 56, June 2007, p. 9, July 2013, p. 16.

[405] *Railway Magazine*, January 2014, p. 64, March 2016, p. 83.

[406] *Sheffield Star* online, 2 January 2014.

[407] *Railway Magazine*, July 2008, pp. 17-24, May 2011, p. 71. *Heritage Railway*, No.132, December-January 2010, pp. 34-8.

[408] *Railway Magazine*, January 2013, p.73. Norfolk Orbital Railway website, accessed September 2013.

[409] *Railway Magazine*, May 1978, pp. 254-5, June 1978, p. 309, November 1988, p. 694.

[410] *Railway Magazine*, May 1977, pp. 214-17.

[411] *Railway Magazine*, July 1976, p. 375, November 1977, pp. 562-3, April 1978, p. 203.

[412] *Railway Magazine*, July 2003, p. 11, December 2004, p. 72, February 2009, p. 23. *Heritage Railway*, No.144, November-December 2010, p. 15.

[413] *Railway Magazine*, February 2009, pp. 20-23.

[414] *Railway Magazine*, September 2010, pp. 14-17, April 2011, p. 62.

[415] *Railway Magazine*, October 2010, p. 55. *Heritage Railway*, No.144, November-December 2010, p. 35, No.146, January-February 2011, p. 25.

[416] *Daily Telegraph*, 13 February 2006.

[417] *Railway Magazine*, February 2007, p. 56. *Railway Magazine*, January 2008, p. 73.

[418] Alan Holmes, *Talyllyn Revived* (2009) p. 13.

[419] *Heritage Railway*, No.94, February 2007, p. 36. All Party Parliamentary Group on Heritage Rail, *Report on the Value of Heritage Railways* (July 2013) pp. 19-20.

[420] For examples of correspondence between preserved railways and the inspectors see Alan Holmes, *Talyllyn Revived* (2009), Peter Johnson, *Immortal Rails: the story of the closure and revival of the Ffestiniog Railway 1939-1983 vol. 1* (2004), *vol. 2, 1964-1983* (2005).

[421] *Steam Railway*, No.318, January 2006, pp. 74-5.

[422] *Railway Magazine*, January 1994, p. 34, October 2007, January 2012, p. 75, April 2012, p. 8. *Heritage Railway*, No.179, August 2013, p.16. Office of Rail Regulation annual safety reports, www.rail-reg.gov.uk.

[423] *Railway Magazine*, January 1974, p. 42, June 1977, p. 299.

[424] *Railway Magazine*, December 2005, p. 41. *Steam Railway*, No.411, February 2013, p. 18. Colin Tyson, ed, *Battle for Bluebell* (2013) p.24.

[425] *Steam Railway*, No.299, July-August 2004, pp. 14, 58-60. *Railway Magazine*, March 2009, p.13, October 2010, p. 60, July 2011, p. 31, September 2011, pp. 12-13.

[426] *Talyllyn News*, 217 (March 2008) p. 32. Robin Jones, *Beating Beeching: Britain's railways fight back from the axe* (2013) p. 10.

[427] *Railway Magazine*, December 1977, pp. 614-15.

[428] *Heritage Railway*, July 2004, p. 31. *Railway Magazine*, April 2004, December 2004, p. 78.

[429] *Railway Magazine*, June 1988, p. 354, December 2004, p. 73, March 2009, p. 6. *Heritage Railway*, No.77, September 2005, p. 5.

[430] *Railway Magazine*, October 2010, p. 56, June 2015, pp. 23-4, July 2015, pp. 43-4. *Heritage Railway*, No.141, September 2010, p. 24.

[431] *Heritage Railway*, No.81, January 2006, p. 22, No.94, February 2007, pp.34-6.

[432] *Railway Magazine*, September 1993, p. 49, August 1994, p. 32, September 2006, p. 62.

[433] *Steam Railway*, No.411, February 2013, p. 28.

[434] *Railway Magazine*, January 2005, p. 74.

[435] *Railway Magazine*, June 2007, p. 67, May 2010, pp. 58-9. *Heritage Railway*, No.94 (February 2007) pp. 35-6, No.135, pp. 8-9.

[436] *Railway Magazine*, December 2005, pp. 42-3, July 2006, p. 57, September 2010, p. 65, December 2013, p. 75. *Heritage Railway*, No.146, January-February 2011, p. 14.

[437] *Railway Magazine*, September 2008, p. 61, May 2011, pp. 7, 64, June 2011, pp. 34-5, 42-4.

[438] Tom Rolt, *Landscape with Figures* (1992) p. 16.

[439] Peter Johnson, *Immortal Rails vol. 1: the story of the closure and revival of the Ffestiniog Railway 1939-1983* (2004) p. 55. R.C. Riley, 'Private Railway Preservation in Britain', *Trains 'Sixty-nine* (1968) p. 17.

[440] *Railway Magazine*, September 1956, p. 633.

[441] *Railway Magazine*, November 1959, p. 799.

[442] *Railway Magazine*, June 1961, pp. 434-5, July 1969, pp. 406-7.

[443] *Railway Magazine*, March 1976, p. 151, April 1979, p. 170. *Steam Railway*, No.300, August-September 2004, pp. 30-1, 37. *The Times Saturday*, 30 July-5 August 1983, p. 1.

[444] *Railway Magazine*, May 1975, p. 248.

445 *Steam Railway*, No.300, August-September 2004, pp. 30-1, 37. *Heritage Railway*, No.123, April-May 2009, p. 73. *Railways Illustrated*, May 2010, pp. 32-3.

446 *Heritage Railway*, No.90 (October 2006) p. 34.

447 For a commentary on some of these themes, see *Heritage Railway*, No.104, November 2007, pp. 36-9.

448 Tom Rolt, *Railway Adventure* (1971 edition) pp. 149-52.

449 N. Pallant, *Holding the Line: preserving the Kent & East Sussex Railway* (1993) p. 27.

450 *Railway Magazine*, November 2014, pp. 16-17.

451 L.T.C. Rolt, *Landscape with Machines* (1992) p. 1. Michael Whitehouse, *Talyllyn Pioneers* (2016) p. 107.

BIBLIOGRAPHY

All Party Parliamentary Group on Heritage Rail, *Report on the Value of Heritage Railways* (July 2013)

John L.H. Bate, *The Chronicles of Pendre Siding* (2001)

Alan Bell, *Branch Line to Hayling* (1984)

Ian Carter, *British Railway Enthusiasm* (2008)

Ralph Cartwright, *The Welshpool and Llanfair* (2002)

W.J.K. Davies, *Ravenglass & Eskdale Railway* (2000 edition)

Dennis Dunstone, *For the Love of Trains* (2007)

Allan Garraway, *Garraway Father and Son* (1985)

Bob Gwynne, *Railway Preservation in Britain* (2011)

Michael Harris, *Keighley & Worth Valley Railway* (1998)

Alan Holmes, *Talyllyn Revived* (2009)

Peter Johnson, *Immortal Rails: the story of the closure and revival of the Ffestiniog Railway 1939-1983 vol. 1* (2004)

Peter Johnson, *Immortal Rails: the story of the closure and revival of the Ffestiniog Railway 1939-1983 vol. 2, 1964-1983* (2005)

Peter Johnson, *An Illustrated History of the Welsh Highland Railway* (2009)

Robin Jones, *Beating Beeching: Britain's railways fight back from the axe* (2013)

Robin Jones, *Great Central: past, present and future* (2014)

Charles Loft, *Lost Trains: Dr Beeching and the Death of Rural England* (2013)

N. Pallant, *Holding the Line: preserving the Kent & East Sussex Railway* (1993)

John Parsons, *Saving the West Somerset Railway: the branch line that refused to die* (2011)

L.T.C. Rolt (ed.), *Talyllyn Century: the Talyllyn Railway 1865-1965* (1965)

L.T.C. Rolt, *Railway Adventure* (1971 edition)

L.T.C. Rolt, *Landscape with Machines* (1971)

L.T.C. Rolt, *Landscape with Canals* (1977)

L.T.C. Rolt, *Landscape with Figures* (1992)

Gordon Rushton, *Welsh Highland Renaissance: the story of the Welsh Highland Railway 1991-2011* (2012)

Rob Shorland-Ball, ed., *Common Roots – Separate Branches: railway history and preservation* (1994)

Strategic Rail Authority, *Community Rail Development: a consultation paper on a strategy for community railways* (February 2004)

Eric Tonks, *Railway Preservation in Britain 1950-1984* (1985)
Colin Tyson, ed, *Battle for Bluebell* (2013)
Michael Whitehouse, ed., *Preservation Pioneers* (2014)
Michael Whitehouse, *Talyllyn Pioneers* (2016)

Articles in books and periodicals
P.N. Grimshaw, 'Steam Railways: growth points for leisure and recreation',
    Geography, v. 61, 1976, pp. 83-8.
Michael P. Jacobs, 'The Isle of Wight's Fight for its Railways', *Trains Annual 1966*
    (1965) pp. 62-7.
O.H. Prosser, 'A New Deal for the Independent Railways', *Trains Annual 1967*
    (1966) pp. 89-96.
R.C. Riley, 'The Bluebell Line', *Railway Magazine*, April 1962, pp. 226-9.
R.C. Riley, 'Private Railway Preservation in Britain', *Trains 'Sixty-nine* (1968)
    pp. 12-26.
Bob Scarlett, 'Management and Finance of Railway Preservation', *Management
    Accounting*, v. 72, No.4, April 1994, pp. 50-1.
Richard Sykes, Alistair Austin, Mark Fuller, Taki Kinoshita and Andrew
    Shrimpton, 'Steam Attraction: railways in Britain's national heritage', *Journal of
    Transport History*, third series, v. 18, 1997, pp. 156-75.
Cliff Thomas, 'The Great Central: at the double', *Railway Magazine*, April 2005,
    pp. 14-20.
Cliff Thomas, 'The South Devon Railway', *Railway Magazine*, March 2005, pp. 45-9.
Susan M. Youell, 'Third Century at Middleton', *Railway Magazine*, April 1961,
    pp. 223-9, 281.

Newspapers and Periodicals
The Daily Telegraph
Hansard
Heritage Railway
Railway Magazine
Railway World
Steam Railway
The Times

Websites
As well as the websites of all the heritage railways themselves, the following have been consulted:
British Heritage Railways: www.british-heritage-railways.co.uk
Heritage Railways: www.heritage-railways.com
The London & North Eastern Railway Encyclopaedia: www.lner.info/
www.legislation.gov.uk/uksi/1987/75/contents/made
Office of Rail Regulation: www.rail-reg.gov.uk

INDEX